Freedom
and
Foreign Policy

Thomas J. Dodd

U. S. SENATOR

BOOKMAILER
New York

Copyright © 1962 by Thomas J. Dodd

Distributed by
THE BOOKMAILER INC.
Box 10, New York 16, N. Y.

The Complete Bookstore-by-Mail Service
Representing all U.S. Publishers

MANUFACTURED IN
THE UNITED STATES OF AMERICA

Table of Contents

I	Our National Purpose	1
II	The Nature of the Enemy	8
III	The Confusion of the West	17
IV	Our Missed Opportunities in Hungary	31
V	Berlin, February 1959: The Khrushchev Ultimatum	42
VI	Khrushchev's Visit to the United States— A Protest	56
VII	Anti-Semitism, the Swastika Epidemic, and Communism	74
VIII	Fallacies of the Nuclear Test Ban	117
IX	Lessons of the Cuban Disaster	159
X	Southeast Asia: The Dangers of Appeasement	173
IX	The Berlin Wall: The Imperative Need for Action	184
XII	British Guiana Heads Towards Communism	197
XIII	Should We Recognize Red China?	208
XIV	The Continuing Danger in the Congo	214
XV	Power in Space and Peace on Earth	229
XVI	Is the UN Worth Saving?	243
XVII	The Indonesia-Netherlands Dispute Over West New Guinea	265
XVIII	Sentimentality and National Policy	275
XIX	The Politics of Liberation	285
XX	Freedom or Communism	302
XXI	Can Liberals and Conservatives Unite For Freedom?	309

PUBLISHER'S PREFACE

The Bookmailer has arranged for permission to publish this collection of speeches by Senator Thomas J. Dodd in book form because it believes they throw a rare and penetrating light on the many critical problems that confront us in the field of foreign policy.

Senator Dodd is in his fourth year in the Senate after serving two terms in the House of Repesentatives. This is a short period of time for a legislator to make a contribution in any field. Yet in this brief period Senator Dodd has achieved a nationwide reputation as an outspoken opponent of Communism and as a thoughtful analyst of the problems posed by the cold war. He is generally recognized, both in this country and abroad, as the principal Congressional spokesman for the cause of those nations which have fallen captive to Communist rule.

Senator Dodd's speeches and statements on foreign policy issues are unique in the annals of the Senate. They are unique for their scope and their scholarship, their philosophical consistency and their non-partisan nature. But they are unique, above all, because they are not post-mortems or afterthoughts —because Senator Dodd has endeavored to address himself to each new crisis as it arose and while it was unfolding, and while our policy was still in the process of formulation. He has done so because he believes it is the duty of the Senate to advise and counsel on foreign policy, and that such advice, if it is to have any meaning, must be proferred before the final die is cast.

Senator Dodd has not confined himself to foreign policy. He has, in fact, been very active on domestic issues. He has sponsored important legislation on such thorny and diverse topics as civil rights, wiretapping, election reforms and juvenile delinquency. But, as he has stated many times, he believes that the overriding issue of our generation is the conflict between Western civilization and world Communism. This has been his major field of action; and it is in this context that his basic contribution must be judged.

Senator Dodd believes that the conflict with communism is mortal; that the Free World has lost battle after battle since the close of World War II because it has refused to face up to this central fact; that we now stand with our backs to the wall; and that the survival of freedom requires nothing less than a basic reorientation of our foreign policy. He believes that concessions and appeasement embolden the Communists and make war more likely; and that a dynamic, affirmative foreign policy, committed to the goal of universal freedom, is the surest way to preserve the peace.

The Senator has, not very surprisingly, become the number one Congressional target of the Communist propaganda apparatus and of the fellow-traveling press. They have found him a difficult target, however, because the Senator has always been so meticulous about his facts, so precise and logical in his arguments, so fair as an investigator.

They have also found him a difficult target because the Senator cannot be neatly pigeonholed, either as a liberal or as a conservative. On domestic issues, his voting record must, by any fair standards, be considered liberal. But he believes that the differences that divide liberals and conservatives on domestic issues are far less important than the basic moral and political values that unite them. He is disturbed by the bitter cleavage in American society today; and he is convinced that liberals and conservatives can and must unite for freedom.

Senator Dodd's non-partisan attitude has won him the respect of Republicans and Democrats, liberals and conservatives. One of the many evidences of the broad respect he commands was a statement made by Senator Paul Douglas in the Senate on March 1. In this statement, Senator Douglas defended Senator Dodd against the charge that he was a reactionary or extremist, praised him for his fairness, and described him as a man who presented the facts about the Communist conspiracy as he sees them.

The speeches contained in this book represent a selection from a much larger body of speeches and statements covering a remarkably wide range of subjects. There were, in fact, many other speeches and statements and articles that we would have liked to include—his speech urging the enactment of a bill to create a Freedom Academy; his speech opposing the ratification of the Antarctic Treaty; his profound analysis of the consequences of the Khrushchev visit, published in the quarterly magazine, *Orbis;* his speech dealing with communist infiltration in the nuclear test ban movement; his statement on foreign aid to communist countries; his Senate speech entitled "How Not to Promote Anglo-American Friendship"; his exposure of the Fair Play for Cuba Committee, etc. But to have included all these speeches and statements would have made this a book of prohibitive size and cost.

Some of the speeches here republished were made two and three years ago. But, allowing for minor changes of detail, they are as pertinent to the problems that confront us today as they were at the time they were made. This is true of Senator Dodd's speech of February 1959 on the Berlin ultimatum; it is true of his speech on the fallacies of the nuclear test ban, which was delivered in May 1960; it is true of his comprehensive analysis of Communist anti-Semitism in March 1960, of his speech on the developing crisis in Laos in May 1961, and indeed of every speech which has been made a part of this collection.

These are speeches to be read and reread and pondered. It is our hope that the publication of this book will give added impact to the views expressed by Senator Dodd, and will help them to achieve the attention they deserve in the great national debate on foreign policy.

LYLE H. MUNSON
President,
The Bookmailer, Inc.

Chapter I

OUR NATIONAL PURPOSE *

I have sometimes felt that some of our friends elsewhere in the world must be a little mystified by the word "Americanism".

They have a strong and fervent patriotism of their own. But we never hear of Canadianism or Mexicanism or Swedenism. To other peoples, the word "Americanism" may seem a boastful affectation, a form of chauvinism, a brash nationalism. But of course it is not.

Americanism is a patriotism that has something necessarily unique about it, because our history has had something unique about it. The love of country which has for centuries drawn peoples of other lands together and welded them into nations was derived from many sources: from a love of things old and familiar, family histories in a town or province which could be traced for hundreds of years, a common tongue, a common nationality, perhaps a common religion, a national literature and music and art, a consciousness of having done certain things together as a people since the days of Charlemagne and Roland.

To the peoples of Europe, then, patriotism has its roots in the past and represents a love of all the similarities and things shared in common with their countrymen. But we in America, in the early years of our nation, had no past. We had more differences than similarities. Our people had no common history except that of escape from the histories of a score of other nations.

* *Veterans of Foreign Wars Magazine*, September 1961. This article received the 1961 award of the Freedoms Foundation at Valley Forge for the best magazine article of the year.

We had no common religion except a heritage of seeking religious freedom. We had no common tongue, no common nationality, no national music or art, no folk tales, no national literature except for the political writings of our founding fathers.

All that we had in common with which to mold a united nation, was a new set of ideas, of attitudes, of institutions; untried, unproved, yet having the universality of expressing the ancient hopes and yearnings of mankind for a better and fuller life. And we shared together a new, virgin continent upon which we could try out our experiment.

It is these concepts, then, none of them fully realized or perfected, yet none repudiated or abandoned, which have ever marked off this nation; concepts that are so familiar to us that perhaps we lose sight of their revolutionary impact upon the world of the 18th Century and their place at the heart of the struggle that is taking place today between the forces of freedom and communism.

These concepts, briefly and inadequately expressed, are, it seems to me, the following:

that the state exists to serve man and that man's liberty, his property, his family and his individual rights are above and beyond the reach of the state;

that every man should have a fair chance to succeed or to fail on his own, a square deal, a clear field;

that every man should be able to speak his piece without fear or reprisal;

that every man should have an equal voice in choosing those who govern him;

that every man should be held innocent of wrongdoing until proved guilty;

that every man should be free to worship as he pleases, or not at all, if he so pleases;

that every man has the right and should have the opportunity to own property and capital and to use these, within reasonable limits, as he chooses, free from tribute to any baron or monopoly, and secure from confiscation by government;

that other men from other lands, with their troubles and with

their hopes, were welcome to come here to our shores and try
their hand at building a new life;
that the normal relationship between men was not one of arti-
ficial division, by class or by trade or by race or by religion,
or by education, but one of democratic equality, of cooperation,
of equal opportunity for all, of working together to tame a
continent and build a nation;
that henceforth the habitual attitude of men need not be fear
and foreboding but confidence and optimism;
that a nation, our nation, could conduct itself toward other
lands with honor, with friendship, without aggression, without
predatory designs.

These ideas are our national patrimony. They took the place of all the unifying forces which centuries of living together had provided for the peoples of other lands. They are the heart of Americanism. They are all that there is to Americanism. And we may say truly that every person who shares these ideals, wherever he may live, is in his heart an American.

These ideas generated a sense of mission which has always characterized our national history. Americanism was not just for home consumption. It was for export. Our people believed that the power of our example would spread freedom across the globe.

And our ideas did catch on, all over the world. By 1917, the American people had decided it was not enough to spread freedom by example alone, that we must defend it with our might and if need be with our blood. We have fought two world wars and are presently engaged in a cold war to preserve the freedom of others in the world and in so doing to preserve our own freedom.

Today we are called upon to support and sustain the forces of freedom wherever they exist in the world. All of our history has prepared us for and guided us toward this moment. Whether or not we rise to the occasion will depend upon whether our people and our leaders understand and embrace the principles of Americanism as they have unfolded in our history.

As the principal bastion of freedom in the world, America

is the principal target for Communist subversion, the first line of Communist aggression. The investigation and exposure of these attempts at subversion in all of their many guises are matters of critical importance.

Along with other Senators on the Senate Internal Security Subcommittee, I have been trying to combat the attempts of our sworn enemies to infiltrate our government, to steal our defense secrets, and to poison the minds of our people, particularly our young people.

This task must be carried on by the FBI, by the Congress and by other groups, and we must have the constant support of the American people. The tragic history of other nations shows us that our cause could be *lost* through the failure to protect ourselves against subversion.

But effective defense against subversion is not enough. For our struggle can be *won* only by a mighty national effort which our history now calls upon us to make, an effort to defend freedom where it exists in the world and to extend it where it does not.

I believe that the vast majority of the American people are prepared and anxious to carry those burdens and make those sacrifices which our destiny now places upon us.

But two political extremes, of the right and of the left, threaten to pull us off the track. The extreme on the right rejects those measures of domestic reform, foreign assistance, military aid and international cooperation which are necessary if we are to preserve and extend freedom. The extreme on the left would have us abandon those outposts of freedom that are now under the guns of communism, and let down our defenses against domestic subversion. The danger from the extreme right is not that it conspires against America or collaborates with our foreign enemies, but that its prejudices and blindnesses may deter us from doing those things that we must do to save our country.

The danger from the extreme left is that it poisons the spiritual and philosophic well which nourishes America, it tangles up our moral guide lines, and softens up our resistance to that extension of leftism which is communism. And the danger from the left is greatly magnified by the fact that its policies so often dovetail and march hand in hand with those of the world Communist conspiracy which is sworn to destroy us.

We live in a period during which many extremists have tried to monopolize the mantle of Americanism, although they have the least right of anyone anywhere to wear it. They speak with the strident voices of intolerance, of bigotry, of accusation, of boastfulness, and of hostility toward others.

They often style themselves as "100 per cent Americans." But they are, in fact, grotesque caricatures, symbols of everything that is essentially un-American. They proceed on the basis that a man is guilty until proved innocent, that the Constitutional rights of suspected persons should be abrogated, that foreigners, foreign goods and foreign ideas should be excluded from our country.

They oppose our commitments and alliances in the defense of freedom abroad. They oppose our aid to the less fortunate peoples of the world, aid intended to help these people to make some of the American dream a reality for themselves. They are bigots. Their magazines and circulars are filled with hatred of Jews, Catholics, Negroes and all other groups except what they like to define as "Americans."

Although this type of "100 per cent American" may like to drape himself in the Red, White and Blue during the daytime, his uniform at night is sometimes the white sheet. This brand of misnamed Americanism is founded upon fear, suspicion, division and malice. These advocates, though they call themselves patriots, are tragic and contemptible examples of the fact that it is possible to live in the greatest of all nations and yet to represent everything that is hostile and inimical to the ideas which give life to that nation.

At the other extreme, we have those who are the products not of a perverted, distorted kind of loyalty, but of no loyalty at all. A small group of our people, some of them articulate and influential in the press, the arts and the communications media, have lost that sense of mission and confidence and optimism which is an essential part of the American story.

The answers of the ultra-leftists in America to the challenge of our time are weasel words justifying the abandonment of Laos, Quemoy, Formosa, Berlin and other critical areas. Their appeals are for disarmament without adequate inspection, for a nuclear test ban without means of detection, for abandonment of the development of crucial weapons on the theory that we can trust the Communists also to forego these developments.

They believe that the history of man is meaningless and that, therefore, the history of our country is insignificant. They feel that there are no absolutes, that nothing is eternally true or false, right or wrong, that nothing is fixed and changeless, that all will change and pass away. And therefore they feel that no issue, no concept, not even freedom itself, is worth risking life to defend.

To them, patriotism is a naive, outmoded superstition of unsophisticated people, nationalism is a menace, and Americanism is a term for scorn and derision. They see the caricature of Americanism which I have tried to describe earlier and they use it as an excuse for ignoring the reality of a true Americanism which has a just claim upon them as it has upon all of us.

They are the American imitators of Bertrand Russell and Philip Toynbee, who argue that it is preferable to surrender now to communism rather than run the risk of world war by taking those steps necessary to our defense.

The story of our country is a story of avoiding the extremes of the right and the left. We may hope with confidence that our people will continue to do so and that we will continue up the road on which we started in 1776.

Americanism, then, is that dedication which leads us to cherish what our fathers brought to the world, to defend it where it has taken root, to extend it where we reasonably can. Americanism is our national conscience, the voice of our history, which speaks to us today and bids us:

to insist on a fair chance for all and a free ride for none;
to encourage all to speak their minds and to protect none from fair criticism of what he has said;

6

to pursue the goal that no man be artificially pushed up nor arbitrarily held back;

to work for the perfection of our process of free choice and for the preservation of our federal system of limited government;

to extend to the homeless refugee from tyranny the hand of welcome;

to resist all appeals which seek to divide our people by race or creed or political partisanship;

to support the investigation and exposure of our country's domestic and foreign enemies, and to maintain with equal zeal the integrity of those methods by which we investigate and expose;

to sacrifice all that is required of us for the defense of our country;

to give and give and give, of our time, of our energy, of our wealth to help the people of the world to grasp for themselves the prize of liberty and opportunity;

to support our leaders when they are strong, and reprove them when they are weak;

to keep ever in our hearts the words of Senator Carl Schurz: "Our country . . . when right to be kept right; when wrong to be put right."

This is patriotism. This is Americanism. There are no 100 per cent Americans. No one can fully qualify for that magnificent accolade. But let us hope that there are millions of ordinary Americans who will humbly and devotedly answer their country's need, millions who will do their best in the faith that a merciful and loving and just God will do the rest.

Chapter II

THE NATURE OF THE ENEMY*

World communism, like a mammoth cloud, darkens the future of individuals and of nations. One-third of the world's people is already enslaved by it; another one-third is teetering on the edge of the chasm; and the lives of all who live in the avowedly anti-communist world are altered and complicated because of it.

You will pay the heavy price of communism whether you realize it or not.

At the least, your lives may be interrupted by military service; you will have to pay the expense of resistance to communism in the form of high taxes and continuing inflation; you must sacrifice the inestimable benefits that could otherwise have resulted from the enormous amount of national energy that must go into resisting communism; and day-to-day anxiety and uncertainty over the future will continue to affect the daily lives of each of us. Thinking and compassionate men and women must be deeply and continually saddened by the knowledge that one billion fellow human beings are at the mercy of a ruthless, conscienceless barbarism. Communism stands in the way of peace, of progress, and of security for all mankind.

At the worst, it poses for all of us the threat of war, of enslavement and even of annihilation.

That is why it is so important that we have a proper understanding of this fearful spectre walking the earth. Unfortunately, there is a great deal of confusion, fuzziness and

---

* Dean Junior College, Franklin, Mass., June 7, 1959.

apathy abroad concerning communism, some of it stemming from academic circles.

There are a number of stock arguments which one hears continuously that tend to obscure the real nature of communism and dissipate one of the principal weapons against it, the moral condemnation of decent people.

We hear repeatedly that nothing is gained by calling Communists harsh names or continually raking over their past crimes, as though it would somehow be better to forget the true nature of the enemy.

We read a lot of newspaper accounts of how things have improved behind the Iron Curtain, but precious little about the essential barbarism upon which communism is founded and which sustains it in power.

There is a philosophy current that many of our difficulties with the communists are due to misunderstanding, which implies that the Soviets and the Red Chinese are perhaps well meaning and that our difficulties could be resolved if we would only look at their side of things and get them to look at our side.

Perhaps the most popular phrase of those who minimize the evils of Communism is that we cannot look at the world scene in terms of "black and white," which of course carries the implication that both the Free World and the Communist World are at fault for the present danger and that each side has its good points and its bad points. I willingly concede our bad points, but I have never been able to discover the good points of communism.

This type of thinking, seeping into the American consciousness from all sides, amounts to a tremendous cumulative attrition which is utterly confusing. People who are weary after long years of anxiety are only too happy to seize upon such news items as the building of children's playgrounds in Moscow as an indication that the Kremlin masters are human and after all that everything is going to be all right. This sort of thing, constantly repeated, causes us to let down our guard, to look for an easy way out; and it eventually leads to fatal concessions to the Kremlin.

So first of all, let's get one thing straight. Let's get communism in true focus.

Communism is total evil. It is all black. There is nothing gray about it. There is nothing good about it. Its ends are evil. Its means to those ends are evil.

If, by force of circumstance, Communists are for something right, it is only as an expedient to advance their evil ends.

If they occasionally appear in a worthy light, it is because they must make some appeal to human needs and aspirations.

When they educate the ignorant, it is to perfect their apparatus of enslavement.

When they industrialize, it is to strengthen their capacity for aggression.

When they talk peace, it is just another means of waging war.

When they allow long overdue improvements in living conditions, it is evidence that even communist oppressors must make some concessions to the wishes of the oppressed.

There is no evil so appalling that communists would shrink from it, if it would effectively advance their ends. There is no atrocity so hideous that they would not willingly commit it if it served their purposes.

The Red Chinese regime, in the ten short years of its existence, has as a matter of governmental policy murdered thirty million men, women and children. The horror contained in this statistic is too great for the human mind to assimilate or the human soul to ponder. And this is but a repetition of the crimes of the Russian Communists, which have been committed on the same scale.

A penetrating *New York Times* editorial pointed out that more shocking than the Red crimes themselves, are the reasons behind them. I quote from that editorial:

"The whole 'commune' system, it comes out, is an attempt to destroy the accepted moral and rational basis of the society.

"Thus the atrocities are directed not merely against the human body. They are aimed at the heart and soul. It is not merely the man and woman who must be killed but the ideas, concepts, hopes, sense of values and traditions that have made the lives of those persons worthwhile.

"The details of the killings as related in the testimony are shocking.

They are, however, not nearly as profoundly terrifying as what underlies them."

Communism is at war with the whole human race. It is based on the blasphemy that a human being is just a particle of matter, without independent mind or spirit. It seeks to destroy the family as an institution. It seeks to wipe out religion. It seeks to blot out the human conscience and to distort all concepts of right and wrong. It seeks to reduce man to a mere beast of burden, without a will, without a personality, without a home, without personal property, without knowledge of God, without hope of eternal life.

Of course, they have not yet been successful in this task. They have found the objective of permanently defacing human nature somewhat beyond them. The task has been too great. There have been many retreats, deviations, new approaches.

But the end goal never changes. We must always remember that; and we must continually renew our understanding of it.

Certainly we must live in the world with them, but we must never forget what they are.

Certainly we must confer with them, but we must never concede to them on any basic principle.

The Western World is presently engaged in negotiations with the Communists. Unless there is a fundamental change in communist doctrine, there is no hope that these negotiations will lead to true peace.

I say this for three reasons:

First, Communism is fundamentally dedicated to the destruction of the Free World and of the ethical and rational bases of that world. Its fixed and unswerving objective is to destroy us. The Communists may have to postpone this destruction, they may have to adopt new approaches to it, but it remains their central objective in foreign affairs. As long as this remains true, there is no hope of any lasting settlement, or of any relaxation of tensions, since such things must be based on some common interest between East and West.

Second, whereas we in the West regard peace as the normal

order of things, and warfare as an interruption of that order, communist doctrine regards warfare, ceaseless conflict and violence as the essential order of life. There is no such thing as peace to them. There is only the absence of armed conflict, an absence which must be utilized for other forms of warfare. Therefore, it is only the West that seeks peace, and the notion that peace is being prevented by mere misunderstandings or resolvable differences is absurd.

Third, there is almost no hope that arguments based on reason and truth will have any effect whatsoever on Communists at the bargaining table. For the true Communist, there is no criterion of truth but communist dogma. While we in the West subject our policies and our principles to many tests of truth which are above, beyond and independent of our political credo, the Communist is incapable of doing so. Argumentation will not move him. Truth will not pierce his dialectical armor. Only the force of events, demonstrating the falsity of communist doctrine, can erode communist certainty.

These facts are fundamental to any successful coping with Communism. It is impossible to exaggerate their importance.

It is all too easy to fall into the error of assuming that the Communists are essentially like ourselves. They look like us; they dress like us; they can be affable and good-natured; their capacity for pretense is infinite.

It is hard to keep our eye on the communist ball continually and to keep in mind the fact that on basic issues we do not have and can never have anything in common with them.

This having been said, I hasten to add that mere rejection by us of communism offers no solution to the world-wide danger. It is not rejection that the world is seeking, but affirmation.

The impoverished, despairing peoples of the world are in search of a prophet, a philosophy, an ideology that promises a way out of their present degradation.

Americans have an old familiar saying "you can't beat something with nothing." We cannot beat false prophets with no prophets. We cannot beat dedication to evil with lack of dedication. We cannot solve the desperate problems afflicting half the world by merely rejecting the communist solution. We must offer a solution of our own.

We must put forward our solution in the face of many disadvantages. The uncommitted peoples of the world are generally so impoverished that they feel a kinship with the communist masses, a kinship that they could not feel with the prosperous and advanced peoples of the West.

The record of colonialism of our European allies stands against us in the eyes of those who do not understand that communism is the most ruthless and total imperialism the world has ever known. The totalitarian Communist bloc can act with a unity, a decisiveness, and a single-mindedness that is impossible for the democratic coalition. And in the nature of things, the aggressor has an initiative that the Free World cannot seem to wrest from it.

But communism possesses one fatal disadvantage. It runs against the grain of human nature. It chokes and destroys the spirit of man.

Communism is essentially evil and man is essentially good. Communism cannot satisfy any of the higher needs of man, the aspirations, the hopes, the yearnings that distinguish man from lower forms of life.

Only ignorance or despair will drive men to communism. Therefore the principal task of the West is to offer light and hope.

But the battleground today is not the higher needs of man. It is the lower needs, the more tangible, the immediate day-to-day necessities of existence.

Freedom, and all the values this term suggests, cannot flourish or have meaning without the existence of certain material conditions.

We in America have become used to a constantly rising standard of living. We have come to expect it, as though it were in the nature of things. The college students of today live better than their parents, and you expect your children to enjoy higher standards than you now have. But for a large part of the world, living standards have actually been declining despite the enormous technical advances of the past century.

It is a commonplace to say that one-third of the world goes to bed hungry at night. But it is not so generally understood that a large portion of this one-third are eating even less than they were ten or twenty years ago. And ten years hence, the outlook for them is even bleaker.

This inevitably feeds the hopelessness upon which communism thrives.

To men who are faced with these basic problems of existence, communism offers a coherent, exciting, tempting body of ideas and programs. And Russia provides the example of a nation which in a short period of time has bridged the chasm from a primitive, agricultural order to that of a highly industrialized state.

The West, despite its primacy in the realm of the spirit, seems unable to offer a convincing ideological antidote.

Nor does the example of our high standard of living or of our flourishing political institutions cause the unfortunate peoples of the world to flock to our colors.

Our talk of democracy, of free institutions, of representative government seems too parochial, too involved, too concerned with forms, to go to the heart of man's basic needs. And in the eyes of millions, our alliances with totalitarian regimes make a mockery of our professed ideals.

We seem unable to make our ideological system intelligible to others.

At a time of crucial importance to Western civilization, we seem unable to produce enough leaders who can so articulate the needs and hopes of men as to inspire the love and admiration and trust that America once enjoyed.

In our history, in our philosophy, in our religion, in the practical programs of assistance already in effect, we have all the needed elements for a new order of justice and peace and plenty—an order that will satisfy the lowest and the highest needs of men. We lack only the vital reserve of statesmen and prophets, who can combine these elements in a form that will rekindle the hope and enthusiasm of the world.

Perhaps the young men and women of your generation will fill this need.

If the Western World, with its unparalleled capacity for producing material wealth, can meet the immediate material needs of men, if we can lead the way to the eradication of social injustice, of poverty, of discrimination, of material degradation, then the battleground for the hearts and minds of the world's people will change to a conflict in which we of the West will have all the advantages.

For man's higher needs are the very things that Western civilization answers and which the cold, merciless dogma of communism cannot supply.

The highest value that Stalin could put upon man was that he was the most precious form of capital. If that were true, if that were the full significance of man, then communism would indeed inherit the earth.

But it is not true. Man possesses mental and spiritual attributes above and beyond the material world. Man has needs and appetites that no material order or philosophy can satisfy.

He needs friendship. He needs understanding. He needs truth. He needs love. Our Judaic-Christian civilization, nourished by contributions from the Greco-Roman world, is in its finest aspects the highest response to these higher needs of mankind.

Whatever may be our weaknesses in the West, we have one great strength. Our universities are free. Our churches are free.

We have preserved unbroken the tradition of free inquiry started by Plato and Aristotle. We have preserved the knowledge of the tradition, the revelation, and the moral law of God.

The people of the West remain free to seek truth and to love God. It is we and not the Communists, who are able to satisfy man's highest needs. This and this alone will save us.

Our alliances, our weaponry, our economic strength, important as they are, will never establish peace on earth. But the Church and the University, in God's good time, will do so.

Ten years ago Dr. Charles Malik, now President of the General Assembly of the United Nations, made one of the most profound statements of our century when he said:

"Communism is a doctrine of despair. Its only and complete answer therefore lies in the existence of hope. If the Western world can show a way to eradicate the shame and scandal of poverty, of exploitation, of oppression, of greed, without resort to social revolution and class-struggle and dictatorship: if it can place these material values in their proper subordinate place within the context of a mighty spiritual movement which will be revolutionary without being subversive, and which will draw its substance from the infinite riches of the Western positive tradition, then the necessity for Communism will vanish, and the spectre which now walks the earth will be laid forever."

The terrible example of communism is having one salutary effect on the Western World. It is purging us of our own follies.

The example of their total materialism is making us rightly ashamed of our own materialism.

The example of their total atheism is calling forth a spiritual rejuvenation in the West.

Their attempt to destroy all moral values is causing us to re-examine our own neglect of those values.

Their record of ruthless imperialism has caused the West to be ashamed of its own imperialism.

Their brutality is enlarging our compassion.

In the sins of communism, we see our own sins writ large.

In our desperate need to overcome evil, we are rediscovering our own capacity for good.

To the young men and women in our colleges, there opens the greatest challenge, the greatest responsibility in the long history of our civilization. If the products of our free institutions cannot refine from our heritage a ringing message, an inspiring, uplifting ideology that will satisfy the universal hunger for truth and justice, then our civilization will have lost the capacity to lead, and leadership will pass on to others.

Perhaps never in human history has so much been staked upon the performance of a single generation. The stakes are mortal, for they are the preservation of all that we have known and cared for, all that is worth preserving.

Chapter III

THE CONFUSION OF THE WEST*

Over the past 15 years, the whole of Eastern Europe, China, North Korea, North Vietnam, and Cuba have been lost to the Communists. On top of the sweeping victories it has scored in Europe, Asia, and Latin America, world communism is today bidding boldly and at an accelerated tempo for new areas of control. Everywhere the free world is on the defensive.

This record of failure and disaster is too persistent to have been the product of the laws of chance. We have lost and lost and lost because we have persistently failed to understand. I would go further and say that we have lost because we have refused to face up to the facts. And facts are the beginning of all understanding.

But we must understand, because time is running out for the free world. Another 15 years like the past 15 years and there may be no more free world to defend.

We have been losing the cold war partly because we have failed to understand its total character, partly because we have been amateurs fighting against professionals. The Soviets have been winning the cold war, first, because they have, from the beginning, accepted it as a total war, to be waged with all their resources and on every plane, and second, because they have, through their specialized training institutions, developed scores of thousands of practitioners in the art of total political warfare.

There is nothing in our previous history and nothing in our experience as free men which might have prepared us to con-

---

* Paris, France, December 1, 1960.

tend with the phenomenon of total war, a war waged by a thousand different means, a war in which the enemy conducts an integrated offensive on every plane of human activity—the economic, the political, the diplomatic, the psychological, the social, the cultural—a war conducted by stealth and subversion and Pavlovian techniques.

With the political warfare weapon, the Communist enemy has moved over and around the military defenses of the free world to secure beachheads deep in our rear areas.

This enemy has a coordinated long-range strategy for victory, in which he uses all methods and means against us.

Never has the situation been as perilous as it is today.

The West has lost its nuclear monopoly, and its ability to deter Soviet aggression has, in consequence, been seriously impaired. The Communists have became more aggressive, more arrogant, more contemptuous than ever. The symbol of this new attitude is Prime Minister Khrushchev pounding his shoe on the table at the United Nations. And this arrogance has been accompanied by a shift in tactics which makes the Communists, in my opinion, infinitely more dangerous than they have been heretofore.

THE INCREASE IN SUBTERRANEAN COMMUNIST ACTIVITIES

Going back to Lenin's earliest directives, the Communists have always planned their activities so that one portion of them has been above ground, another portion under ground. But in recent years, the Kremlin has been placing an increasing emphasis on subterfuge and subterranean operations.

In the old days, Communist movements, while they conducted part of their operations under ground, nevertheless used to identify themselves as Communist movements. The Chinese Communists never pretended that they were anything else but Communists, even though a lot of wishful thinkers in the Western World insisted that they were really agrarian reformers. Under the deposed Arbenz regime in Guatemala and under the Castro regime in Cuba the international Communist movement succeeded in coming to power in countries that were strongly Catholic and basically anti-Communist. They did this by exploiting certain legitimate grievances and by encouraging the people to believe, yes, and encouraging the American State Department to believe, that they were not really Communists.

In the old days, too, the Communists would conduct most of their front operations in a manner that made them clearly discernible and identifiable. There was the League Against War and Fascism, there was the World Peace Congress, there was the Stockholm Peace Petition, and there were many other operations like these where Communist initiative and Communist control were apparent to all but the willfully blind. Today, instead of creating front organizations of their own, the Communists are operating increasingly through infiltration in organizations established under non-Communist auspices.

The Communists must be combated on two levels, therefore: above ground and under ground. But increasingly the battle has become one against their subterranean forces.

The free world has had a limited success in fighting the Communists in the open, fighting them, that is, when they are clearly identified as Communists. In my own country, the Communists have been forced out of control of a number of important trade unions. In France and Italy, operating against very great odds, the anti-Communist trade-union organizations have made some modest headway. But even in the open phase of the struggle, we have not really done very well.

In the United States, key unions like the Harry Bridges' Longshoremen's Union, the United Electrical Workers Union, and the American Communications Union are still under Communist domination, despite all the efforts of independent trade unionists and of government.

In France and Italy, the Communist-dominated CGT and CGIL, respectively, still embrace by far the majority of the organized workers. Nor has any serious dent been made in these countries in the vast apparatus of Communist-dominated cultural, social, fraternal, and benefit organizations which play so important a role in the Kremlin's manipulation of Western public opinion.

In England, known Communists either control or exercise a large measure of control over the powerful Mine Workers Union, the General Transport Workers Union, the Electrical Workers Union.[1] The dangerous degree to which the Communists had succeeded in infiltrating and taking control of British trade unions was dramatically revealed at the recent Labor Party conference where the Communists and pro-Communists pushed through a motion calling for unilateral disarmament.[2]

In Japan, the Communists are also the single strongest force in the trade-union movement. Through the Teachers Union, which they dominate completely, the Communists are teaching young Japanese children that the U.S.S.R. is their real homeland and that the United States is an aggressive imperialistic power.

The subterranean communist attack on the free world, as it is being executed today, displays five major prongs.

There is the infiltration in the organs of government, through which the Kremlin obtains much of its intelligence and through which it frequently succeeds in inducing the governments of the free world to do precisely what the Communists would like them to do.

There is the infiltration in press and radio and television and entertainment, which the Communists use to confuse Western public opinion, to exercise pressure on government policy, and to turn one Western country against another.

There is the infiltration in organizations established under non-Communist auspices, which the Communists then use as pressure groups in support of a nuclear test ban or some other Soviet foreign policy objective.

There is the street mob, organized around fraudulent na-

---

[1] Since this speech was delivered, the anti-Communist elements in the British Electrical Workers Union have, with the aid of the British courts, succeeded in liberating their union from Communist domination.

[2] Shortly after this speech was delivered, Mr. Hugh Gaitskell and the other moderates in the British Labor Party succeeded in reversing the unilateral disarmament motion.

tionalist and non-Communist slogans, which is becoming an increasingly important instrument of Soviet policy. The terrible power of this weapon was driven home to the whole world, Soviet and non-Soviet, when a Communist-organized mob prevented the President of the United States from visiting a friendly foreign country. [Japan]

Finally there is the new type of crypto-Communist movement best typified by Castro[3], a movement which operates behind an innocent facade of nationalist and reform slogans. If such a movement could come to power 90 miles from the shores of America, in a country as unlikely for a Communist take-over as Cuba, then its possibilities are almost unlimited.

THE MANIPULATION OF PUBLIC OPINION

Communist propaganda, when it is clearly identified as Communist propaganda, the free world can counter. But the trouble is that 99 percent of the articles and publications and radio and TV programs that serve the Communist cause cannot be clearly identified as Communist propaganda.

In certain cases some doubts can be raised by proof that some of the principals involved have long records of affiliation with Communist-front organizations. But, far more often than not, those who are used to transmit the Communist propaganda line are not Communists or pro-Communists, but simply "innocents."

The "innocents" include sentimentalists; wrong-headed, soft-headed, and muddle-headed intellectuals; and the so-called "angry young men," the neurotic rebels against parental and governmental authority who always exaggerate tenfold the faults of their own country. But "the innocents" also include many decent, intelligent people, fundamentalist humanitarians whose very humanitarianism makes it impossible for them to conceive of a regime that is utterly without morality or totally evil.

There are no "innocents" under Communism. This peculiar

---

[3] In December, 1959, there were still many people who believed that Castro was not a Communist. Since then, Castro has openly proclaimed that he has always been a Marxist-Leninist.

phenomenon exists only under Democracy. And it is exceedingly difficult to cope with the "innocents" in freedom-loving societies. They cannot be prosecuted because they do not violate the law. They cannot be accused of conniving with the Communists because, except in rare cases, they do not consciously connive. And there is no way of muting them without violating the basic principles of our free society.

The "innocents," in fact, are just about untouchable. If you criticize a Communist, the brickbats will come mostly from the fellow-traveling claque and fellow-traveling press. This, one can ignore. If you criticize a fellow traveler, all the "innocents" will join the assault upon you. This can be serious. And if you dare to criticize an "innocent" for giving aid and comfort to the Communists, almost the entire press, from left to right, will charge that justice and decency have been affronted. This can permanently mar a man's public reputation.

Let me give you an illustration of how the Communist propaganda operation is sometimes unwittingly assisted by publishing houses that are certainly not Communist, but which are influenced by authors, editors, or personal contacts who, in a few instances, harbor sympathies for the Soviet Union *in toto,* but far more frequently sympathize with some aspect of Communist policy, or for Communism in a specific geographic area.

In December, 1960, two books on Cuba were about to come off the press. One was a book by a former Communist, Nathaniel Weyl, an expert for several decades on Latin American affairs. It is a solid, carefully documented yet dramatic work that tells the story of Castro's rise to power and of the manner in which he was abetted by naive American sentimentalists, deluded liberals, and open philo-Communists. The other book, entitled "Listen Yankee," was written by C. Wright Mills, a Columbia University sociologist with no particular expertness on Latin America, a charter member of the "Fair Play for Cuba" Committee. "Listen Yankee," as you probably guessed from the title, is a scurrilously anti-American and pro-Castro diatribe. But it was printed by the highly reputable, even conservative, publishing house of McGraw-Hill, and the chances are that it will enjoy a circulation many times greater than the anti-Castro book.

"Listen Yankee" was printed simultaneously in hard-cover and paperback edition. I am told that the initial printing will exceed 150,000. The advance advertising was on a scale generally reserved for works of the first magnitude, works like Churchill's memoirs. The December (1960) issue of *Harper's* Magazine contains a lengthy reprint from "Listen Yankee" as its No. 1 item; and *Harper's* has advertised its December issue in the New York *Times* and other papers with full-page reproductions of the cover of "Listen Yankee."

In a free society, one does not forbid the publication of pro-Castro or pro-Khrushchev books. This situation, however, goes beyond the act of publication. Despite the fact that the Castro regime has now been openly exposed as Communist, despite the fact that it has been denounced by the American Government and that the governments of all the other American States have turned against it, despite the open embraces between Khrushchev and Castro, despite the berserk anti-American propaganda conducted by Castro, despite all these things, it is still possible in America to get a pro-Castro book printed by a highly reputable publishing house, advertised and distributed on the scale of a top best seller, and favorably reviewed in some of the great pillars of the American press.

There is nothing new about this situation, of course. When the Chinese Communists were bidding for power, the only books on China that became best sellers were the ones that portrayed the Reds as agrarian reformers. And when Castro was bidding for power, there was no dearth of reputable commentators and reputable newspapers to assure us that he was not a Communist, but an idealist.

Among the most prominent expounders of the myth that Castro was really a reformer was Herbert L. Matthews, New York *Times* correspondent in Cuba for a brief period of time. Castro, said Mr. Matthews in the early days, believed in—I quote—"liberty, democracy, social justice, the constitution, and free elections." He likened him to Abraham Lincoln.

Many months after Castro came to power, Matthews said, and again I quote: "This is not a Communist revolution in any sense of the word, and there are no Communists in any positions of control." Mr. Earl Smith, former U.S. Ambassador to Cuba, told the Senate Subcommittee on Internal Security that Mr. Matthews' articles in the New York *Times* "served to inflate Castro to world power and world recognition." Mr. Matthews may have acted in innocence. But he permitted himself to be influenced by people who did not act out of innocence.

There are some who will say that the confusion that has at various times characterized our attitude toward the Chinese Communists, toward the Arbenz regime in Guatemala, toward the Castro movement in Cuba—that our confusion in these instances and so many other instances has all been a matter of accident. For my own part, I do not think it is an accident. There is pattern here, there is organization, and there is purpose; and despite all the innocence that certainly prevails in the foreground, I am certain that in the background, if you delved deeply enough, you would find the real organizers of public confusion in the free world.

COMMUNIST INFLUENCE ON GOVERNMENT POLICY

It is almost as difficult, but for other reasons, to deal with the problem of Communist infiltration in government. There are many people in my own country and, I am afraid, even more people in other countries, who will raise the cry of "McCarthyism" at the mention of Communist infiltration in government. Let us review a few pertinent facts.

Alger Hiss, one of the top officers of the State Department and the secretary of the founding conference of the United Nations, was identified as a Communist agent and was convicted of perjury for denying that he turned over state secrets to Whittaker Chambers, a self-confessed Soviet agent.

Harry Dexter White, who, as the energetic assistant to Secretary of the Treasury Morgenthau, in effect ran the American Treasury, has also been proved, beyond any reasonable doubt, to have been a Communist agent.

Frank Coe, one-time assistant to White, was compelled to resign as head of the International Monetary Fund when he claimed protection of the Fifth Amendment in refusing to reply to the question: "Are you a Communist agent?" Mr. Coe is as of this date (December 1, 1959) in Communist China.

Think of the implications of this: Communist agents have at different times directed the American Treasury, the International Monetary Fund, and one of the key offices in the U.S. State Department.

It would be foolish to believe that all the Communist infil-trees have been removed from the U.S. Government, that the problem of infiltration no longer exists. On the contrary, there is reason to believe that in our country and in every other country of the free world, the international Communist movement has greatly stepped up its infiltration of government offices. The Communists, moreover, do not infiltrate in a haphazard way. Their infiltration is planned and directed. Intelligence is the lesser part of their purpose; their major purpose is to mess up, to misdirect, Western foreign policy. If China happens to be the area of interest at a given moment, they will try to achieve positions of influence in government that will enable them to influence its policy vis-a-vis China. If plans are made for a Castro-Communist takeover in Cuba, then it can be taken for granted that, simultaneously, the Communists will endeavor to direct intellectual adherents with backgrounds in Latin American affairs into various desk positions where they can exercise their talents.

All this can be taken as axiomatic. But the free world is asleep to this danger.

I have the greatest admiration for British law and the fairness and respect for law that pervade British society. Let me, however, draw the attention of my British friends to a few disturbing facts. Bruno Pontecorvo and Burgess and Maclean were able to defect safely to the Soviet Union. Alan Nunn May was apprehended and sentenced, but on the basis of information provided by Igor Gouzenko in Canada. Klaus Fuchs was also imprisoned; but here the FBI provided the lead. On their own, the British security forces have not apprehended a single major Communist agent. What reason can there be for this? I can think of no other reason than a general lack of awareness, at both public and governmental level, of the extent of the danger. [See Postscript, page 30].

I do not say this in reproach. I believe that my own country is somewhat more alert. But even in my own country only a small part of the job has been done.

The question is sometimes asked: What difference can one Communist or several Communists in government make? I shall answer this with a few examples.

During World War II, for reasons which have never been properly explained, the British Government abandoned the nationalist forces of General Mihailovich in Yugoslavia and threw its support behind the Communist army of Marshal Tito. Not a single one of the British or American officers attached to Mihailovich recommended that he be abandoned; on the contrary they all strongly recommended that we support him. How did it come about that the West abandoned Mihailovich and, in effect, installed Communism in Yugoslavia?

It has recently become a matter of public record that Maj. James Kluggman, the officer in charge of the Yugoslav and Near Eastern Desks in British Intelligence during the war, was a British Communist, who later became a member of the Central Committee of the British Communist Party. Perhaps this helps to explain the British switch to Tito, which we supinely followed.

In 1943, the U. S. Government decided to make $200 million in gold available to the Chinese Nationalist Government to be paid upon demand. The gold was urgently needed by Chiang to maintain the value of the Chinese currency, to pay his troops, and for other pressing obligations. But despite repeated requests from Chiang, two years later, in 1945, only $27 million had been paid over. Why?

The Senate Subcommittee on Internal Security has been engaged in the examination of the voluminous diaries left by former Secretary of the Treasury Morgenthau. In these diaries, there is recorded a frank exchange between Harry Dexter White and Frank Coe, both now identified as Communist agents. In this exchange, which took place on May 10, 1945, they make it clear that they have sabotaged the transfer of gold to the Chiang government with every artifice and excuse at their disposal.

In the privacy of his own office White admitted that the United States had "absolutely no legal grounds" for delaying shipments. He said—I quote: "We have been successful for over 2 years in keeping them down to 27 million."

THE CONFUSION OF THE WEST

Deploying their various infiltrations and their psychological warfare weapons with great skill, the Communists have frequently been able to manipulate Western public opinion and Western policy in the manner of Pavlov conditioning his dogs.

There has been a whole series of critical situations in which the Communists have succeeded in persuading the majority of the people in the non-Communist world to believe what the Kremlin wished them to believe, and in persuading Western governments to do what it wished them to do.

The Communists achieved one of their first major successes in the realm of psychological conditioning at the time of the 1944 Communist insurrection in Greece. If you look back through the American newspapers of that time, you will find that a great majority of our editors, our public officials, and public opinion molders in general, attacked Prime Minister Churchill for his courageous decision to put down the Communist insurrection. They did so because, in one way or another, they were led to believe that Churchill was intervening against the heroic Greek resistance fighters, and not against a Communist insurrection which had already gone to the point of mass executions of anti-Communist citizens. Today, of course, everyone agrees that Prime Minister Churchill did the right thing. In fact, he did the only thing. But very few people stopped to consider how it was that the Communists were able completely to befuddle our mental processes and destroy our sense of balance.

They achieved a success of even greater magnitude when they succeeded in persuading so many people in the free world that the Chinese Communists were not really Communists but simple agrarian reformers.

We should have learned from China: but we did not. Ten years after the Communists seized power in China, we fell for precisely the same shell game in Cuba: Castro was not a Communist but a simple reformer. So said Herbert Mathews in the New York *Times,* and so said many people in our own State Department.

As the recent and perhaps most striking example of the psychological manipulation of public opinion and Government policy, we have the West's calamitous retreats in the negotiations for a nuclear test ban, retreats clearly induced by the international hysteria which the Kremlin has so cleverly fostered and exploited.

First, we said that the question of nuclear weapons and nuclear testing could not be separated from that of general disarmament, because of the enormous Soviet advantage in conventional arms. We said, too, that there could be no disarmament without inspection.

Then, under the public clamor for a test ban, we agreed to a voluntary moratorium and to negotiations for a test ban in isolation from the problem of general disarmament.

We originally said that the moratorium would be a temporary 18-month arrangement, and that our decision at the end of that time would be dependent on the progress of the Geneva negotiations for a test ban. Having failed to make any serious dent in the Soviet opposition to adequate inspection, we extended the moratorium for another year.

Worse than this, in the Camp David announcement of March 29, 1960, President Eisenhower and Prime Minister Macmillan accepted the principle of a voluntary moratorium on undetectable tests—that is, on tests below the size of a Hiroshima-type bomb—if the Soviets are willing to accept inspection of tests of detectable magnitude. This, I submit, makes a mockery of the principle of inspection, on which the free world had previously based its entire approach to disarmament.

And while these concessions were being made by the West, the cries and lamentations echoed through the press and the meeting halls and the Government corridors of our country, openly or implicitly urging still further concessions to the Soviet viewpoint in an effort to achieve a test ban agreement.

Most of those in the ranks of the test ban movements are unquestionably decent, well-meaning people, who are properly horrified at the thought of nuclear war, and of the mutations that might conceivably—although no one is really certain— result from continued atmospheric testing.

It is a measure of Communist adroitness in psychological warfare that they are still able to use the specter of fallout from nuclear testing to stimulate the test ban hysteria, although it is clearly apparent to every sensible person that the nuclear powers need not conduct any tests that contaminate the atmosphere. The tests can be under ground or above atmospheric altitude.*

WHAT CAN BE DONE

How do we extricate ourselves from our defensive posture? How do we cope with Communist infiltration in Government and the press, with the Communist manipulation of pressure groups, with Communist psychological warfare, with the fraudulent nationalist movements masterminded by communism in Asia, Africa, and Latin America?

Let me close my presentation with one concrete proposal. I have said we have been losing the cold war because we have been amateurs fighting against professionals. So long as this situation persists, we shall continue to lose the cold war. To help overcome this handicap, a group of U.S. Congressmen,

---

* *Author's note:* At the time this speech and my speech on nuclear testing (Chapter VII) were made, the best available scientific information was to the effect that our nuclear weapons development program could be adequately served by underground tests and tests in space. This evaluation, in turn, was conditioned by the prevalent belief that the moratorium on testing, in one form or another, was bound to be extended. On this one point, I have had to revise my position in the light of the massive series of atmospheric tests conducted by the Soviet Union in September and October of last year, and in the light of new scientific evidence that important aspects of our nuclear weapons development program were critically dependent on atmospheric testing.

I am convinced, however, that the development of cleaner warheads will limit the fallout from our atmospheric tests to a level that does exceedingly little, if any, damage to public health.

and I am proud to be a member of this group, have proposed the creation of a Freedom Academy.

The function of the Freedom Academy would be, first, to develop systematic knowledge of all aspects of the Communist conspiracy; second, to develop a science of counteraction against Communist subversion that will see us through the perilous period ahead and ultimately pave the way for victory; and, third, it would train Americans and nationals of other free countries in the science of total political warfare, as it must be waged by free men.

With every day's news it becomes clearer that the old methods of defense against communism are not enough. The free world and, in particular, the great Western Powers, must master the new dimensions of conflict the Soviets are employing against them and they must go over to the offensive, using all of their strength and wisdom. We must have a total mobilization of our minds and wills and spirits.

If we fail, let us have no illusions about the penalty, for ourselves and for our children.

The universal triumph of freedom, on the other hand, would open the way to the utmost heights for mankind as a whole.

[*Postscript:* Since this speech was made, the British people have been aroused to the need for tighter security measures by a series of events, the most famous of which was the so-called "Portsmouth spy trial." A British Parliamentary Committee has recently submitted a report urging stricter security in the Civil Service.—T. J. D.]

Chapter IV

OUR MISSED OPPORTUNITIES IN HUNGARY *

We in the United States, we in the Free World, have talked much, but we have done little, about liberation. "Liberation," as we have used the word, has not been a guide to a meaningful course of action in the conflict between freedom and world Communism. It has been, on our lips, a political catch-phase, a hypocritical shibboleth.

To the extent that the concept of liberation has been kept alive, to the extent that it has been given meaning, it is not ·we of the free world who deserve the credit, Mr. Chairman, but the dedicated representatives in exile of the captive European peoples.

You have kept the concept of liberation alive despite the frequently negative and discouraging attitude of those who should assist you. You have sought to arouse the Free World from a lethargy which, if continued longer, points the way to doom. It has, I am afraid, been a thankless and unrewarding and sometimes bitter task. You have been accused, I know, of adventurism and war-mongering, of subordinating the interests of the entire Free World to your own selfish little national interests. But I say to you and I say to my fellow-Americans that the interests of the captive nations and of the Free World community are one. I say that the captive nations, even in captivity, protect the Free World and protect the peace because they constitute the chief deterrent against Soviet aggression. I say that the Free World in its own self-

* New York, N. Y., October 19, 1960.

interest must seek the liberation of the captive nations by every peaceful means at its disposal: or else it will pay for its moral and political delinquency by forfeiting its own freedom.

We can not, we must not, seek refuge in the ancient alibi of Cain: "Am I my brother's keeper?" In the world of today we must observe the biblical injunction to regard our neighbor's welfare as our own, because this basic moral attitude has become the price of our own freedom.

A few days from now we shall be celebrating the fourth anniversary of the great Hungarian Revolution. The Hungarian Revolution presented the Free World with an opportunity—an unparalleled opportunity—to restore the frontiers of freedom to their pre-war limits. Our failure to react to this opportunity was, in my opinion, one of our gravest policy failures of the post-war period. It is to this opportunity and this failure that I wish to address my remarks tonight.

If we are to reverse the trend of recent years, if we are to force the communist world back on the defensive, if we are to set our sights on the victory of freedom over tyranny, we must first of all restudy the strategy and tactics of world communism and we must draw all the hard, bitter lessons of the post-war era. We must decide where we have erred and where we have failed and what we might have done to avoid this failure. We must conduct this reappraisal without partisan rancor. We must all be brutally frank with ourselves—nothing less than this will suffice.

In particular, I believe that we must examine the lessons of the Hungarian Revolution, that we must try to determine what we did that we should not have done and what we might have done that we did not do. It is imperative that we make this examination because, with or without an active liberation policy, there will be more Hungarian Revolutions.

Who can deny this, after East Germany, Poznan, Budapest and Tibet?

Whether these revolutions culminate in disaster or in the triumphant restoration of freedom to the captive peoples, may very well depend on how well we learn our lesson.

We were all inspired by the heroism of the Hungarian Revolution. We suffered with the Hungarian people when the Red Army reinvaded the country and assaulted Budapest. We opened our hearts to assist the scores of thousands of Hungarian refugees who fled across the frontiers to escape from Soviet terror. But at the time of the Revolution, how many voices were there in either Party who urged a more resolute course of action, who took the stand that compassion and charity were no substitutes for courage and moral conviction?

For the timidity and inaction which characterized our policy at the time, we must all share responsibility.

Before the Hungarian revolution, there were many who scoffed at all talk of liberation. Not very surprisingly, those who had lost all hope were inclined to favor some form of military disengagement, combined with a guarantee of the *status quo* in Europe.

The chief accomplishment of the Hungarian Revolution was that it proved that liberation *is* possible, given a favorable conjuncture of circumstances. Such a conjuncture occurred in the months preceding the Revolution. The Kremlin had been wracked by a series of power struggles; the entire Communist world had been thrown into further disarray by Khrushchev's denunciation of Stalin's crimes at the 20th Congress of the Soviet Communist Party; the weakening at the center had resulted in a weakening of control in the satellites; and the growing evidences of discontent in each of the captive nations communicated themselves like electric impulses to the other captive nations. It is not inconceivable that a similarly favorable conjuncture of circumstances will arise within the next several years.

There are those who read a different meaning into the Hungarian Revolution: who see in it conclusive proof that liberation is impossible and that the West has no alternative but to accept the *status quo*. To them I say that the Revolution was neither a completely foredoomed undertaking nor a tragic defeat.

The Hungarian Revolution might have been successful if the United States and the United Nations had taken a few affirmative measures. It might have been successful if the Western alliance had not been rent asunder by the Suez crisis.

And, even without moral support from the UN and the West, it might still have been successful.

At the time of the Hungarian Revolution, Poland and East Germany stood on the brink. Had either one gone over the brink, the chances are that the entire satellite empire would have erupted in the flames of a super-revolution. The Soviet Army would not have been able to cope with such a situation.

The Hungarian Revolution was a completely spontaneous national uprising. But even if it had been organized and calculated, it would have been a justifiable risk from a military and political standpoint. If we weigh the consequences, the Hungarian Revolution, in defeat, ranks as the most significant victory for the forces of freedom since the end of World War II.

From their own history, the Russians know something of the concept of victory in defeat. Napoleon won the Battle of Borodino. But General Kutuzov, as Tolstoy recounts in *War and Peace,* insisted that the battle, in terms of its ultimate consequences, was a decisive victory for Russia. The outcome, as every schoolboy knows, was Napoleon's disastrous retreat from Moscow.

Khrushchev was able to crush the Hungarian Revolution by massing his armored divisions against the people of Budapest. But the Revolution, in defeat, exposed the lie of Communism for all peoples to see. Overnight, it converted the Warsaw Pact from a diplomatic asset into a military and diplomatic liability.

The Revolution destroyed for all time the myth that Communist regimes can enjoy at least a measure of popular support. Until several months before the Revolution, the people of Hungary, like the other peoples in the Soviet empire, gave the impression of passive acceptance of their regime. But underneath this appearance of passive acceptance there lay a smouldering hatred. When the volcano of this hatred erupted, one had to look around and ask: "Where are the Communists?"

Most significant of all, the younger generation, the students and workers who had known no other world and who had been indoctrinated since childhood in Marxist dogma—these were in the forefront of the fight against the regime. The Hungarian Revolution has demonstrated, if this needed any further demonstration, that neither one generation nor three generations nor ten generations can produce a breed of men who will accept as natural and proper the complete abrogation of human freedom. There is, in short, no such thing as a Communist generation.

Even in defeat, therefore, the Hungarian Revolution was a many-sided victory for the cause of freedom. But the Revolution need not have failed. I am convinced that we had it in our power to assure its success. The trouble was that we were completely unprepared. And there was no excuse for this lack of preparation because there had been ample warning.

Throughout the spring and summer of 1956 there had been rumblings in the satellite countries. In August, the Poznan revolt brought radical changes in the Polish government and resulted in the removal of Marshal Rokosovsky as Commander in Chief of the Polish forces.

But when the Hungarian revolution erupted two months later, we had prepared no policy to deal with such a contingency. In consequence, our response to this historic opportunity was laggard, unimaginative, and timid.

The Eisenhower Administration could think of nothing better to do than to assure Khrushchev that we regarded Hungary as part of the Soviet sphere and that he could therefore intervene with impunity.

Let me suggest some of the things that might have been done with just a bit more foresight, a bit more preparation and a bit more courage.

The Hungarian revolution began on October 23, 1956, with a student demonstration in Budapest in front of the statue of the Polish hero, General Bem. When the police opened fire on the crowd, what had been a peaceful demonstration turned into an armed insurrection. Fighting against Soviet tanks with small arms and Molotov cocktails, the Freedom Fighters, in several days of fierce fighting, forced the withdrawal of Soviet military units from Budapest and other major centers.

On October 27 the formation of a new government, headed by Imre Nagy was announced.

On October 30th, Prime Minister Nagy proclaimed the abolition of the one-party system and publicly recalled the Hungarian representative to the UN, Peter Kos.

On November 1st, Prime Minister Nagy announced Hungary's withdrawal from the Warsaw Pact, proclaimed Hungarian neutrality, and urgently appealed to the United Nations to put the question of Hungary on the agenda.

His message to the United Nations read—and I quote: "Reliable reports have reached the government of the Hungarian People's Republic that further Soviet units are entering into Hungary . . . therefore, I request your Excellency promptly to put on the agenda of the forthcoming General Assembly of the United Nations the question of Hungary's neutrality and the defense of this neutrality by the Four Great Powers."

Nagy's appeal reached the UN at 12:27 p.m., Thursday, November 1. Note this time well. Fifty-eight hours remained between the moment the message arrived and the hour on the early morning of November 4 when the Red Army treacherously struck. But so absorbed was the UN in the debate on Suez, so unprepared were we, so determined to avoid "provocation" of the Soviet regime, that no action was taken on Prime Minister Nagy's urgent appeal.

The text of the Nagy cable was circulated to the UN delegates at 2:30 p.m. But it was simply one mimeographed document among numerous mimeographed documents, and many delegates did not read it until late that night.

I believe that it was a great misfortune for the Free World that John Foster Dulles suffered his first collapse at this critical juncture. In the early morning of November 2nd, after an all-night session on Suez, Dulles interrupted the debate to say that he hoped the UN would "not be preoccupied with the Middle East to the exclusion of assisting the state of Hungary to regain its independence." Hours later, John Foster

36

Dulles was on a surgeon's table, undergoing an emergency operation for cancer.

On the afternoon of Saturday, November 3, the Security Council met again to consider the matter of Hungary. It met, to our eternal shame, not at the request of the United States, but at the urgent insistence of Dr. Emilio Portuondo of Cuba. At this meeting, the Yugoslav delegate, Dr. Brilej, stated that negotiations between the Hungarian and Russian governments seemed to be proceding in a satisfactory manner, that it would therefore be unwise to intervene. He moved for adjournment.

Ambassador Lodge supported the proposal! "We believe," he said, "that adjournment for a day or two would give a real opportunity to the Hungarian government to carry out its announced desire to arrange for an orderly and immediate evacuation of all the Soviet troops."

I shall never be able to understand what motivated Ambassador Lodge to make this statement. For this, let me emphasize, was 48 hours after the receipt of Premier Nagy's appeal in which he made it clear that, far from making progress on the withdrawal of Soviet troops, new Soviet units were pouring into the country.

And so the matter dragged on and on, while the sands of time were running out.

Just before midnight of November 3 the UN received the text of Prime Minister Nagy's final dramatic message, informing the world of the Soviet attack on Budapest.

The Security Council approved a U.S. resolution calling upon the government of the USSR to desist forthwith from intervention in Hungary, and affirming the right of the Hungarian people to a government of their choice. This resolution was promptly vetoed by the Soviet Union.

But for the people of Hungary, in any case, the hour was already too late.

This is what happened in the United Nations in the critical days preceding the Red Army's final assault.

Let me suggest some of the things that might have been done. and should have been done.

First, without waiting for the formal communication from Prime Minister Nagy, we should have made it demonstratively clear that we recognized the Nagy government as the legitimate government of Hungary. Among other things, we should have established contact with his government the moment it took office and suggested an immediate appeal to the UN.

Second, between the time of the establishment of the Nagy government on October 28 and the receipt of Prime Minister Nagy's appeal on November 1, we should have lined up support for a motion urging the immediate dispatch of a corps of UN observers to Hungary, and this resolution should have been introduced in the General Assembly within hours of the receipt of Premier Nagy's communication.

Third, until the arrival of these observers, the ambassadors of the UN countries in Budapest should have been asked to serve as *pro tem* observers.

Fourth, Secretary General Hammarskjold should have been notified in advance that any communication received from the Nagy government was to be marked "urgent" and instantaneously transmitted to the members of the Security Council.

Fifth, reacting to the repeated report of Soviet troop movements, we should have let it be known that any attempt by the Red Army to reinvade Hungary and depose the lawfully appointed government of Premier Nagy would be looked upon with the gravest concern by the United States government; that the State Department would immediately respond to such aggression by demanding the imposition of the most stringent economic and diplomatic sanctions; that, beyond this, the consequences, including the military consequences, were completely unpredictable.

Sixth, as a routine defensive precaution at a time of crisis, we should have placed the United States Forces in Europe on alert and asked for an emergency session of the NATO Council.

If we were not prepared to issue the same kind of warning to the Kremlin that the Kremlin has issued to the West over Suez, Berlin, the U2, Cuba and the Congo, then we should at least have said nothing and kept them guessing.

How different the world situation would be today if we had pursued the course of courage in Hungary!

The liberation of Hungary would, of course, have made the liberation of the other satellite countries unavoidable. There are many who say that Khrushchev would have risked war rather than accept this prospect.

I challenge this assertion.

The Kremlin has always backed down from a showdown. At the time of Hungary, it would have shunned a general war like the plague. It would have been impossible to conceive of circumstances more disadvantageous from its own point of view.

If war had come over Hungary, the Kremlin would have entered it with its satellite empire in open revolt or on the brink of revolt, and with the Soviet hierarchy still bitterly divided. The Red Army troops in Hungary had shown serious signs of disaffection. In the USSR itself, there was manifest unrest among the students of the University, and there had been the great uprising of the Vorkuta slave laborers. Finally, the United States at that time still had an overwhelming preponderance in nuclear weapons, while the Soviet Union had still not tested its first ICBM.

There is clear evidence that, when the Red Army withdrew its forces after the first round of battle in Budapest, the Kremlin was divided and uncertain about the course to be followed. In his speech in Budapest on December 2, 1959, Premier Khrushchev admitted frankly that some of his Kremlin cronies had opposed his decision to use the Red Army to crush the revolution. They opposed it because they feared both Western reaction to intervention and the potential impact of intervention on their own Empire. Emboldened by Western assurances, however, Khrushchev and the interventionists won the day in the councils of the Politbureau.

For a period of four years, from the death of Stalin until the events in Hungary, the Free World had within its grasp an unparalleled opportunity to seize the political offensive, to force communism back with measures short of war, to recreate the political equilibrium in Europe which is essential to a stable peace. But we did nothing. We played the Cold War according to the communist rules.

These rules, as the authors of "Protracted Conflict" have pointed out, demand that the Cold War always be fought on the territory of the Free World and never on the territory of the Soviet Union or the countries it has annexed through aggression. They demand that we do nothing to exploit Soviet weaknesses, while taking it for granted that the Kremlin will mercilessly exploit each and every weakness it may find in the West's protective armor.

If we continue to fight the cold war according to these rules, it goes without saying that we shall lose it.

If we are ever to extricate ourselves from the fatal paralysis of our defensive posture, it is essential, in my opinion, that we study and restudy the lessons of our lost opportunities in Hungary and in Eastern Europe. Only when we have digested these lessons, will we be able to respond intelligently to the opportunities that will again present themselves in the not too distant future.

I have said there will be more Hungarys. Of this I am certain. In the evolution of the hatred of tyranny, there is a point where it becomes a blind and all-possessing passion. And no regime in history has been so outstandingly successful in fostering this special breed of hatred as has the communist regime in Russia and its satellite regimes in other countries.

There will be more Hungarys because of this hatred, because of the eternal will to freedom, because totalitarian societies *do* undergo crises, and also because any crisis in a totalitarian society tends to be a major crisis.

We must ask ourselves "What will we do next time?" But we must ask ourselves another question: "What practical measures can we take to encourage the spirit of resistance among the captive peoples, and to keep alive the hope of liberation and faith in the Free World?"

There are some who say that the development of nuclear

weapons makes it necessary for the Free World, as a matter of self-preservation, to abandon "liberation" as a reckless pipe-dream. The converse is true.

The emergence of a nuclear stalemate means that we do not now possess, or will not possess in the near future, the deterrent of nuclear superiority. Given the massive superiority of the Soviet Union in conventional forces, this creates a highly dangerous situation. In this critical period upon which we are now entering, there is only one serious deterrent available to us: the continuing spirit of resistance of the captive people. It becomes more necessary than ever before, therefore, that we encourage the will to liberation and support it by every practical means.

The crimes of Soviet imperialism must be spread on the record at every appropriate opportunity. Our propaganda must be sharpened. Our diplomacy must seek to raise the issue of the captive nations at every session of the UN and at every major diplomatic conference. NATO'S ground forces in Europe must be strengthened. A Freedom Academy must be created, where representatives of the Free World receive concentrated training in the science of counteraction to Soviet aggression. But above all we must persuade the captive peoples of Europe, by our actions, that we shall never reconcile ourselves to their subjugation.

And it would be enormously helpful if we could also persuade them that we have learned the lessons of the Hungarian revolution.

Chapter V

BERLIN, FEBRUARY 1959:
THE KHRUSHCHEV ULTIMATUM *

Mr. President, a week ago today I submitted a resolution concerning German reunification and the present Berlin crisis. I wish to speak today on that resolution. I join in the debate on this crucial question almost with a sense of regret. I realize my own limitations and the inability of any of us to keep fully abreast of all the shifting developments on the world scene. And surely no new Senator relishes the prospect of pitting his views in opposition to the views of wiser men whom he respects and admires.

Even the most senior Senator cannot study these grave and complex questions without a weariness of mind and of soul that must come to all who seek solutions to seemingly insoluble problems.

What we do and say here is bound to have some influence, for good or ill, in our country and in the world. What we do may be misunderstood. What we say may be misrepresented. What we believe may be in error. All of these misgivings loom large in the mind of one so new to this Chamber as I.

But the Berlin crisis approaches, and the historic responsibility of the Senate to advise and give counsel on questions of foreign policy now devolves upon us. The Senator from Montana [MR. MANSFIELD] has rightly urged us to fulfill that duty and bring these problems before the Nation while there is still time for meaningful discussion.

The people of this country are entitled to a sincere public discussion of the problem which, if not properly resolved, may

---

* United States Senate, February 26, 1959.

lead them to disaster or to war; and the views of the people must be given expression through debate on the floor of the Senate.

And so I wish today to write into the public record the position of at least one Senator on this matter of such vast import for the future of mankind.

Let us first review the simple facts of the situation confronting us.

On November 27, 1958, the Soviet Union demanded that the United States, the United Kingdom, and France abandon West Berlin. Each subsequent Soviet statement has made that Soviet ultimatum ever more rigid and unyielding. The free world has been given a deadline, May 27, 1959. Moscow says that on that date, Soviet responsibility for guaranteeing free-world access to West Berlin is at an end. Russian troops are to be withdrawn from East Germany and replaced with East German troops. The Western Powers must then, according to Moscow, make all future arrangements with the East German puppet government.

We are told that if we attempt to maintain our right of access to West Berlin without the approval of the East German puppet regime our forces will be fired upon. If they defend themselves, Russia will call it an act of war and will rush to the defense of the East Germans, thus presumably touching off World War III. This, in brief, is the official Russian policy.

There have been two types of reaction to this Soviet ultimatum. The President and the Secretary of State have responded to it by reaffirming their belief in the soundness and rightness of our policy. They have upheld the basic principles of that bipartisan policy, while suggesting a number of subordinate questions upon which we are willing to negotiate, if the Soviets are really interested in negotiation. The position of our Government, as I understand it, is this:

The Four Powers must make the basic decision on German reunification but representatives of East and West Germany may sit in as advisers. Ultimate free elections are an absolute necessity, but there is room for negotiation over what form these elections will take. I certainly hope that we will call on the United Nations before we use force and before the deadline of May 27. The Western Powers insist upon their right of free access to West Berlin, but they may call for United Nations counsel before using force, and they will use careful forbearance in exercising those rights. Western troops must remain in Berlin, but only so long as the West German Government and people desire them to stay.

This is the policy of our national administration. It is, in my judgment, a policy that is sound, enlightened, and morally right.

Critics of this policy have responded to the Soviet ultimatum in a far different vein. They attack our policy as too rigid and inflexible. They say that "free elections" and "standing fast in Berlin" are slogans, not policies. They argue that a divided Germany threatens the peace of world and see continued German partition, and German reaction to it, as a certain cause of war. They say that the Soviet ultimatum makes it essential that we reexamine our policy and come forward with compromises and concessions. They insist that because our policy has not produced a settlement in 14 years, it has failed and should therefore be scrapped. They advocate a withdrawal of Western troops because they feel that some accident or chance border incident could set off World War III. They maintain that even token agreements would be a great step forward because they would relax tensions and change the diplomatic atmosphere. They contend that we ought to join in a European security pact that would recognize Red control of Eastern Europe as a permanent fact of history and thus allow the Russians to feel secure. They maintain that the Russians are looking for a face-saving way to withdraw troops from Eastern Europe, and that we should make compromises that will help them to do so.

My purpose today is to examine these assumptions.

Is our Berlin policy too rigid and inflexible? I think not. There is no peculiar virtue in the concept of flexibility. To me, flexibility implies compromise and concession. When applied to fundamental principles, right principles, flexibility is not only without virtue; it becomes a vice. What concessions or compromises can we make on the basic principles of our Berlin policy?

Can we abandon the principle of free German elections? To do so would be to abandon the principle that our country has lived by and kept alive for almost two centuries.

Can we withdraw our troops from West Berlin? To do so would leave it at the mercy of Communist encirclement and attack.

Can we submit to a Communist blockade of West Berlin? To do so would mean slow but certain starvation and destruction.

Can we surrender the concept of four-power responsibility? To do so would be to surrender the reason for our presence in West Berlin and to shirk responsibilities which grew inevitably out of our combined victory over Germany in World War II.

These are the concessions the Soviets demand. I say that we cannot grant any one of them. Let those who complain of our inflexibility address themselves to these basic principles and tell us which one of them is subject to flexible compromise.

If they say that I am setting up a straw man, and that they do not mean to yield on any of these points, then it is they who are sloganizing, not we.

"Free elections" and "stand fast in Berlin" are expressions of principle, not slogans. But cries of "inflexibility" and "rigidity" are indeed slogans unless they spell out the points upon which we should make concessions. If the critics of our present policy advocate compromise on any of the basic points of that policy, they should say so. If they do not, they should give up their slogans and join forces with those of us who stand behind the fundamental principles of our foreign policy.

Mr. Khrushchev stated, only a few days ago, that the Soviet policy is absolutely inflexible; that the Kremlin will make no concessions; that they do not even want a foreign ministers' conference.

The Communists have remained intransigent in their unjust position for 14 years. Must we therefore retreat from our just position? Whenever the Soviets continue to say "No" so long that a crisis becomes imminent, there are always cries from well-intentioned people in our camp that our policy is too rigid, too inflexible, and too unrealistic, and that we should turn to compromise and accommodation. These criticisms should be directed at the Soviet Union. But instead "the righteous are called to repentence instead of the sinners."

When we have resisted these slogans, as we did during the first Berlin crisis, we have made progress. When we have listened to them, we have sunk further into the swamp of compromise on basic principle that has in the past led from disaster to disaster. Have we forgotten the lessons of the Hitler era with its compromises, concessions and flexibilities?

There are others who, while remaining silent as to basic concessions, maintain that we ought to make token agreements, that we ought to make our tone of voice more friendly, because small agreements and friendly words would establish a new climate of opinion, an atmosphere of good feeling and mutual trust that would usher in an era of real agreement on basic issues.

On the surface this argument may seem appealing. No one would suggest that we should be brash, or rude, or discourteous in our diplomatic negotiations. These are the hallmarks of Communist diplomacy.

Our diplomatic representatives have not been guilty of these things. On the contrary, American representatives have traditionally conducted themselves with a courtesy and a dignity which is born of dedication to right principles and confidence that they will ultimately prevail.

But the etiquette of diplomacy solves nothing in this Communist age. At the Geneva Summit Conference in 1955, our leaders indulged themselves to the full in soft words, smiles, and geniality, to an extent we should perhaps like to forget now. And while all this was going on, the Communists were shipping guns to Nasser in Egypt to touch off new violence in the Middle East. The belief that soft words, or agreement for the sake of agreement, will make any change in the basic facts of international life is a folly which is incredible in this forty-second year of Russian communism.

Such thinking seems to be based on the belief that the great division in the world between freedom and slavery is caused by a great misunderstanding; that we do not really understand the Russian leaders; that they do not understand us; and that if we could only start understanding each other our differences could be resolved.

This insipid sentimentality flies in the face of four decades of history. The Russian leaders understand us only too well. Sometimes they understand us better than we understand ourselves. They understand us and seek ceaselessly to destroy us and everything we stand for. If we could understand them better we would quickly see that this is their sole objective.

Secretary of State Dulles dealt with this question in testimony before the House Foreign Affairs Committee on January 28 of this year, in words that I would like to quote now:

It would be easy to devise a form of words which could be agreed to between the United States and the Soviet Union and which would give many unwary people a sense of relief, and a feeling that our Nation need no longer make the effort and sacrifice that are now called for. The Soviet Government has, for a long time, been trying to get that result. It is, however, my deep conviction that the cold war cannot be ended in any such way and that to take that step would merely make it probable that the cold war would end in victory for international communism.

Mr. President, any artificial accommodation which gives the appearance of agreement without the substance is a dangerous folly that can only disarm us and send us to our doom, comforted, and reassured that all is well.

Another assumption which enjoys wide currency is the argument that a divided Germany threatens us with World War III. This assumption is usually accompanied by reference to Germany's responsibility for two previous world wars.

Such reasoning, I think, overlooks the basic source of tension in the world. World communism and world communism alone, threatens us today with world war. Germany can be no more than a pretext for war, if and when the Kremlin decides that it wants war.

There are some who fear that the proximity of Communist and free-world troops in Germany could give rise to an accident, or an incident, that would touch off war. They contend that the pulling back of atomic weapons and troops from this area is essential.

There is a danger always present when armed forces face each other across a thin line.

We should try, we are trying, and we will continue to try, through disarmament and other negotiations, to reduce and ultimately to remove this hazard.

But this is not the imminent and critical danger. It is the effect, not the cause, of Communist hostility.

We are willing, and indeed anxious, to reach a sound agreement on these questions. The Russians are not. So we come back to the esential point. It is the hostility of the Communists that threatens us with war.

If war comes this year—God forbid—over the Berlin crisis, it will come as a deliberate, calculated stratagem of Red aggression. Berlin is just another phase of their long-term plan to subjugate the free world. The Berlin question is just a pawn in their hands and will certainly not determine, of itself, whether there shall be peace or war.

There is, however, one circumstance which could give rise to a world war that no one wanted. If we, through the appearance of division, through weakness and lack of purpose, encourage the Communists to attempt some new act of aggression, this may well trigger off a war—a war for which we are tragically unprepared. The hazards of flexibility and vacillation are far greater than those of strict adherence to right principles.

The critics of our present Berlin policy argue that our position has failed for 14 years to bring either German reunification or free elections, and therefore, they say, it is a failure and should be reversed.

But we cannot put a time limit on how long we shall stick with a right policy.

Fourteen years is a short time in the history of freedom. The struggle between freedom and communism is not one of months or even years. It may be a matter of decades or of generations. It may be that generations of Americans will have to stand on the present line in West Berlin in order to prevent the Communists from standing on the Rhine River. Our enemies understand this, and it is about time that we do.

Permanent partition is preferable, I think, to Communist enslavement of West Germany.

Assuming that our German policy is morally right and practically sound, as I believe it to be, we must persevere in it with the same tenacity with which the Communists pursue their evil program for world domination; that long, and then one day longer.

Some of those who are demanding a new policy argue that Russian policy is based on a feeling of insecurity and fear of attack. They contend that if we would scrap NATO, pull back our defenses, and enter into mutual security arrangements which recognize and acquiesce in permanent Moscow control of the captive nations of Eastern Europe, then Russia would cease its aggressive acts, and a new day of peace would dawn.

How can this be true? Who threatens Russia with attack? Can we believe that the Communist rulers, who are able to decipher our most carefully guarded scientific and military secrets, could be so completely deceived about this question? Of course not. They know that we will never attack. They know it from our history, from the traditional attitude of our people. They know it from every newspaper in this country, from every issue of the CONGRESSIONAL RECORD, from every statement that bears upon this subject by any official in the land, from the highest to the lowest.

The historical truth is that Russian policy is based, not on fear of attack, but on a planned deliberate policy of world Communist domination and complete extermination of all that we represent. Failure to grasp this is to miss the central fact of the world we live in.

Finally there are those who contend that Russia is trying to force a solution of the German problem, because it fears another Hungarian-type revolt in Eastern Germany. This is an interesting thesis. Those who offer this argument contend that Russia fears such an uprising, because it would force Russia to take reprisals that might touch off World War III. Then they move on and conclude that Russia wishes to avoid this prospect and that we should help her avoid it by entering into agreements that would lessen the probability of revolts and, therefore, lessen the probability of general war.

This, at last, I think, brings us face to face with the basic issue of our foreign policy.

In my judgment, to make concessions which strengthen the Kremlin's hold over its enslaved peoples on the false assumption that we thus lessen the probability of general war is only to make certain a general war, one that we cannot win because we will have bartered away every position of strength from which to fight such a war.

One more concession may seriously sap the will of the enslaved peoples to resist. One more disaster may so shatter free-world confidence in our leadership that each ally will seek to save itself through some foredoomed accommodation with world communism.

Will we see a repetition of the 1930's, concerning which Winston Churchill said:

Each one feeds its neighbor to the crocodile, hoping the crocodile will devour it last.

The problem of Berlin is, of course, the problem of all free peoples everywhere. If we fail in this, what hope is there for all of the enslaved peoples now held in subjugation behind the Iron Curtain? If the Communists, with their capacity for ruthless organization, ever gain control of the vast resources of Germany and add those resources, that technical know-how, that skilled manpower to their own great power, they would at that moment become superior to the free world in economic strength, in industrial might, in scientific capacity, and in military force. That is something to think about.

No; we must stand firm, doing everything we can honorably and peacefully do to stimulate the dissolution of the Russian Empire, confident that constant internal troubles, springing from man's thirst for freedom, will prevent Russia from launching World War III and will eventually force the Kremlin to grant concessions to its peoples that will mark a decisive step away from tyranny and toward freedom.

I say we should stand fast; persevere in the truth; make Russia solve its internal problems through concessions to its captive peoples, and not through free-world concessions to their Kremlin masters.

There are, in my judgment, four ways in which Communist tyranny can be pulled down.

It can be pulled down by an attack from the West; but we rule out that possibility, and rightly so.

It can be pulled down by violent revolution. But the example of Hitler and the example of previous attempts at revolution convince us that under present conditions any such mass rebellion to be successful, requires an exceptionally favorable conjuncture of circumstances.

It can be pulled down, piece by piece, through the steady attrition of hundreds of millions of subjects who, in every way short of open and reckless rebellion, resist the evil philosophy that seeks to reduce them to mere beasts of burden.

And, finally, it can be pulled down by internecine warfare within the Communist high command, by a falling out of the thieves, which is made all the more probable by reverses in the world and continued resistance at home.

The third and fourth approaches to the dissolution of Soviet tyranny provide the policy which I believe the free world ought to be pursuing.

How do we increase the will to resist of the captive peoples behind the Iron Curtain? How do we increase the likelihood of another split within the Communist high command?

Certainly we cannot accomplish these ends by making it easy for the Russians to get through this difficult period. We can advance these causes only by sticking to our principles in Berlin and by making it crystal clear that we are prepared to face whatever consequences may follow from our action.

For more than a decade we have been living in an era of Communist advance through the device of partition. We have a divided Europe, a divided China, a divided Germany, a divided Korea, a divided Indochina.

The Chinese threat to Formosa and the Communist threat to West Berlin may signify that we have passed into a new era, one in which communism, having consolidated the gains made through partition, will now seek, through piecemeal aggression, to end partition and to make what is half free, all slave.

If that be true, we must meet this plot head on in Berlin.

To the end that the United States may approach this crisis united and determined to stand firm on basic principles, I submitted a resolution a week ago today. The resolution lists six basic principles upon which there is preponderant agreement, and from which there can be no retreat.

These principles are their own best explanation, and I should like to read them now:

(1) No plan or treaty calling for German reunification is acceptable which does not provide for a free government, ultimately freely selected by the people of West and East Germany.

(2) Until an acceptable settlement of the German reunification problem is achieved, the continued presence of Western troops in West Berlin, which has proved agreeable to the German people, is, under present conditions, essential.

(3) The interests of the free world and of the German people are better served by a free West Germany within the Western Community than by a superficially reunited Germany afflicted with a Communist East Germany.

(4) No plan of German reunification or confederation is acceptable which would join a free democratic West Germany with a slave Communist East Germany, except through the free choice of the peoples of West Germany and East Germany.

(5) Whoever may be in nominal control of East Germany, the United States should enforce its right of free access to West Berlin, in concert with its allies, by whatever means necessary.

(6) Recognition can only be accorded to an East German Government which is truly independent and truly representative of the wishes of the people of East Germany.

Mr. President, I believe that this resolution provides an expression of support for the policies of the President and Secretary of State that is needed and deserved, and that will strengthen their hand in these difficult days and in coming months.

My friend and colleague the Senator from New York [MR. JAVITS] submitted a week ago today another resolution which I commend to all. I was particularly impressed by his suggestion that there be appointed a group of Senators who personally would bring the encouragement of the United States Senate to the people of West Berlin, and who would be in West Berlin on May 27, as an unmistakable symbol of our determination to stand by our pledges.

Mr. President, the hour is late. Our friends in Europe already are discouraged by our appearance of division and vacillation. The dismayed reaction of West Germany's Adenauer and Brandt, of France's Poncet, of Belgium's Spaak, and of other staunch friends in Europe indicate the danger of this appearance of division in the face of the Communist ultimatum.

I ask, Mr. President, with all urgency, that the Senate Foreign Relations Committee promptly consider my resolution or Senator JAVIT'S resolution, or that it submit its own resolution, expressing the unity and determination of the American people to stand fast in Berlin. I believe it important that we do this now. I beg my colleagues in the Senate to act favorably and without delay.

Mr. President, I have not always agreed with our Secretary of State, Mr. Dulles. But I have always been thankful that this great man understood the essential nature of the conflict of our time. Mr. Dulles sees this conflict as a great moral struggle between the forces of good and the forces of evil. He has had the courage to describe it as such and to treat it as such in his official acts. This significant fact, more than any other, explains his impact upon world affairs and the sense of loss all of us feel at his tragic illness.

We live in an age so poisoned with the false doctrine of secularism and materialism that even God-fearing men seem strangely embarrassed and ashamed to acknowledge publicly the role of morality in international relations. John Foster Dulles deserves the gratitude of mankind, because he based his policies on moral ground; and because he has, through the example of his dedication and self-sacrifice, become a living symbol of a foreign policy that is morally right.

Abraham Lincoln believed that the Civil War was an inevitable consequence of the perpetuation of, and acquiescence in, the injustice of slavery, by both North and South.

Lincoln believed, and so stated again and again in his state papers, that continued and unredeemed violations of God's moral law led inexorably to catastrophe. If the continued acceptance of slavery for millions resulted in a terrible Civil War, what will be the result of the continued acceptances of slavery for hundreds of millions?

The Berlin question is more than a question of policy, of diplomacy, or of military posture. It poses an inescapable moral question.

With respect to almost every nation that has fallen victim to Communist aggression, there was one point in time, one occasion, when a courageous and vigorous free world policy based on the unselfish application of moral principles could have frustrated Communist aggression.

That point in time for the Ukraine was 40 years ago. For Poland it was 13 years ago. For China it was 10 years ago. For Indochina it was 5 years ago. For Germany it is today.

This may be our last chance to redeem our past errors. In a record filled with failures, compromises, and concessions that spelled slavery for millions of people, we have preserved one last outpost of freedom within the Communist slave empire.

That outpost is West Berlin. It must never be surrendered.

It may be that the Soviet tyrants mean what they say this time, and that our devotion to freedom and our determination to protect our own security is now faced with the supreme and ultimate test.

If that is true, this is no time to reexamine our principles. Our principles are right principles and need, not reexamination, but reaffirmation. It is our state of national preparedness which must be reexamined. Mr. President, I think we should embark today upon a 90-day program of the utmost urgency that will prepare the American people, the American economy, and the American defenses for whatever demands that may be made upon them.

If we are in fact facing the ultimate test, let us approach May 27 not as a divided people, seeking ways to avoid our responsibility, asking ourselves if the price of freedom is too high, resentful of our fate.

Let us, rather, approach this date as a united America, proud of our ideals and traditions, conscious of our great mission in the world, and confident that if we but act aright, the hand of God will sustain us to the ultimate victory.

[*Editor's note:* This was Senator Dodd's maiden speech in the Senate. TIME magazine treated it as a page 1 story. The speech and the bipartisan reaction it evoked in the Senate were generally credited with having dampened a growing sentiment for compromise and with having encouraged a firm Administrative reaction to the Khruschev ultimatum.]

Chapter VI

KHRUSHCHEV'S VISIT TO THE UNITED STATES— A PROTEST *

The long road to futility and failure, upon which man has journeyed for so much of his history, is marked with familiar tomb stones, such as the Munich Conference, which have come in popular thought to be regarded as separate, independent events, turning points which ushered in great periods of tragedy and defeat.

But historians recognize that events such as Munich cannot be rightly judged, of themselves, as clear turning points. They were rather the culmination of a whole series of less spectacular events, which led to and foreordained those tragic happenings which became symbols of an age.

The appeasement at Munich was foreshadowed by a whole series of lesser appeasements. The failure to oppose Nazi rearmament, the failure of courage, of sacrifice, of patriotism, the failure of the free world to rearm itself morally and militarily, the failure to oppose Hitler's march into the Rhine, the failure to oppose the seizure of Austria, the support given Hitler by free world industrialists and financiers, the deference and homage paid to Hitler by free world leaders, all these formed the pattern of which Munich was the logical and perhaps inevitable outcome.

I believe that in our own time we are repeating the same pattern of concessions to insatiable tyranny which 20 years ago reached the point of no return at the conference table in Munich.

---

* United States Senate, August 13, 1959.

For the past several years, our national policy has lacked the positive, virile, and resourceful characteristics that are necessary if we are to make progress against the Communists. We have not succeeded in projecting our system as the wave of the future. But while John Foster Dulles was at the helm, there was a steady and unyielding determination to avoid concession and appeasement.

While it cannot be said that we made forward progress, we did avoid appeasement. We held the line.

The role that Dulles played in resisting the forces of concession and compromise did not become fully apparent until his tragic illness and death removed him from the direction of affairs. Since his passing, there has been a slow but perceptible retreat. We are now observing the early examples of that retreat. It is imperative that we fight this trend at the outset. Tomorrow may be too late.

We have not yet committed a final, irremediable act of appeasement from which there is no return.

There is, therefore, hope that it can be averted and so long as there is that hope, I feel there is the duty to speak out, however unpopular or unwelcome my words may be.

I need not attempt to retrace the entire pattern of this mid-century appeasement; the record is sufficient to point up the danger.

On November 27, 1958, Communist Dictator Khrushchev issued an ultimatum to the United States, Great Britain, and France to get out of West Berlin or face the consequences of war.

Our immediate response to this challenge was one of apparent strength and firmness. But month by month, the Communists have chipped away that strength and firmness and a new pattern of appeasement has unfolded.

A most significant concession, a most striking retreat from previous policy, was President Eisenhower's invitation to Nikita Khrushchev to tour the United States as an official and honored guest of the American people.

The Khrushchev invitation was announced to the American people almost before there was any official indication that it was being contemplated. The President's swift and secret consummation of the Khrushchev visit was obviously aimed at preventing any opportunity for prior public discussion of the merits of such a proposal. Previous samplings of public opinion in this country had indicated that a considerable portion of the American people was flatly opposed to a Khrushchev visit. But there had been very little public discussion of the question and surely no organized attempt to stimulate public opposition.

If President Eisenhower's timing was designed to choke off public controversy, it was remarkably successful. The Members of Congress, suddenly presented with an accomplished fact, with only a few exceptions, either approved the President's action or remained silent.

The Nation's press was faced with the choice of either supporting the President's action or of appearing to embarrass and thus hamper the official foreign policy of our country.

The American people, confronted with exhortations to give Khrushchev a friendly reception, were propagandized into a position of either applauding the Communist dictator or of appearing to hinder efforts to "relax tensions."

The tens of millions of Americans who opposed the Khrushchev visit were, therefore, almost without spokesmen in the Congress and in the press of the United States.

The full measure of the triumph we accorded Khrushchev by inviting him to our country as a state guest can only be understood in the light of what happened at the Geneva Conference.

We said that we would not negotiate under ultimatum; but we have gone to Geneva twice without insisting on a formal retraction of the Khrushchev ultimatum which created the Berlin crisis.

We insisted that we would never recognize the East German puppet regime; but in according their representatives equal observer status with the West German representatives, we granted them a partial *de facto* recognition.

We said that our right of presence in Berlin derived from the occupation statute and could be terminated only by a treaty of peace with Germany; but we have now backed down to proposals which speak only of right of access, which make no mention of the occupation statute and our right of presence, and which, in effect, concede to the Kremlin the right to terminate or rewrite any Berlin agreement whenever it is so disposed.

We said that a solution of the Berlin impasse could be negotiated only as part of an overall German settlement, but we abandoned that concept and agreed to discuss Berlin as a separate question.

We insisted that the President would not go to a summit conference unless there were genuine progress at the Foreign Ministers' conference; but he agreed to White House summit meeting with Khrushchev nonetheless. Anyone else can describe it as he may, but I tell the Senators it will be a White House summit conference in fact.

There are many people who had misgivings about the Eisenhower-Khrushchev exchange but who felt that they should withhold judgment at least until after the Soviet dictator's visit. To these I would suggest that they look more closely at the fruits of the invitation—because these fruits provide us with a foretaste of the bitter harvest to come.

The invitation to Khrushchev was extended in early July, 1959. The first result of the invitation was that the Soviets became more demanding and more insolent in the negotiations at Geneva. In the first session they insisted that the question of Berlin be discussed by itself and not within the framework of the Western package, which provided for the staged reunification of Berlin and Germany through democratic processes. In the second session, which convened on July 14, 1959, *after* the invitation to Khrushchev had been extended, they not only insisted that we accept their terms on Berlin; they took the stand that they would refuse to discuss the question of Berlin unless we accepted their proposal that the four great powers abdicate their responsibility for the reunification of Germany and turn the matter over to an all-German committee in which East and West would be equally represented.

Even more disturbing than their stepped-up demands was

the personally arrogant manner of Soviet Foreign Minister Gromyko. Whereas during the first session, before the invitation, he had at least observed the diplomatic proprieties, in the course of the second session, after the invitation, he treated the Western Foreign Ministers with open contempt. It was, to put it mildly, a cat-and-mouse game in which the West was the mouse.

There were reports, according to the July 30, 1959 issue of the *Christian Science Monitor*, which I consider to be a responsible newspaper, that "Mr. Herter in recent weeks has lost all patience with and respect for the Kremlin's policy as executed here by Mr. Gromyko and has at times bluntly informed the Soviet Minister he will not tolerate the calculated Soviet denigration of the Western Foreign Ministers."

It is some consolation that Mr. Herter protested in strong terms. But the fact nevertheless remains that he did tolerate it and continued to tolerate it for 3 solid weeks.

This was the first fruit of our invitation to Khrushchev.

The second fruit was equally bitter, equally a portent. President Eisenhower, prior to announcing the invitation, had time and again stated that there could be no meeting at the Summit unless there were some progress at Geneva to justify it. In an effort to make things as easy as possible for the Russians, our definition of what constitutes progress was watered down until it was understood to mean nothing more than a retraction of Khrushchev's Berlin ultimatum. Personally, I would question this definition of progress, but for the purpose of this argument I am willing to let it stand. Instead of retracting his ultimatum, Khrushchev repeated it—without a deadline but in more threatening terms—in the joint statement he issued with Polish Communist Chief Gomulka on July 22:

If, despite the good will of the German Democratic Republic

by which, of course, he meant the East German Communist puppet regime

and other Socialist countries

meaning other Communist satellite countries—

liquidation of the abnormal situation in West Berlin is not effected, then

Poland and the Soviet Union will support East Germany in the measures which it may recognize as appropriate within the framework of its sovereign rights, to liquidate the abnormal situation in West Berlin.

The third fruit that matured in the brief interval after the invitation was issued was the invasion of Laos by guerrillas based in Communist China and Vietnam, with Vietnamese and Chinese participation. I believe that it is of more than passing significance that at the very moment of President Eisenhower's consent to a new meeting at the summit, Khrushchev thus brazenly reopened a crisis that was supposed to terminate with the signing of the Geneva Convention of 1955.

In all of these things I see unmistakable harbingers of the things to come, I read a portent of potential disaster unless we rally from the paralysis of understanding and of will which seems to afflict us.

Thus, the first objection to the President's invitation was that it represented a major diplomatic defeat and was recognized as such in the Communist and non-Communist worlds alike. To the uncommitted nations of the world, so often pictured as watching to see who is winning the East-West struggle, Khrushchev appeared the dominant personality in the world.

More compelling to me is the fact that the Khrushchev invitation was indefensible on moral grounds. Why is this so?

Vice President Nixon, in a peculiarly inept statement, has described Khrushchev as a man who "worked his way up from the bottom." Before we accept the Vice President's "rags to riches" summary of Khrushchev's career, let us get the facts into the record.

If Khrushchev's rise to power can be described as working up from the bottom, it should also be added that he did so through a singular career of murder, treachery, and betrayal.

Khrushchev first appears in history as a Communist official in the Ukraine in the early 1930's helping to direct the program of planned starvation which resulted in the death of 5 million Ukrainians.

In 1938 Khrushchev was appointed Communist chief in the Ukraine. He was appointed to that position as a reward for his previous ruthlessness and cruelty. His task was to direct the great Ukrainian purge of that year.

It is all a matter of history. I fear that some of our young people have never learned it. Some of our older people have forgotten it, and some of our leaders do not now want to remember it. Authorities on Ukrainian history estimate that 400,000 men, women, and children were murdered under Khrushchev's overall direction in that single year.

Perhaps a fully documented account of the purge in one of the districts of the Ukraine will give a graphic picture. I have the documentation. It is here, if anyone questions it.

Three months after Khrushchev rose to power in the Ukraine, 12,000 people were murdered in the small city of Vinnitsa; each of the victims was shot in the back of the neck —in some cases two or three times. They were thrown into mass graves. Their fate was unknown to their families and townspeople until the graves were accidentally discovered several years later.

The documentation on Vinnitsa is complete, with hundreds of photographs, reliable details of eyewitness accounts, and authoritative medical records. This is what Khrushchev did in one small city. The atrocities of Vinnitsa were repeated throughout the Ukraine.

He continued to rise in Communist ranks through his participation in other purges in the Ukraine, right up to the German conquest of that area in 1941.

Following the war, he was sent back by Stalin to direct the crushing of the resistance of the Ukrainian people to the reimposition of Communist rule.

We have lived in an era of totalitarian regimes, regimes which have perpetrated crimes on so gigantic a scale that people cannot comprehend them, crimes so often repeated that our sensibilities become fatigued and our reaction dulled. Many who would be shocked by an individual murder in their home town have come to accept organized murder, the organized annihilation of distant millions as a fact of 20th century life. And when these crimes are obscured by the passage of 20 years, many cease to respond altogether. I cannot explain this, but I know it to be a fact. Perhaps someday psychologists will be able to explain it. Nevertheless, it remains a fact in our time, and it greatly assists the Communists and all other totalitarian regimes in carrying out their plans.

If there are those who feel that the mass murder of thousands of human beings loses its relevance after the passage of 20 years, I point out Khrushchev's role in the massacre of the Hungarian patriots in 1956. Perhaps in this way I can help them to understand a little more clearly. If time is at the root of their trouble in comprehending, understanding, or reacting to crime on an enormous scale and distant in time, then let us take a recent period, 1956.

It was Khrushchev who in 1956 ordered the Red army to invade Hungary, depose the legal government of Imre Nagy, and ruthlessly massacre Hungarian civilians in all areas where there was open opposition. It was Khrushchev who invited the Hungarian commanding officer and patriot, Gen. Pal Maleter, to negotiations under flag of truce—historically, traditionally, from ancient times, a custom of honor—and once he got him under the flag of truce, he then had him arrested by the chief of the Soviet secret police, General Serov. It was Khrushchev who lured Premier Imre Nagy and his colleagues out of their sanctuary in the Yugoslav Embassy by perfidiously offering them an assurance of safe conduct and then kidnaped them as they emerged from the Embassy.

It was Khrushchev who in 1958 horrified the conscience of the free world by ordering the murder of General Maleter and Prime Minister Nagy after secret trials on fraudulent charges.

Nikita Khrushchev rose to Communist prominence as the hangman of the Ukraine.

He has maintained himself in power as the "butcher of Budapest."

He has on his hands the blood of countless thousands of

innocent people who were murdered under his personal direction.

He is responsible for the continued suffering of millions in slave labor camps.

He is the principal world spokesman for the ruthless attack on religion under which Cardinal Mindszenty, Archbishop Beran, and countless other churchmen of various faiths have been persecuted.

He is the sponsor of the dreadful persecution of Jews within the Communist empire. He maintains the iron grip of tyranny over a dozen captive peoples.

In addition to his personal crimes he is the principal representative of the system of concentration camps, mass murder, brainwashing, militant atheism, the organized promotion of falsehood and lies, and the planned ultimate enslavement of the entire non-Communist world.

This is the man whom the President invited to our country as an honored guest. This is the man to whom we were asked to extend all of our courtesies, our kindnesses, our tokens of honor and esteem, our symbols of approval.

To those who deny that a state visit by Khrushchev implied approval for Khrushchev by our Government and people, let me point out what was involved in such a visit.

I doubt that our people have fully comprehended what was involved, and I doubt that my colleagues in Congress fully comprehended what was involved.

The same edition of the *Washington Star* which published the account of the President's invitation to Khrushchev carried also a story about NATO in the 10th year of its existence. That story pointed out that the free world has never taken the necessary steps to build up NATO to the point where it could carry out its mission of defending Western Europe against Russian attack. The Western Alliance, despite repeated provocation by Stalin and Khrushchev, has an unbroken record of failure in reaching the stated goals of NATO strength. Even in the past months of tension over Berlin, there has been no perceptible buildup of NATO strength.

If our effort has proved unequal to the task even in periods of recognized danger, what will happen to free world defenses after the phony Khrushchev peace offensive has really gotten off the ground during his American tour? How bad will the danger get? How far can it go?

A few days ago the Secretary of the Army, Mr. Brucker, deleted from a major address those portions of his speech which realistically described the evil, aggressive nature of our Communist opponents. The Secretary of the Army of the United States wrote the truth in a speech and then took it out, presumably in an attempt to say or to do nothing which would be offensive to Mr. Khrushchev. This is the sort of thing which, repeated in a hundred different ways, will weaken our resistance, confuse our people, reduce their awareness of the danger, and therefore weaken the spirit of opposition to Communist aggression.

Perhaps nothing can do more to perpetuate a false feeling of security or to promote the mirage that everything will come out all right, than a visit by Khrushchev to the United States. It will be an easy thing for him to demonstrate glowing friendship, affable qualities, and peaceful intentions for 2 weeks.

But it will be a hard thing, and it will take a long time for us, to overcome these deceptions and the false sense of safety they will give to the American people.

Those who have been soft on communism will grow softer. Those who are unconcerned about the Communist menace will become even more indifferent. Those who have been sounding the alarms will find their difficulties multiplied. Those in the world who understand the nature of communism, and who have looked to the United States as the citadel of resistance, will become further discouraged. Advocates of the Khrushchev visit have advanced a number of reasons in its favor, reasons which I would like to discuss.

The most frequently quoted argument is that it is better to talk with Khrushchev than to fight a nuclear war with him. This is, of course, a complete *non sequitur*. Anyone trained in logic will not dispute my statement.

In the first place, we are not necessarily faced with either alternative, as the President has maintained for 4 years. Time and time again he has said that is not the position we are in and, of course, he has been correct. But now, all of a sudden, as a reason for inviting this Red tyrant to our country, this excuse, which the President has denounced for 4 years, is trotted out in support of the intention.

How much must our people learn, how much history must be written, how much tragedy must be revealed, before they will awaken to this awful, simple, all-important, supreme fact of our time?

The question of Khrushchev's state visit to America should not be confused with the question of the feasibility or the necessity for negotiation. I think this is an important point. I would not object to a meeting between Eisenhower and Khrushchev under proper conditions. I* hope I am realistic and practical; and I think I understand and recognize fully, as well as anyone else, the necessity for negotiations. But the point is that negotiations should never take place under conditions that imply concessions, under threats and conditions which imply approval of, or indifference to, Communist tyranny.

There are many who maintain that the complete failure of the Geneva conferences created an emergency which made President Eisenhower's invitation a necessity in a last great effort to avoid war. That is an intriguing thought. But can that be true? Have we already forgotten that the Berlin crisis was manufactured by the Communists, for the very purpose of forcing free-world concessions? To say that, in order to avoid war, we must yield to Khrushchev on the question of a summit conference, leads inevitable, in logic, to the conclusion that, to avoid war, we must reach an agreement with Khrushchev, and must choose between appeasement or surrender. Up to now, our policy has been based on the proposition that sufficient military, economic, political, and moral strength would deter the Communists from attack. But the Communists have already won half the battle, if we now adopt the philosophy that peace is dependent on agreements with Khrushchev, agreements forced by the threat of war or by threat of attack.

It is held that when Khrushchev comes here and tours this Nation he cannot fail to be impressed by the size and strength of our country and the determination of our people to defend what we have.

I feel that no brief visit, crowded with all the functions inherent in state visits, can give any visitor a real opportunity to assess the strength of our country, even if the visitor came with an open mind.

I suspect that Khrushchev, like other Soviet visitors to this country, will see here only what he wants to see. I am sure that he will not be impressed by tours of a few military bases or scientific establishments, even if he agrees to visit them. He is too used to staging guided tours and demonstrations of strength in Red Square to be impressed by them here.

We know that the Kremlin maintains constant surveillance of our magazines, newspapers, scientific journals, and statistical publications. The Kremlin has all that information. It is not hard to get. Khrushchev has at his fingertips exact information as to the capacity of our economy, the state of our scientific progress, and the status of our military strength. He can learn more about these subjects in a 2-hour briefing in the Kremlin that he can during a 2-week tour of the United States. I am confident that Khrushchev is already accurately informed as to the economic and military potential of the United States. There is every indication that he fully recognizes our industrial superiority. He talks about it all the time. As a matter of fact, he has publicly acknowledged it on many occasions.

Nor is the geographical size of this country likely to impress one who is used to traveling in the far larger Soviet Union.

He will doubtlessly be impressed by the standard of living here, the conveniences and the luxuries. But will he interpret them as signs of strength; or will he, with his cunning and canniness, interpret them as signs of weakness?

He may be impressed, not by the attractive features of our society, but by the absence of an effective civil defense program, by the absence of discipline, by the absence of dedication and sacrifice.

It is in the tradition of Communist dictators to mistake

friendliness for fear, to mistake kindness for softness, to mistake courteousness for submissiveness. That has happened time and time again. It is not only in the tradition of the Communist dictators; it is likewise in the tradition of all other dictators. Dictators have made those mistakes throughout history.

Will the American people appear to him as determined and strong, or will they appear as luxury-loving, frivolous and incapable of the sacrifices that his own people are forced to endure? We cannot know.

In any whirlwind tour of the United States Khrushchev is likely to see only what he wants to see and to carry home the impressions that he had when he arrived. There is just as much danger that his interpretation of what he sees here will encourage him in his aggressive designs as there is cause for hope that he will be discouraged, or that what he sees will deter him from his course.

It is often said that the free world can only gain from exchanges of this kind with the Communists and that if the price for having our President visit the Soviet Union is to have Khrushchev here, then the benefit is well worth the cost.

I dispute this. The Communist system is fully able to control any impressions that American visitors might make there. Any momentary personal triumphs which one or another of our representatives might score in various spots of the Soviet Union can be easily isolated and a variety of propaganda can be let loose to distort the words and actions of our visitors. The obstacles which were placed in Vice President Nixon's path, the planted hecklers, the distortions and misrepresentations of his words and acts prove this.

Four decades of Communist tyranny and propaganda have cowed the peoples of the Soviet Union, reduced them to fearfulness and docility, and robbed them to a great extent of the capacity for independent thinking. And above and beyond this, the actions of the Soviet Government are not governed by the moods or wishes of the people.

Everything is reversed in the United States. There is no attempt to control or distort the news accorded Communist visitors and there is no means to do so even if there were the will. These visitors are great novelties; they have tremendous news value and they are given every opportunity to make exactly the kind of impression they want to make. Their attempts to disarm the American people, to disguise Communist motives, to erode away our moral indignation against communism are carried out under ideal circumstances.

Their visitors, their exhibits are calculated to weaken the basic resistance of the American people to communism. The greater their success, the greater likelihood that more and more Americans will cease thinking of communism as a dread, monstrous tyranny which seeks to destroy all that we stand for and begin to think of it as just another way of life that differs somewhat from our own, but which has its own good points.

The further this false doctrine spreads in this country, the stronger will be the clamor for foolhardy unilateral disarmament, the greater will be the resistance to continuing sacrifices to maintain our strength, and the easier will be the path of Communist infiltration and subversion.

There are those who say that after Khrushchev comes here he may be convinced of the true desire of the American people and its Government for peace in the world. Does anyone seriously contend that the tensions in the world are caused by Khrushchev's honest doubt that America seeks peace?

If the long record of our deeds throughout the six decades of Khrushchev's life has not convinced him of the desire of the American people for peace, then I am sure that no 2-week visit will do so. We do not have to prove our peaceful intentions.

What we must avoid, rather, is a mistaken estimate by Khrushchev, that the American people are so peaceloving they do not have the will to fight for Berlin or for other free world territory and are prepared to surrender piecemeal rather than stand up against Communist aggression. Khrushchev knows the American people are peace loving. He is counting on that as one of the elements of weakness in the Western camp. There is no need to bring him here to find out what he already knows.

There is no need to encourage him to demand further concessions that the American people must not grant.

For all these reasons, I am raising my voice today against the invitation to this infamous Red dictator to ply his wares on American soil.

The Governments of Norway and Sweden recently invited Khrushchev to visit their countries. To Moscow, these little nations so close to Soviet Russia, so relatively defenseless against Communist might, with their long tradition of neutrality, must have appeared inviting targets for Khrushchev's softening-up policy. Yet a wave of public opposition to Khrushchev's visit swept these countries. The opposition was spearheaded by churchmen, prominent intellectuals, Nobel Prize winners, university professors, writers, and student organizations.

When it became obvious that Khrushchev's Scandinavian visit would result in a propaganda defeat, instead of the expected victory, Khrushchev abruptly called off the trip.

The world's spiritual leaders are beginning to be heard on this question. Bishop Jonzon of Sweden told his countrymen:

Inviting Khrushchev to our country is the same thing as letting the enemy through the frontline in a shooting war. Every word and action of his serves a definite purpose. It was shaking to see with what supreme skill Mikoyan played on every string during his visit to America—idealism, love of peace, sentimentality, naivete, sensation, vanity, business sense, mammon.

In our own country, Cardinal Cushing recently issued a statement which I would like to repeat:

In behalf of millions of people in Russia and in countries held in bondage and slavery under the tyranny of Khrushchev and company, who cannot speak for themselves;

In memory of the martyrs of Poland, Hungary, East Germany, and other countries murdered by the men of Moscow;

In honor of our American boys killed in Korea, shot out of the skies, and suffering in prisons;

I raise my voice against the proposed invitation to Khrushchev to visit our country and I call upon others who share the same sentiments to do likewise.

Mr. President, I wish there were more such voices raised, and I hope there will be.

I must confess that as my first session in the U.S. Senate

moves toward an end, I feel ever more strongly an unavoidable conviction that the Government and people of our country are not measuring up to the challenge of our age.

Faced with the clear need for a vastly enlarged national defense effort, we have come forth with an inadequate defense budget.

Faced with the necessity for a more vigorous and dynamic mutual security program, we have failed almost completely to make any substantial improvement.

Faced with startling Communist advances in scientific technology and in education, our own plans for the revitalization of our education have fizzled and died out.

Faced with the crying need to communicate an ideology around which the peoples of the world can rally, we have seen our Vice President in Russia, in his presentation of the American way of life, place primary emphasis upon the luxuries, the appliances, and the conveniences which our people enjoy. This is not the essence of America, as the New York *Times* pointed out last Sunday. The essence of America is freedom. We need leaders, we need spokesmen, we need representatives who understand freedom and who understand tyranny, and who can articulate with respect to both.

If our failure to meet these challenges continues, the eventual result will be defeat. But we hasten the day of that defeat when we go beyond failure to do the right thing and begin again to do wrong things.

Bringing Khrushchev to this country is a dreadful wrong.

It is bound to hurt us and the causes we represent. In the interest of salvaging something from this debacle, in the hope of limiting the harm wherever possible, I have some recommendations to make. I never believe it is enough to say "no" in the face of reality. I do not believe that the invitation can be withdrawn. I have no illusion that any such thing will happen. It will stand. It was issued by the head of our country, the President.

What can we do in the midst of this situation? First, the President should take up with Khrushchev the issue of the captive nations, pointing out to him that the American people will regard further agreements as meaningless until there is evidence that the Soviet Government intends to respect its past agreements. That is one thing we ought to do.

Second, our Government should insist on a clear-cut retraction of Khrushchev's Berlin ultimatum before we engage in further negotiations.

Third, all of the concessions offered by the West at the Geneva Foreign Ministers' Conference in the hope of obtaining an agreement should be considered null and void since the conference ended without agreement. Any future negotiations should have a fresh start.

Fourth, wherever possible, every attempt must be made by leaders of both parties who come into contact with Khrushchev to emphasize our firm resolve never to abandon the people of West Berlin.

Fifth, the American representatives and people who will meet Khrushchev during this tour should understand that their actions will be watched everywhere in the world.

The eyes of the world will be on us. What we do, what we say, how we conduct ourselves, will have an effect. Khrushchev must be accorded no ovations in the citadel of freedom. The conduct of the American people should be governed by restraint and dignity. It would be wrong for our Government to ask our people to pretend to an enthusiasm which violates their religious beliefs and political convictions.

Sixth, those officials who are charged with planning Khrushchev's visit should draw a clear distinction between Khrushchev and between the legitimate leaders of free nations whom we have welcomed to our shores.

I earnestly hope that this great body will never be disgraced by being summoned in joint session to hear Nikita Khrushchev address the Congress from the same rostrum which has so often been graced by the great leaders of our own country and by the decent God-fearing men who have come here from the other free nations of the world to receive the tribute and the recognition which they and their nations deserve.

I hope that during Khrushchev's visit we shall hear church bells in the land, tolling their remembrance for the murdered millions behind the Iron Curtain. I hope that there will be public observances of prayer for the deliverance of the captive nations. I hope there will be peaceful demonstrations of our dedication to that true peace which can only be achieved by spreading freedom and justice throughout the earth.

Let there be no cheers for the Red dictator, no crowds assembled to greet him, no flattery or flowers. Let our people be civil but silent.

Our Government has presented Khrushchev with an opportunity for a tremendous victory. It is my hope that the good sense of the American people will limit the proportions of that victory.

Chapter VII

ANTI-SEMITISM, THE SWASTIKA EPIDEMIC, AND COMMUNISM *

Last Christmas night, swastikas and anti-Jewish inscriptions were painted on the synagogue in Cologne. The incident was the signal for an epidemic of swastika painting on synagogues and Jewish institutions throughout Germany and the free world. There were incidents in almost every West European country, in the United States, Canada, and Latin America, and in Australia. Day after day for a period of weeks, the American press and the press in other countries carried headline stories on the swastika epidemic.

Freemen everywhere were horrified by the reappearance of this symbol of intolerance and persecution, under whose aegis 6 million Jews had been brutally murdered by the Nazi regime. At the close of the war in Europe, an incredulous world had recoiled from the fact of this crime: a crime that can never be completely understood, completely explained, or properly requited. Slowly, almost unwillingly, sadly, mankind moved to the acceptance of this terrible truth.

The reemergence of the swastika not only brought back to memory the most terrifying act of Nazi bestiality: it again posed the question of anti-Semitism before the conscience of the entire world.

For anti-Semitism is not a specifically German problem—it is a world problem. It exists both in the free world and in the Communist world, in all those countries where there are

---
* United States Senate, March 15, 1960.

Jewish communities and, for that matter, in many countries where the Jewish communities are tiny or nonexistent. It varies in degree and in quality from one country to another. In most countries of the free world it has been reduced to residual proportions. In other countries, it is a massive and current phenomenon. But its existence is something that must be combated, no matter what the degree or quality, because prejudice can lead to hatred; and hatred, unbridled, can lead us once again to a totalitarian Gehenna.

It must be combated because it contradicts the doctrine of universal love which is the heart of our religion and because it does violence to the foundation of our society.

It must be combated because, even in its milder forms, it constitutes a danger to our sanity and moral probity.

It must be combated because it is a tool of the Communist conspiracy.

It is a problem with many parts. To combat it effectively, we must view these parts in proportion, so that our actions may be governed by an intelligent assignment of our energies.

The need for a sense of proportion is something that cannot be overemphasized.

A sense of proportion is the key both to sanity and morality. In the world in which we live today, it may very well be a key to our survival.

Our everyday judgments, our code of morality, our legal system, our political decisions—all are governed, or should be governed, by our sense of proportion.

It is not enough to be able to distinguish right from wrong. There are many gradations of evil, and the civilized society distinguishes between them in its structure of laws. Similarly, it is not enough to be able to distinguish the beneficent from the harmful, the safe from the dangerous.

Without a sense of proportion we should find ourselves equating petty larceny with rape, measles with leprosy, a toy chameleon with a crocodile.

In the balanced mind, in the sane society, everything is scaled, everything has its measure or its value.

When an individual loses his sense of proportion, he can no

longer cope effectively with the problems of everyday life. When a nation loses its sense of proportion, it courts disaster.

In the light of our reaction to the swastika epidemic events, I wonder whether the free world has not already lost much of its sense of proportion, whether it is not suffering from some kind of mesmeric condition that has destroyed its capacity for judgment. If this is so, then the Kremlin's experts in psychological warfare have achieved a signal victory.

Now that the headlines generated by the epidemic have disappeared from our front pages, and now that the hysteria that accompanied them has died down, I believe we can learn much from a careful analytical postmortem.

What were the origins of this international rash of anti-Semitic incidents? Does the neo-Nazi movement really constitute a serious danger? Did the Communists instigate the epidemic or did they simply exploit it for cold war purposes? What effect has it had on the Western Alliance? Does anti-Semitism still remain a major problem? And, if it does, how does it manifest itself in various countries and at what points is the problem most acute? These are some of the questions we ought to try to answer.

But I believe the free world has most to learn from a self-analysis of its own reactions to the epidemic. I believe that such an analysis will reveal that, at the height of the outbreak, the free world was afflicted with an almost total collapse of its sense of proportion, so that, in our eyes, small dangers became big dangers while massive and imminent dangers were ignored; so that scattered violations of human dignity in country "A" made us roar our protest at the top of our lungs, while, in country "B," violations of human rights and human dignity a thousand times as grave and ten thousand times as numerous commanded our total silence.

We would be less than human if we did not react with indignation to the persecution of the Jews in any country. My argument is that our indignation, to be meaningful, must also be governed by a sense of proportion; and it was not so governed at the time of the swastika epidemic. I do not argue for less indignation; I argue for more indignation, for indignation that responds in proper measure to every crime and every injustice.

In country "B"—the Soviet Union—there are some 3 million Jews. In a land where all minorities are persecuted, they are the most persecuted of all minorities. They have been the victims of a policy that can only be described as physical and cultural genocide. They are without political representation, without community organizations, almost without religious or cultural rights and without opportunity for higher education or employment.

Summing up the plight of the Soviet Jews, the Anti-Defamation League of B'nai B'rith said in 1958:

> The prospects for Soviet Jewry are dire and gloomy: at best, the extinction of a once-flourishing and rich cultural tradition and life; at worst, the completion by the Communists of the heinous work begun by the Nazis—the liquidation by forcible assimilation of this community of 3 million Jews.

Between the brutality of Soviet anti-Semitism and the brutality of Nazi anti-Semitism, there is little to choose. About all that is lacking so far in the U.S.S.R. is the gas chambers. For this deficiency, the Communists have made up, at least in part, by employing Siberia and the firing squads as substitute instruments of death.

The crimes that have characterized Soviet anti-Semitism have not been perpetrated by hotheads or juvenile delinquents.

They have been perpetrated, or else instigated, by the Soviet state itself, first under the command of Josef Stalin and then under the command of the present Prime Minister, Nikita Khrushchev. In my opinion, this fact makes these crimes a thousand times more damnable.

How does the free world react to the merciless persecution of the 3 million Jews in the Soviet Union? It closes its eyes to it. Instead of protests and indignation, we witness demands for increased trade with the Soviet bloc, for stepped-up cultural exchange programs, for State visits by the Soviet terrorist in chief.

In country "A"—Germany—there are some 30,000 Jews who enjoy complete freedom of religion, complete equality before the law, complete acceptance. While there is a residue of anti-Semitism from the terrible days of Hitler, the Government has done its utmost to combat this residue and to make restitution to the Jews for their suffering under nazism.

Suddenly there is a rash of swastika smearing and of other minor acts of vandalism, perpetrated, for the most part, by juvenile delinquents. No Jew is physically assaulted, no Jewish building seriously damaged. The Government moves with the utmost vigor to punish those responsible. The press, pulpit, and political parties join in unanimous condemnation of the hate smearers.

And how does the free world react to this situation?

Overnight, the West German democracy was placed in the pillory, rendered suspect, morally isolated from its Western allies, and this in the critical period preceding the summit conference.

The reaction was strongest in Great Britain. Forty thousand Londoners marched in a protest parade; German maids were dismissed by their employers; orders for German goods were demonstratively canceled by a number of British concerns; and some editors even suggested a reexamination of Germany's role in the Western alliance.

In our own country, although the reaction was milder and more mixed, the swastika campaign brought a flood of protests from U.S. editors, from Members of Congress, and from religious leaders. "The fact that acts of anti-Semitism can take place under present circumstances," said one of our most respected newspapers, "is a clear indication that the sickness still lurks deep in the German soul."

One of my old colleagues in the House said that it was high time the President and Congress considered whether our massive economic and military assistance is making a contribution to the sad events in Germany.

It is to the eternal credit of the Jewish leaders that they kept their sense of proportion while so many people, who had far less reason to fear the reemergence of the swastika, were losing theirs. Heaven knows, no Jew could have been blamed for reacting strongly, even excessively, to the news of the swastika epidemic. Instead, the recognized leaders of the Jewish community, in this country and abroad, spoke with statesmanlike restraint and balance. By their sanity, by their morality, by their abjurence of vengeance and hatred and racism, they showed an example to the entire free world.

Dr. Nahum Goldmann, president of the World Jewish Congress and Premier David Ben-Gurion of Israel, both told their coreligionists that the record of the Bonn Government toward the Jews was beyond reproach and that it would be nazism upside down to hold the German people guilty in perpetuity for the crimes of the Hitler regime.

Mr. Ben Epstein, director of the Anti-Defamation League of the B'nai B'rith, in an interview over the German radio on January 14, rejected the theory that some international Nazi organization was responsible for the epidemic. He said that while two members of the neo-Nazi party had been responsible for the original incident in Cologne, the epidemic which followed was essentially a wave of imitative behavior by juvenile delinquents and other irresponsible elements.

Dr. Hendrik G. van Dam, president of the Jewish community in Berlin, in an article entitled "Anti-Semitism Without Jews," assailed "the merciless anti-Germanism" in other countries and the tendency to seek any evidence in support of a collective judgment of the German people, and he warned against those journalists who "attempt to prove that the Germans never change, that the Federal Republic, therefore, is not fit to be a member of an alliance, and indeed cannot be trusted."

But in the general hysteria that existed for several weeks, these voices of reason were swallowed up. Only the most assiduous readers of the press noticed them.

The swastika epidemic was something that lent itself intrinsically to sensationalism, and the democratic press cannot be blamed for treating it as a matter for page 1 reportage. But in doing so, in my opinion, it served, unwittingly, as a vehicle for a Soviet campaign of saturation propaganda.

After several weeks of swastika headlines and exaggerated reactions, the threat of world communism and the Berlin crisis became items of minor importance in the public mind. If the headlines and the hysteria could be taken as a guide, the real menace confronting the free world was not Communist aggression, but the revival of nazism and anti-Semitism in Germany.

Encouraged by the reaction of the free world to the swastika incidents, the Communists propaganda apparatus had a field day. No charges were too extreme, no language too extravagant. *Pravda* on January 8, for example, charged that "this organized racist campaign had been launched as if at a signal given by Adenauer" and it said that its purpose was to "clear the road for a wide propaganda in favor of a nazi ideology, openly fascist."

The following day the Communist German radio charged that the entire campaign had been organized by the West German office of psychological warfare under the direction of Defense Minister Strauss.

The orgy achieved its peak on February 1, when Mr. Khrushchev wrote in an open letter to Chancellor Adenauer: "People are prosecuted in your country for their thoughts, for their progressive ideas. You actually occupy the same position occupied by Hitler." It would be difficult to find a comparably insulting letter from one head of state to another, even on the eve of war.

The purpose of all this propaganda was obvious. It was designed, very simply, to further isolate West Germany, to further divide the Western Alliance, and to soften our policy, by appealing to our still vivid memories of Nazi brutality. In particular, it was designed to appeal to the people of Britain, where anti-nazism is frequently combined with a strong general dislike of Germans and Germany.

The ultimate goal of this propaganda is the city of West Berlin.

GERMANY'S POSTWAR RECORD

The questions of neo-nazism and anti-Semitism in West Germany have been posed, and these questions can only be answered by a detailed evaluation of Germany's postwar history.

Anti-Semitism, the Swastika Epidemic, and Communism

As executive trial counsel at the major Nuremberg trial, I had spread before me in nightmarish detail the whole incredible story of Nazi barbarism and of its fiendish persecution of the Jewish people. Almost equally incredible, was the story of how this party of madmen and fanatics had achieved power over a nation of 70 million people, and enslaved their minds and warped their characters.

To those of us who were close to the problem in the immediate postwar period, the problem of denazification seemed almost insurmountable. How could tens of thousands of administrators be dismissed, and an administration still be maintained? How could minds be purged of the Nazi virus and a sense of morality and civic responsibility restored? How could teachers be found so that the new generation of Germans could be schooled in dedication to the ideals of democracy? There were many of us who felt at the time that the restoration of Germany would be a work of generations.

I have seen the bottom of the abyss from which the German people had to come; and, for my own part, I cannot help marvelling that they have traveled so far in so short a period of time. There is still much to be done. There are certain hard unpleasant facts that must be confronted. But when we compare the Germany of today with the Germany of yesterday, there is every reason for optimism and confidence.

For the great progress that has been made, I believe that Germany and the free world will remain eternally indebted to the statesmanship and humanity of Chancellor Konrad Adenauer and of men like Mayor Brandt of Berlin and his predecessor, Mayor Ernst Reuter. But one leader or a few leaders by themselves could not explain the rate of recovery in Germany. The fact is that there were in Germany far more anti-Nazis and non-Nazis than we had been inclined to believe.

For more than a decade now, West Germany has had a freely elected parliamentary regime, a free press, and a free society which is watchful of individual liberties.

In successive elections, at Federal, State, and municipal levels, the overwhelming majority of the German voters have given their support to the Christian Democratic Party or to the Social Democratic Party. Both of these parties are completely dedicated to democratic ideas, are staunchly anti-Nazi, liberal in their approach to social problems, solidly pro-Western in their orientation. Of the long list of splinter parties, the largest is the Free Democratic Party, which in 1958 won the backing of 7.7 percent of the electorate. These splinter parties are also, for the most part, essentially democratic in orientation, some of them liberal, some of them middle-of-the-road, some of them conservative.

The one significant exception, the German Reichspartei, is neo-Nazi in outlook, and is led by a group of diehard ex-Nazis. But it has a national membership of only 13,000 and obtained only 1 percent of the vote in the last election. This means that it has no representation in parliament, because under German electoral law, a party must obtain a minimum of 5 percent of the popular vote before it is given representation. In addition, there are half a dozen other ultranationalist reactionary splinter groups which, between them, were able to obtain 1.32 percent of the total vote.

On the basis of the electoral record of the past decade, it is obvious that there remains a core of unregenerate Germans who are prepared to vote to resurrect the past. But it is a very tiny core, representing no more than about 2.5 percent of the total electorate.

The important thing is the trend. Before the Nazi Party came to power, it obtained an increasing percentage of the German vote in successive elections: 18.3 percent in 1930, 37.1 percent in 1932, 44.2 percent in March 1933. Has the trend since the end of the war been toward a revival of Nazi extremism, or toward the parties of moderation? Here, I believe, the proof is conclusive: In 1949 the Christian Democratic Party and the Social Democratic Party between them polled 60 percent of the vote. In 1953, the figure rose to 74 percent, in 1957 to 82 percent.

These, in my opinion, are the basic facts, the central criteria, in appraising Germany's political evolution since the end of the war.

What remains to be done?

EX-NAZIS IN GOVERNMENT: EAST AND WEST

There is still a problem of former Nazis in government. The Jewish organization, the B'nai B'rith, speaks of some 900 of them, of whom several hold high office. This is a relatively small number compared with the scores of thousands of Nazis who were dismissed from office; but it is still reason for concern. There is also a number of ex-Nazis who hold positions of importance in private life as editors, writers, publishers, bankers, and industrialists.

It is proper that the problem of ex-Nazi officeholders should be openly discussed by the West German people and by their allies. But it becomes a trifle outrageous when Khrushchev and his German quislings mount their pulpits and prate self-righteously about ex-Nazis in the West German Government.

In Communist Europe there was no process of denazification. In East Germany and in every European country where the Communists have taken power, they have opened their ranks to the most vicious Nazis and Nazi collaborators. Their past was no handicap; quite the contrary, for the dirty work which the Communist regime had to do, a gangster past constituted a decided recommendation.

I have in hand a documentation compiled by the Investigating Committee of Free Jurists in Berlin. In it are listed some hundreds of former Nazis who now hold important posts in the Communist government of East Germany, or in its armed forces. Here are their photographs, their Nazi party numbers, the record of their date of entry into the Nazi party, the lists of their awards and decorations from the Hitler government. In it you will find such names as that of Dr. Kurt Schumann, president of the East German Supreme Court; Siegfried Dallmann, chairman of the Law Committee of the People's Chamber; the chief editor of the official Communist theoretical periodical "German Foreign Policy," Hans W. Aust; and a long roster of political leaders, leading judges, officers, publicists, and educators.

When the Berlin Jurists Association first printed its list of ex-Nazis in the service of communism, the German Communists—unable to deny the truth of the charges—replied with the assertion that all of these people had realized their past political errors and had developed into "upright democrats and fighters for peace." By this they mean to say that these people have now become Communists. Such a statement I would not be prepared to dispute. For a Communist to become a Nazi or a Nazi to become a Communist requires no real transformation. They are blood brothers.

PROBLEMS OF DENAZIFICATION

In West Germany, as a result of the denazification process, the apparatus of government was purged of virtually every Nazi who was personally guilty of crimes against humanity. In an operation which involved scores of thousands of people, it was inevitable that there should be some errors of judgment. A number who were guilty escaped punishment, while some who were innocent were wrongly punished. But, in general, the denazification courts made exceptions only for those former Nazi Party members who could prove that they used their positions for anti-Nazi purposes, or that their party membership was a simple formality necessary to protect their positions or livelihood.

On the basis of the evidence I have seen, I am inclined to believe that while there is still a fair amount of house-cleaning to be done, many of the ex-Nazis at present employed by the West German Government have demonstrated their innocence. Each case must be considered on its merits; no sweeping judgment could possibly be fair.

About Refugee Minister Oberlaender and Interior Minister Schroeder I have serious doubts. They were not personally involved in any crimes against humanity; Oberlaender, in fact, has voluntarily submitted himself to an examination by a committee of former resistance fighters. Both men have strongly opposed the neo-Nazi movement. But the fact remains that they did belong to the Nazi Party and not to the opposition. In the case of Dr. Hans Globke, secretary of the Chancellor's office, however, I have examined a documentation which completely persuades me of the man's innocence.

The story of Dr. Globke illustrates how exceedingly complex

the business of making judgments can be. The Communists raise his name at every opportunity. They charge that he was co-author of a legal commentary on the infamous Nuremberg racial laws. This is true. This information in itself would predispose most decent people against Globke. How, they would ask, could such a man be innocent?

In the terrible politics of our time, men have frequently been confronted with choices that torture the soul. If one sees an opportunity to serve the cause of freedom in the ranks of the Nazi movement, does one reject the opportunity because it is morally repugnant, or does one accept? It is not an easy choice; and if one accepts, it is not an easy thing to explain or live down. In fact, during World War II more than one resister posing as a collaborator was shot down by fellow re-sisters to whom his identity was unknown.

As a functionary in the Ministry of the Interior, Dr. Globke was given the task of preparing a legal commentary on the Nuremberg law. He was not a Nazi; he was by tradition a devout Catholic who abhorred the brutality and godlessness of the Nazi regime. The specific choice which confronted him was whether to resign and leave the drafting to some fanatical Nazi, or to assume the responsibility and draw up the com-mentary in a manner which would leave the greatest number of loopholes for Jews, half-Jews, quarter-Jews, and one-eighth Jews. In a torment of conscience, Globke at one point came to Cardinal Konrad von Preysing, then Bishop of Berlin, and suggested that he resign his post. The Bishop urged him not to resign because he was in a position to render invaluable services to the anti-Nazi cause.

The loopholes existing in Globke's legal commentary were effectively utilized by thousands of German Jews, many of whom have written letters in his defense. Among other things, according to this testimony, Globke served as their chief go-between with the Ministry of the Interior. Dr. Wal-ter Jellinek, a Jewish professor at Heidelberg University, has written to him: "You belong to the very few men of the Hit-ler era whom I remember with gratitude and with pleasure."

Under Secretary of Justice Walter Strauss, himself a "non-

Aryan," has stated that he can prove Globke saved the lives not only of thousands, but of tens of thousands of German Jews. Dr. Jacob Kaiser, chairman of the Christian Democratic Party and a veteran of Hitler's concentration camps, has testified that Globke played a key role in the anti-Nazi resistance from the beginning of the war, that he helped draw up plans for the overthrow of the Nazi regime, and that he had been slated to take over the post of Minister of Education if the plot of July 20 had succeeded. Cardinal von Preysing has testified that over and above his fundamental opposition to nazism, Globke always "sought to obstruct or prevent unlawful actions and acts of injustice and violence on the part of the Nazis to the fullest extent possible to him." And there are many more such testimonials from people of unimpeachable anti-Nazi records.

Perhaps the most important testimony comes from Dr. Hans Gisevius, Allen Dulles' chief contact with the German resistance and author of the book "To The Bitter End." Dr. Gisevius has stated repeatedly that few people rendered more decisive services to the resistance than Globke. I met Gisevius during the course of my duties in Nuremberg, and like everyone else who met him, I was enormously impressed. Perhaps better than any other man he knows the moral dilemma which confronted Globke because he himself served the resistance in the ranks of the Nazi secret police.

I have been greatly impressed by the fact that, as a result of the growing body of evidence in Globke's defense, key Jewish organizations concerned with the German situation no longer list his name among the ex-Nazis whose presence in government they consider suspect.

This has been a rather long digression. But since Dr. Globke has been wrongly accused not only by the Communists but by uninformed Western editorialists, I wanted to take advantage of this opportunity to set the record straight.

RESTITUTION AND REEDUCATION

There have been many articles in the Western press dealing with the continuing prevalence of anti-Semitic attitudes among the West German people, the inadequate treatment of the Nazi era in German history textbooks, the unwillingness of the older generation to confront or speak openly about the so-called recent past, the ignorance of German youth concerning the crimes of the Hitler era.

There is a good deal of validity to these criticisms.

But on checking back through a number of such articles I have discovered that, almost without exception, they have been based on public opinion polls or studies conducted by German organizations or on articles or statements by prominent German educations and political leaders. This demonstrates, in my opinion, that there are substantial numbers of Germans who understand the weaknesses in their society, who are doing their utmost to expose them, and who are endeavoring to devise remedies. The severest critics of the weaknesses in West German society have, in fact been the West German people themselves. This is as it should be in a democracy. What is more, it proves that the West German system, despite certain weaknesses, is essentially healthy.

According to a report shortly to be made public by the American Council on Germany, there is a growing trend in West Germany toward public castigation of what happened during the Nazi period. The trend is becoming more and more evident in the press, in the TV programs, in the movies, and, most important of all, in the schools.

"It has taken 15 years," says the report, "but this year marks the beginning of a really noticeable awareness of Nazi crimes and a determination to bring them out into the open, to examine the developments which led up to 1933 and to answer the demanding questions of this generation of youth about the period in their country's history which they did not know."

The report quotes instance after instance of new school programs designed to teach the terrible truth about the Nazi era to German students. It also describes the rapidly expanding program of adult education now being conducted by the Institute on Current Events, the People's High Schools, and other bodies.

87

The horrors of the Hitler regime are also being brought home to the German people by the series of so-called concentration-camp trials involving former camp directors. These trials have been front-page news throughout the German press. In general, I am not a believer in gory details when it comes to newspaper reporting. But in this case I believe the German press has rendered a service by its detailed and graphic reporting.

Incidentally, the Bonn Government has been so assiduous in tracking down Nazi criminals and bringing them to trial that hundreds of Nazis have fled the country. Certainly no Nazis with criminal records have dared to return to their fatherland. In Egypt, alone, there is a colony of some 600 Nazi refugees from anti-Nazi Germany, where many of them are working hand-in-glove with Communist agents in spreading anti-Semitic propaganda and exacerbating Arab-Israeli relations. Those who believe that West Germany is some kind of paradise for former Nazis, might do well to ruminate on the meaning of this inverted historical situation.

Among the older generation, who supported the Hitler regime either through their action or inaction, there has admittedly been a tendency to forget the past or at least not to talk about the evils of the past. Frankly, I do not find this surprising. It is only human to want to put painful memories out of one's mind. But even this older generation has given many evidences of understanding and of contrition. Indeed, it has been remarked that the hundreds of thousands of Germans who came to performances of "The Diary of Anne Frank," sat through the play in a stunned silence more eloquent than any spoken repentance.

But most indicative, in my opinion, of the vast progress Germany has made was the reaction of the German people to the incident at Cologne and the rash of anti-Semitic incidents which followed it. The rabbi of the Cologne synagogue received thousands of wires and letters from individual Germans, expressing their personal indignation and their shame. The Protestant churches, the Catholic bishops, the trade unions, the student and youth organizations joined in condemnation of the desecrations. Virtually every newspaper in the country thundered editorially against the delinquents and criminals who were fanning the evil embers of the past and thus defaming their country, and they demanded the most stringent measures against them. In Berlin, 15,000 students marched in an anti-Nazi protest demonstration. So great was the public pressure that even the Mutual Society of SS Veterans adopted a resolution threatening expulsion of anyone guilty of an anti-Semitic act. The Federal Government and the Land governments acted with the utmost vigor to track down the perpetrators and to punish them.

On January 20, Prof. Carlo Schmid, vice president of the Bundestag, made a remarkable statement to the Bundestag in the name of all four parties. I quote one paragraph from this statement:

It is a disgrace that this could happen in our country. This disgrace is not mitigated by the fact that in other countries, too, walls have been smeared with swastikas and abuse of the Jewish people. We Germans have no right to point our fingers at others. It is true that in other countries there has been ruffianism under the sign of the swastika; but in our country 6 million Jews were murdered in the name of this symbol. For this reason, what has happened in Germany during these weeks is a greater disgrace than it would be elsewhere. And for the same reason, our reaction against it must be stronger and must proceed from greater introspection.

When Professor Schmid concluded his statement, the entire Bundestag rose and applauded enthusiastically. No more significant statement of contrition has ever been spoken in a parliamentary body.

The attitude of the German Government on the question of restitution provides perhaps the most concrete evidence of its determination to extirpate the evil vestiges of the past and somehow atone for the terrible crimes that were committed in the name of the German people.

When they are completed, Germany's payments of restitution and reparations to Jewish victims of nazism and to the State of Israel will total almost $6 billion. Dr. Nahum Goldmann, president of the World Jewish Congress, has declared that Israel has received more money from Germany than from all the Jews in the world put together.

Germany's commitment to pay restitution was entirely voluntary. This in itself is remarkable. Indeed, I believe it is unique in history. But Germany's restitution program is remarkable in many other ways.

It is remarkable because the commitment was made not at a time of general prosperity, but in the year of 1951, when the Government was still attempting to cope with the gigantic problems of reconstruction and with the equally gigantic problem of the 9 million refugees and expellees from the Soviet zone.

It is remarkable for a generosity that refused to be limited by an already generous initial commitment. As Dr. Goldmann pointed out, Germany's restitution payments will amount to two or three times as much as the figure German and Jewish experts had originally agreed upon.

It is remarkable because this onerous voluntary burden was assumed by unanimous vote of the Bundestag, with the complete support of the German press, with the backing of a clear majority of the German people, and in defiance of a threatened Arab boycott of Germany.

This is Germany's postwar record.

THE ORIGINS OF THE EPIDEMIC

Who was responsible—what was responsible—for the swastika epidemic? The white paper issued by the Bonn Government has, I believe, presented a frank and careful analysis of the epidemic. The white paper found that, of the 234 culprits apprehended, 8 percent had clear records of either neo-Nazi or Communist association, while 24 percent acted out of subconscious Nazi or antidemocratic motives. The German police uncovered no evidence to prove that the outbreak was controlled or centrally directed. On the other hand, the white paper made it clear that the neo-Nazi movement could not escape moral responsibility for the individual actions of its members.

It had been suggested by sources both inside Germany and

abroad that the entire outbreak was the work of the Communists, bent on discrediting the Adenauer government. The white paper found that, once the epidemic got underway, the Communists got in on the act. Of those apprehended, at least seven had proven records of Communist affiliation. Members of Communist youth organizations were found smearing swastikas and pasting up anti-Semitic placards, and agents of the East German police were found operating in Berlin and in some of the neo-Nazi organizations. But it found no proof of Communist masterminding. On the basis of the evidence available, the West German authorities concluded that the epidemic was essentially the work of nonpolitical elements —of hoodlums and juvenile delinquents.

I believe the German white paper did the right thing in bending over backward to avoid any accusation that could not be conclusively substantiated. I cannot escape the feeling, however, that the evidence of Communist involvement unearthed by the West German authorities tells only a small part of the story. And I am surprised that there should have been people who felt that somehow the charge of Communist instigation constituted a heinous libel against the Kremlin.

The specific charge that the Communists instigated the swastika epidemic may not be provable. But, from a strictly legal standpoint, is it libel to suggest that a many-times convicted rapist may be guilty of still another act of rape, or that a notorious forger and perjurer may have pulled off another act of deception? Where a crime of a specific type has been committed, is it not common procedure in every country to suspect those criminals whose records show a long list of crimes that are similar in purpose and method?

Whether or not the charge was intrinsically libelous depends on whether or not the Kremlin has a record of collaboration with Nazis or Nazi elements or a record of anti-Semitic instigation which might be relevant to the charge. Such a record does exist: and what a long and terrible record it is.

History records that when the League of Nations imposed economic sanctions against Fascist Italy in an effort to hamper or, if possible, prevent its rape of Ethiopia, the Soviet

Government stepped into the gap and provided Mussolini with vast quantities of oil and other commodities essential to the conduct of his war.

History also records that when the Nazi Party in 1931 called for a plebiscite to oust the democratic government of Prussia, the Communist Party voted with the Nazis, even though the ousting of the government would have brought the Nazis to power.

History also records that in 1939 the Soviet state concluded a treaty with Hitler which made it possible for Hitler to unleash his war against the West; that this treaty contained secret annexes providing for the division of Europe between Nazi Germany and Soviet Russia; that at the signing of this treaty, Stalin toasted Hitler with the words, "I know how much the German nation loves its Fuhrer"; that Molotov gloated over the dismemberment of Poland with the shameful words, "One blow from the German Army and one blow from the mighty Red Army, and this ugly duckling of Versailles ceased to exist."

History also records that until the Soviet Union itself was invaded, the Communist Parties throughout the world did their utmost to support the war efforts of Nazi Germany and to obstruct and sabotage the war efforts of the Allied democracies; that Walter Ulbricht, the present head of the East German Communist Party, said to his followers on November 23, 1939: "Not only the Communists, but also many Social Democratic and National Socialist workers regard it as their task not in any circumstances to permit a breach of the pact. *(By this he meant the Hitler-Stalin pact).* Those who intrigue against the friendship of the German and Soviet people are enemies of the German people and are branded as accomplices of British imperialists."

History also records that the Kremlin turned over to Hitler's Gestapo certain German Communists who were on the Nazi wanted list. Among those thus turned over was Margarete Buber-Neumann, widow of the German Communist leader, Heinz Neumann, who had been executed by Stalin in 1937. Not even the limited, perverted sense of honor that is customary among thieves was evident in this practice.

History records that the Soviet regime has practiced anti-Semitism in its own territory, has engaged in a genocidal campaign against Jewish culture, has exported anti-Semitism to its satellite countries, and is currently employing the anti-Semitic motif in its broadcasts to the Arab countries. The Kremlin has conducted, and is conducting today, an anti-Semitic propaganda strongly reminiscent of Goebbels and Streicher and that infamous forgery 'The Protocols of the Elders of Zion." The general theme of this propaganda is that Jewish bankers and Zionists have combined with the American capitalists and imperialists to plot an attack against the Soviet Union and that Jewish religious and humanitarian organizations are all agents of American intelligence.

How can one possibly "libel" a government with such a record! That the Kremlin is morally capable of having instigated the swastika epidemic is, therefore, indisputable; and while moral reputation does not constitute proof, it does constitute justification for suspicion.

If we accept the finding of the white paper that the outbreak was essentially a psychological epidemic, I feel that the Kremlin still deserves a much larger share of the blame than the white paper has attributed to it. An epidemic is caused by a virus. The swastika epidemic may have been caused in part by the latent virus of anti-Semitism which exists in small pockets in Germany. But since the end of the war the chief breeding place of the virus of anti-Semitism has not been Germany nor has the chief instigator been the neo-Nazi movement. The chief breeding place has been, and remains today, the Soviet Union. The chief instigator is the international Communist movement.

No one can tell me that the Soviet state can encourage internal anti-Semitism on a massive scale, and can direct its exportation to the satellite countries and to the Arab world, without somehow spreading the infection to the peripheral areas. In this sense, even accepting the psychological epidemic theory without reservation, the Kremlin bears an inescapable moral responsibility.

THE RECORD OF SOVIET ANTI-SEMITISM

There should be no secret about Soviet anti-Semitism. The terrible ordeal of the Jewish people under the Kremlin's rule has been painstakingly set forth and documented in a whole series of studies by scholarly authorities. In addition to several full-length books on the subject, there have been studies by the American Jewish Committee, the Anti-Defamation League of the B'nai B'rith, the Jewish Labor Committee, the authoritative Jewish magazine, *Commentary*, the internationally respected weekly, *The New Leader*, the Select Committee on Communist Aggression of the 83d Congress, and by the Senate Subcommittee on Internal Security. Scattered over a period of 2 decades, moreover, there were some dozens of carefully researched articles in newspapers like the New York *Times* and New York *Herald-Tribune* and in magazines like *Life*.

But for some strange reason, the terrifying story of the persecution of the Jews under communism has not penetrated the public consciousness of the free world.

Perhaps the scholarly studies were too esoteric, too limited in distribution.

Perhaps the newspaper and magazine articles were too scattered and infrequent to be effective.

Perhaps the Jewish communities in the Western countries did not speak up as loudly as they should have for fear of further endangering their coreligionists behind the Iron Curtain.

Perhaps our minds are conditioned far more than we ourselves are prepared to admit by the most powerful and most subtle propaganda apparatus the world has ever known.

Whatever the reason may be, I am convinced from many conversations that, in the public mind, anti-Semitism is far more closely identified with Germany than it is with the Soviet Union. I do not blame the public for this. I try to be a reasonably assiduous reader. I was aware before I began preparing this analysis that anti-Semitism existed on a very substantial scale throughout the Soviet sphere. But as I checked through the available documentation, I found myself constantly appalled.

Anti-Semitism, the Swastika Epidemic, and Communism

I was appalled by the totality of Soviet anti-Semitism, by its utter ruthlessness, by its doctrinal and practical similarity to Nazi anti-Semitism. I was even more appalled to discover how little I knew, how little my friends knew, about this terrible crime against humanity which has been going on for more than two decades now.

Let me set forth here the full record of this crime.

For many years after the Bolshevik revolution, it was commonly believed, by conservatives as well as liberals, that, despite all its evil features, communism did not practice discrimination on racial or religious grounds. It was equalitarian in the sense that all men, regardless of race or religion, were equally persecuted. Personally, I question this conception of equalitarianism; but there were, and still are, many people who seem to see some peculiar virtue in equality of persecution.

The myth that all men are equal under communism remains to this day one of the Kremlin's chief propaganda weapons in its appeal to the Negro, Jewish, and other minorities in this country, to racial minorities in other countries, and to the colonial peoples.

The fact is that the Soviet Union is a gigantic prison house of nations where minorities have been persecuted and exploited, and where genocide has been a common instrument of state police. It is an imperialist empire which, for its cold-blooded ruthlessness, has no equal in history.

The fate of the Jews under communism is most illustrative.

The treatment of minorities, historically, may be considered a gage of social and moral progress; and in modern times, it has become a gage of social sanity. Wherever minorities have been oppressed in Europe, the Jews have generally been among the first to suffer and they have often suffered the most acutely. This is so because they are dispersed and more helpless, and because differences of custom and religion and the survival of ancient prejudices make them convenient scapegoats for despotic regimes.

On the specific question of anti-Semitism, the Communist

leaders, in the early days, made some very strong statements: "Anti-Semitism," said Stalin, in an interview with the Jewish Telegraphic Agency of America in January 1931, "is an extreme form of racial chauvinism, is the most dangerous survival of cannibalism. Anti-Semitism as a phenomenon hostile to the Soviet system, is severely punished by law. Active anti-Semites are punished by capital punishment under the laws of the U.S.S.R."

Thus spoke Stalin in 1931. But, in reality, anti Semitism is as inherent in Marxist totalitarianism as it was in Nazi totalitarianism. Karl Marx himself was, in many of his statements, as virulently anti-Semitic as Goebbels. Over the decades, the Communists have done their utmost to conceal this fact. Marx's translators into English and the European languages carefully eliminated his anti-Semitic diatribes from editions of his books and writings. But the proof exists.

I have in hand the first English translation of the unexpurgated papers of Karl Marx on the so-called Jewish question. It was printed only last year. In it, you will find that Marx referred to the distinguished German Social Democratic leader, Ferdinand Lasalle, whom he considered too moderate, as, I quote, "Judel Itzig—Jewish nigger." In another letter, Marx made the statement: "Ramsgate is full of Jews and fleas." In still another statement he said, and I quote again: "Emancipation from usury and money, that is, from practical real Judaism, would constitute the emancipation of our time."

This was not Hitler speaking. It was the recognized ideological father of Soviet communism. This was Karl Marx.

The persecution of the Jews in the Soviet Union can only be understood within the context of the Marxist ideology and of the Kremlin's broad general policy toward all minorities.

In the period immediately after the revolution, when they were still endeavoring to consolidate their regime, the Bolsheviks attempted to purchase the support of the national minorities by preaching the freedom and equality of peoples. The appointment of native Communists to party and Government posts was encouraged. The use of the various minority languages, which had been restricted under the czar, was also encouraged.

By the early thirties, Stalin had achieved absolute power. At this point, the toleration and encouragement of national cultures gave way to a massive campaign against the languages and cultures of all the national minorities.

The development of a totalitarian state requires total-conformity, it requires the reduction of all peoples to a single norm. The Russian language was selected as the instrument for the new cultural straitjacket because it happened to be the language of the largest national group and was the most widely spoken.

In the Ukraine, for example, Russian was again made the main language of instruction in almost 80 percent of the universities. Ukrainian specialists and scientists were assigned to other areas of the Soviet Union while increasing numbers of Russian specialists and scientists were imported into the Ukraine.

The apparatus of government was ruthlessly purged of all those who were suspected of the sin of bourgeois nationalism. Ukrainian intellectuals, party leaders, and administrators were the chief targets of this terror. The terror reached its zenith during 1937-38 when, it is estimated, some 200,000 persons were executed in the course of 1 year. I have documentary evidence concerning the massacre in the city of Vinnitsa alone of 12,000 persons; and there is evidence that similar massacres occurred at many other points in the Ukraine.

The man in charge of the Ukraine during this period, I might point out, incidentally, was a certain N. S. Khrushchev, who last summer was invited to visit our country as an honored guest.

What happened to the Ukrainian people happened, with variations in pattern and degree, to all the other national minorities in the Soviet Union.

The imposition of Russian Communist control was even more marked in the case of the minor Moslem nationalities of central Asia. In all of these central Asian Republics, Russians held the key posts in the ministries of security and of the interior and, in general throughout the apparatus of party and government. In the so-called autonomous Kazakh Republic, for example, native Kazakhs, according to a report published in 1948, held only 2 percent of the administrative posts in the ministries of local industry and public health; 4 percent in light industries; 6.7 percent in textiles; and so on down the line.

The Negro in America unquestionably suffers from serious restrictions on rights and opportunities. He is now on his way up. But in the darkest days after emancipation, he enjoyed far greater rights than do some of the Asian minorities in the Soviet Union today.

In certain respects the persecution of the Jews and of Jewish culture in the Soviet Union has been even more severe than that endured by other minorities. Physically their persecution is on a par with that of the Ukrainians. In terms of denial of opportunity, their treatment is even worse than that of the Kazakhs. Culturally, their persecution is total. Instead of being permitted a restricted representation in the apparatus of party and government, the Jews today are virtually excluded from all administrative positions of any importance. While all religion is persecuted and regulated, the Jewish religion is persecuted with particular ruthlessness.

Why is this so? I can think of several reasons. First of all, there is the fact that the Jews have both their own religion and their own national culture; this makes them eligible for persecution on both scores.

Secondly, the rulers of the Kremlin have apparently suspected them of mass disloyalty to the Soviet state. This is not surprising, for no Jew could be expected to enthuse over things like the Hitler-Stalin pact or Moscow's incitation of the Arabs against the State of Israel.

Perhaps even more important, the great majority of the Russian Jews have relatives in America. This makes them suspect, in Khrushchev's eyes, of harboring pro-American sympathies.

Finally, Communist anti-Semitism, like czarist anti-Semitism, exploits the Jew as a scapegoat—a convenient outlet for popular resentment which might otherwise be directed against the regime.

A major shift in Soviet policy toward the Jews first became apparent in 1937-38. Zinoviev, Radek, and a few of the other old Bolsheviks who were liquidated in the great purges of the thirties had been born Jews. Of course, they could no more be considered Jews than Stalin and Khrushchev could be considered Christians. But there is reason to believe that in Stalin's paranoid mind, party opposition to his one-man rule somehow became identified with the accident of Jewish birth.

Perhaps more important, there seemed to be a growing possibility of a deal with Hitler. If this deal were consummated, every Jew in the Soviet Union would have to be considered an enemy of the regime.

Surreptitiously, the Soviet Government began to encourage anti-Semitic propaganda. Secret directives went out to the civil service to restrict recruitment of Jews and to demote or remove many of those who held office. Jewish schools and newspapers and community organizations were forcibly closed down. Thousands of the Jewish communal leaders were physically liquidated.

The Nazi invasion of the Soviet Union did not persuade the Kremlin to abandon its persecution of the Jews. Jews in the Red Army fought heroically against the Nazi invader and, in many cases, rose to fairly high rank. But Stalin by this time apparently shared Hitler's psychopathic hatred of the Jews. The result was a policy of passive cooperation with the Nazi enemy in permitting their extermination.

When Hitler invaded Russia there were more than 5 million Jews in the Soviet Union proper and in the territories it had annexed under the Hitler-Stalin pact. More than 3 million of these vanished during World War II. Scores of thousands of those who vanished were victims of mass deportations to Siberia. The great majority, however, were captured by the Nazis and perished in their infamous extermination camps.

But the question arises: How is it that more Jews were not able to flee before the Nazi army? How is it that the Nazis were able to capture virtually intact the large Jewish communities in so many cities in Soviet territory?

Jewish organizations in this country are convinced that the Soviet Government did nothing to facilitate the evacuation of the Jews from areas that were threatened by the Nazi army, even though they knew the fate that awaited the Jews under Nazi occupation. According to eyewitnesses before the House Select Committee on Communist Aggression in 1954, those Jews in the occupied territories who succeeded in escaping did so by fleeing individually or in small groups through the swamps and forests. They testified that Jews attempting to flee from threatened areas en masse or in large groups were turned back by Soviet guard units.

The attitude of the Soviet press during the war also deserves some comment. The Kremlin editorialists could find no words strong enough to denounce Nazi inhumanity. But they spoke always of "crimes against Soviet citizens." The systematic extermination of the Jews by the Nazis was, apparently, a crime that did not call for special mention or display of moral indignation.

For several years after World War II, Soviet policy toward the Jews continued to manifest two faces. In its propaganda to the free world, the Kremlin continued to pose as an opponent of anti-Semitism and all forms of racial discrimination. At home, the persecution was intensified. In increasing numbers, the Jews were forced out of administrative positions. Public hostility toward them was encouraged by a hundred subtle devices.

During the period of Soviet occupation, at least 40,000 Jews were deported to Siberia from Hungary alone and many thousands more were deported from Rumania.

Other terrors awaited the Jews of the satellite countries. In the immediate postwar period the Communists did not yet have complete control of these countries. They were either in the process of consolidating control or preparing to seize power. What more convenient smokescreen could there be for them, what more effective diversion, than a campaign against the Jews, with a few old-fashioned pogroms thrown in?

In Poland during the course of 1946 there was a whole series of murderous attacks on Jews which cost several hundred Jewish lives. In the pogrom at Kielce alone, 41 Jews were killed by a mob, while the Communist militia stood idly by, or else arrested the Jews.

In Czechoslovakia there was also a series of bloody anti-Semitic incidents. The Communists tried to blame these incidents on the Fascists, but there is considerable evidence that they themselves instigated them. The Communist Minister of Propaganda during this period, Vaclov Kopecky, referred to the Jews in his statements as "those bearded Solomons" or "this Jewish scum." In this propaganda he was abetted by the present Prime Minister of Czechoslovakia, Antonin Zapotocky.

In Hungary, local Communist leaders organized bloody attacks on the Jewish people in the cities of Miskolcz and Kunmadaras. According to the testimony of Dr. Zoltan Klar, a Hungarian Jewish leader, and of Mr. Irving Engel of the American Jewish Committee, the Communist police did nothing to prevent the riots and in many cases they protected the instigators. Those responsible for the riots, moreover, were never punished.

But in 1948 Stalin apparently became impatient with the limited, gradual anti-Semitism of the previous decade. The cold war had sharpened. Tito had defected from Soviet control. The Jews of the Soviet Union and the satellite countries had shown unconcealed enthusiasm over the establishment of the State of Israel. In the warped mind of Stalin this situation called for an all-out offensive against everything that might be considered a "foreign" or "Western" influence. Anything which suggested adherence to a non-Russian group was automatically guilty of "bourgeois nationalism;" and friendship for anything outside the Soviet Union was stygmatized as "cosmopolitanism."

In the fall of 1948, with one sweeping administrative decree, Stalin and his cultural commissar, Andrei Zhdanov, completely eliminated what remained of Jewish cultural and communal life in the Soviet Union. Nominally, the campaign was directed against the Zionists. Of course, everyone who considered himself a Zionist had long previously perished in Stalin's concentration camps. In reality, the new Soviet anti-Semitism was directed not against Zionism, but against everyone of Jewish origin, even if they were Communists.

In this respect, I see nothing to distinguish the anti-Semitism of Stalin from the anti-Semitism of Hitler.

At one stroke, all Jewish schools were closed. Jewish newspapers were shut down. The Yiddish publishing house, Emes, was also closed. The Jewish Anti-Fascist Committee in Moscow was dissolved and its leaders arrested. More than 450 Jewish writers, artists and intellectuals—the cream of the Jewish intelligentsia in the Soviet Union—were executed.

Despite restraints and persecution, Russia under the czar had been the world center of Yiddish culture. In the early period of cultural tolerance, the Soviet Union had the largest number of Yiddish schools in the world, the greatest number of Jewish pedagogical institutions, the only Jewish institution of higher learning in Yiddish, and Yiddish departments in many universities. There were 4 Yiddish state publishing houses and 14 state theaters. And there were 35 periodicals and newspapers, 4 of them dailies.

Some of these institutions and publications had ceased to exist during the anti-Semitic purges of 1936-38. Others had ceased to exist during the war. But with the Zhdanov decree, everything ceased. Where there had once been a flourishing Jewish culture, there was now a desert.

One year after the Zhdanov decree, in September 1949, there took place the first of a whole series of spectacular Communist show trials involving Jewish defendants. The scene of this first trial was Budapest. The chief defendant was the former Minister of the Interior, Laszlo Rajk.

Rajk himself was not a Jew. In fact he was generally considered anti-Semitic. He had used his post to instigate the pogroms in Miskolcz and Kunmadaras, or else to protect those Communists who had instigated them. Three of Rajk's co-defendants, in this trial, however, were Jewish, and they were forced to sign confessions that they had served as Zionist spies. These so-called Zionist spies had, according to the charges, conspired with America, England, and Tito's Yugoslavia to overthrow the Communist Government.

To the accompaniment of an ominous propaganda about the "world Zionist conspiracy," Rajk and his chief codefendants were sentenced to death.

A few years later, it was the turn of Czechoslovakia. In November 1952, there took place the great Prague trial of Rudolf Slansky, former secretary-general of the Party, and his alleged confederates. In this trial, 11 of the 14 defendants, including Slansky, were Jews. To make sure that this fact was not missed by the public, the official indictment bore the words, I quote, "of Jewish origin", after the name of each Jewish defendant.

As Communists, it goes without saying, all of these defendants had long previously renounced their Jewish religion and they were violently opposed to Zionism. This apparently was not considered any serious obstacle by the professional brainwashers who prepared Slansky and his colleagues for their appearances in court.

The trial, from the first, was an obscene anti-Semitic orgy. The defendants confessed that they had been participants in a worldwide Jewish conspiracy operating in the service of American and British imperialism. For variety, their conspiracy was sometimes referred to as a "capitalist-imperialist Trotskyist-Titoist plot." Involved in this plot, if one were to believe the confessions, were former U.S. Secretary of the Treasury Henry J. Morgenthau, Mr. Bernard Baruch, Israeli Prime Minister David Ben-Gurion, and the Yugoslav Communist leader Moshe Pijade.

All of the evils of the Communist regime and all of the suffering of the Czechoslovak peoples were charged to the account of Slansky and his codefendants and their American and British masters. They confessed to planning the disorganization of the Czechoslovak economy, to contriving artificial scarcities of food and fuel, and the inflation of the national currency. The commentaries of the Czechoslovak press, referring to the Jewish defendants, employed such adjectives as "huckstering," "profiteering," "bloodsucking," "Judases," "scum with a dark past."

On November 28, 11 defendants, 8 of them Jews, were sentenced to death by hanging. The sentences were carried out a few days later.

There is a footnote to the stories of the Rajk trial in Hungary and the Slansky trial in Czechoslovakia. In the fall of 1956, after Khrushchev's denunciation of Stalin's crimes, it was announced that the Rajk trial had been a frameup from beginning to end and that the confessions had been extorted. The rehabilitation of some of Slansky's codefendants implied a similar admission.

What a commentary on the practice of justice under communism!

Needless to say, the Slansky trial was accompanied by a wholesale dismissal of Jews from all public office. The trial also served as a signal for a further intensification of the campaign of official anti-Semitism throughout the Soviet empire. This campaign reached perhaps its lowest point in the infamous "Moscow doctors' plot."

On January 13, 1953, the Soviet Ministry of Internal Security announced that nine prominent doctors, six of whom were Jews, had been arrested on the charge of murdering two Politburo members, Andrei Zhdanov and Alexander Scherbakov, by medical mistreatment. They were also accused of having attempted the murder of a number of top-ranking officers of the Soviet armed forces. The arrested doctors, said the Kremlin, had all confessed that they had carried out their crimes on orders of the world Zionist conspiracy and that these orders had been transmitted from Israel by the American Jewish Joint Distribution Committee.

According to the American Jewish Yearbook for 1954, the so-called doctors' plot resulted in a universal orgy of denunciations, demotions, and arrests of Jewish citizens throughout the Soviet empire. All this, it said, was accompanied by a barrage of propaganda designed to prove that all Jews were apt to be traitors, spies, imperialist agents, embezzlers, and outright murderers.

On March 5, 1953, Stalin died. The public campaign against the arrested Jewish doctors and against the Jews ceased. On April 4 the Ministry of the Interior made the startling announcement that the doctors' plot had been a frameup; the evidence had been falsified and the confessions extorted. This seemed to be a step in the right direction. It caused many people to hope that, with Stalin's death, anti-Semitism in the Soviet sphere had also perished.

Everything that has happened since 1953, however, proves conclusively that Moscow has never abandoned its anti-Jewish campaign.

In Moscow the 13 doctors were released, but this was the only concession granted. The thousands of Jews in prison remained in prison. Zionism remained illegal. Jewish culture and communal life and Jewish emigration remained under total ban, the Jewish religion under a near-total ban. And the basic charges made in the Slansky trial and in the Moscow doctors' plot were repeated and repeated until they achieved the status of articles of faith for all Communists.

Two weeks after the Moscow doctors were released, on April 16, 1953, the head of the Czechoslovak delegation to the U.N., Foreign Minister Vaclav David, upheld all the charges that had been made in the Slansky trial and reiterated the accusation that the Zionists and other Jewish organizations were hotbeds of American sabotage and espionage. Soviet Foreign Minister Andrei Vishinsky backed his Czechoslovak protege to the hilt on this occasion.

In Czechoslovakia, Hungary, and Rumania, the rash of anti-Jewish show trials continued for more than a year after the release of the Moscow doctors. In Czechoslovakia alone there were four such trials between May of 1953 and April of 1954. The last of these trials, which took place in Bratislava, had a new twist. None of the defendants were Jewish, but they were charged with the crime of having protected Jews or having failed to punish them.

These show trials, involving amalgams of Jewish and non-Jewish Communists, received considerable international publicity. The persecution of the Jewish community leaders and

Zionist leaders unfortunately, received far less publicity. Litterally thousands of these leaders had been imprisoned in the satellite countries, in particular in Czechoslovakia, Hungary, and Rumania, during 1948 and 1949. During the course of 1953-54, some hundreds of these were brought to trial, charged with Zionist activities and aid to Jewish emigrants.

These trials were secret, but some of the details inevitably leaked out. Writing in the magazine "Commentary," Peter Meyer reported that in the spring of 1954 the secret trials in Rumania reached such numbers as to constitute a mass terror. Not less than 100 Jewish leaders were tried and sentenced in one month, he said. One of the trials involved 22 members of a Socialist Zionist youth group. Its leader defied the Communist court with these words: "You have tortured and killed many of our members in your dungeons. This crime will never be forgotten." He and his comrades were all sentenced to 20 years in prison.

The 5-year period that followed the Zhdanov decree of 1948 is remembered by the Jews of the Soviet Union as "the black years." The facts about this period were documented as early as 1951 by the Jewish scholar, Dr. Solomon Schwarz in his book, "The Jews in the Soviet Union." But despite such documentations and despite the blatant anti-Semitism of all the show trials that took place during this period, the Kremlin was able to pretend to its followers in the free world, as late as 1956, that there was no anti-Semitism in the Soviet Union.

Even high-ranking Jewish Communists, who should have had access to the facts, assured their followers, and assured themselves, that the charges of anti-Semitism made by Jewish organizations were slanderous fabrications.

In February 1956 there took place the 20th Congress of the Communist Party of the Soviet Union, at which Khrushchev made his famous denunciation of the crimes of the Stalin era. A slackening of control inevitably followed this speech. In his speech to the party congress, Khrushchev said nothing about the persecution of the Jews. But shortly after the congress, on April 4, 1956, the Polish Jewish paper *Folkshtimme* confirmed the fact that the hundreds of Jewish writers who

106

had disappeared in the wake of the Zhdanov decree, had been executed.

To the scattered Jewish following which the Communist Party still maintained in the free world, the article in *Folkshtimme* struck a shattering blow. Some of the most eloquent condemnations of Soviet and anti-Semitism have been written by former Jewish Communists and by official Communist Party delegations who went to the Soviet Union to check on the facts. Their eyes were opened by what they saw.

I want to quote a few paragraphs from one of the many revealing articles that appeared in the world Communist press during the period of disarray that followed these revelations. These paragraphs are extracted from the report of a delegation of the British Communist Party to the Soviet Union and they were printed in the London Communist weekly *World News* in October, 1956:

For some years prior to the death of Stalin, rumors began to spread that all was not well in the Jewish field, and that well-known Jewish writers and intellectuals had disappeared. Then came the revelations of the 20th Congress, and later, specific charges in the *Folkshtimme*.

Naturally these charges created consternation and bewilderment in the ranks of Jewish Communists in all countries, so that it became a matter of urgency and of importance to expose their truth or falsehood.

The first piece of concrete information came from a visit to the Lenin State Library. Here there exists a Yiddish and a Hebrew section. It turned out that there is nothing in Yiddish later than 1948, when publication of Yiddish papers and journals must therefore have ceased.

The Soviet Encyclopedia, which in its 1932 edition devoted about 160 columns to the Jews, reduces this in the 1952 edition to four columns. The biographies of many eminent Jews had been removed. Marx was no longer referred to as a Jew.

The first task, therefore, was to meet a few Jewish writers and to examine their reactions to this. Official requests to this end were made, but we were informed that this was not possible as they were all on holiday, while Halkin (a Jewish writer who survived), who was at home, was too ill to receive anyone.

Then came the discovery from private conversations by Comrade Levy with Jews that the years 1948-52 were known among them as "The Black Years," the period during which many Jews were dismissed from their posts, Jewish poets and writers were arrested and charged with treason and executed, Yiddish disappeared from the street and market place, the population closed up together, becoming tense and nervy, and young Jews who might otherwise have merged with the general population and have forgotten that they were Jews, awoke to a new sense of unity in distress.

But let it be said that this fear did not emanate from any general feeling of antagonism from among the Russian population, but from official or quasi-official sources; from the security police, in fact.

This report, I want to emphasize was written not by critics of the Soviet regime, but by members of the British Communist Party.

The furor which such articles caused in the world Communist movement resulted in a few minor concessions. In the course of 1957, for the first time since the revolution, the Jews were permitted to establish a small theological seminary in Moscow. Permission was also granted for the publication of a small number of prayer books in Hebrew, for the staging of some Yiddish music recitals, for the printing of a few works of Yiddish writers in Russian translation.

But this is as far as the concessions went. Despite repeated promises to Communist delegations which visited the Soviet Union after 1955, the reestablishment of a Yiddish theater and Yiddish press and Yiddish publishing house was never permitted. Instead, there was an accelerated discrimination against Jews in public life, in the national economy and in the educational field.

The Jewish population of the Soviet Union represents approximately 1.4 percent of the country's total population. In 1958, only 3 of the 1,336 members of the Supreme Soviet— one-fourth of 1 percent of the total—could be identified as Jews. On a per capita basis, this would signify that the Jews had only one-sixth the political representation to which they were entitled.

So far as is known, no Jew is to be found in the foreign service, among the higher ranks of the armed forces, or in the various military academies. Jews are also excluded from leading posts in the Communist Party, from the central party newspapers and the foreign section of the Soviet press. Jews are progressively being excluded from admission to the universities.

The facts which I have just listed here were part of a statement issued by the American Jewish Committee in conjunction with their meeting with First Deputy Premier Anastas

Mikoyan in January 1959. Since that time, there seems to have been a further deterioration in the position of the Soviet Jews.

What is the situation today in the Soviet Union? Let me list only a few items from the current catalogs on Soviet anti-Semitism that have been compiled by the *New York Times,* the *New York Herald Tribune,* the *New Leader,* and other publications.

A few months ago the synagogue in the town of Malachovka near Moscow was set on fire.

The synagogues of Chernovtsky, Bobruisk, Korosten, Baranovich, Kharkov, Novoselitsa, Orenburg, Chernigov, Staline, Babushkin, and other cities have been closed down by the security authorities.

In the city of Kharkov, where there are 70,000 Jews, there is not a single synagogue to serve their religious needs.

The synagogue at Voronezh has been taken over by the authorities for use as a grain warehouse. The Jewish community has been unable to raise the money required to redeem it.

In Yevpatoriya, in the Crimea, the authorities confiscated 25,000 rubles raised by the Jewish community to rent a building for a synagogue.

Deprived of synagogues, the Jews have attempted to pursue their worship in private prayer meetings. Such prayer meetings have been reported forcibly dispersed in the cities of Kharkov, Olevsk, Tula, Bobruisk, Vitebsk, and other places. In Vitebsk the Jews were threatened with 10 years in prison if they resumed their meetings.

In Bendery, Baranovich, Minsk, Kishinev, Voronezh, and Kiev, Jewish cemeteries have been desecrated and memorials defaced.

In Kiev, Kharkov, Kuibyshev, Rostov, Kishinev, Odessa, and Lvov, a ban was imposed on the baking of matzoh, the unleavened bread which plays a central role in the Passover observance. To my mind, there could be no more pitiless or more pointless deprivation than this.

For the Jewish population of almost 3 million, there are

only 60 rabbis in the whole of the Soviet Union. Their average age is well over 70. In the case of the Orthodox religion in Russia, there is 1 priest for every 5,000 faithful. This is bad enough. But in the case of the Jewish religion there is only 1 rabbi for every 50,000 Jews. With virtually no replacements in sight, the situation is bound to become worse over the coming years.

The Orthodox church and the Moslem religion have been permitted to maintain a number of seminaries. The only Jewish seminary permitted is limited to an attendance of 20 students. Patricia Blake, in her article in Life magazine last December, has described how these 20 students pursue their studies in the corners of the Moscow synagogue, because no space has been made available for their seminary.

The teaching of Hebrew remains under the ban imposed at the time of the revolution. In the 40 years of Soviet rule, no more than several thousand Hebrew prayer books have been printed; only several hundred distributed.

Openly anti-Semitic books and publications are appearing with increasing frequency. The villains in this literature all adhere to a single stereotype. They all have unmistakably Jewish names; they are all moneygrubbers, without human feeling, dishonest in their relations with the state and their fellow men.

Whether a Jew is religious or non-religious, whether he is pro-Communist or anti-Communist, he has no way of escaping the fate which the Soviet regime has ordained for his people. The word "Jew" is stamped on his internal passport—the document which is the key to a man's existence in every Communist country. This inscription is not intended as a religious identification because the members of no other religious groups are thus identified. The Soviet internal passport does state the nationality of the bearer; but the Kremlin apparently does not recognize the Jews as a nationality because it refuses to grant them the most elementary communal rights enjoyed by the smallest and most primitive national groupings in the U.S.S.R. The marked passports of the Soviet Jews serve only one purpose: the same purpose served in its time by the yellow badge which the Nazis compelled the Jews to wear for the purpose of self-identification. To every factory manager, to every university president, to every party bureaucrat, to every minor official, it constitutes a directive to treat the bearer as a member of a hostile and inferior breed; it constitutes a command to hate and to persecute.

As I was winding up the work on this analysis, I received a communication from a group of professors of the Social Sciences Division of Fairleigh Dickenson University, who had toured the Soviet Union last summer. Appalled by the many evidences of Soviet anti-Semitism, they wrote letters last November and December to 10 leading Soviet educators and editors, including Aleksei Adzhubei, editor of *Izvestia* and son-in-law of Nikita Khrushchev. Their letters pointed out that the Jews do not appear to enjoy the rights guaranteed by Soviet laws and professed by the Communist philosophy, and they asked for a detailed explanation of this anomalous situation. To date only one Soviet editor has deigned to reply. The reply said that their letter had been forwarded to somebody else.

In their letter to me, the group of American professors wrote: "Our observations have led us to the unhappy conclusions that anti-Semitism in the U.S.S.R. is not an atavistic remnant of czarist Russia, but is the official policy of the Government of the U.S.S.R."

In Rumania, in Hungary, and especially in Poland under Prime Minister Gomulka, there appears to have been limited improvement in the treatment of Jews. In these countries, while they still suffer from discrimination and economic disabilities, Jewish cultural and religious life now enjoy somewhat increased freedom. This limited improvement in the satellite countries is, of course, subject to instant recall if it ever serves Communist purposes.

Why is there this difference between Soviet policy toward the Jews and the policy presently pursued in some of the satellites? I can think of two reasons.

The first reason is that the Soviet Government is more directly interested than are the satellites in influencing Arab opinion in the Middle East and in preventing any settlement between the Arab States and Israel. Soviet anti-Semitism and Soviet strategic objectives in the Middle East complement each other. Arab nationalism must be wooed and fanned by constantly identifying Israel and Zionism with British and American imperialism.

Let me give you one example of the Kremlin's propaganda to the Arab world. I quote from the publication "The State of Israel—Its Position and Policies," printed by the Soviet state publishing house in 1958:

> The Zionist movement represents a form of the nationalistic ideology of the rich Jewish bourgeoisie, intimately tied to imperialism and to colonial oppression of the people of Asia. Zionism has tied itself to American and other Western capitalism and, with Jewish terrorist tactics, attacked its Arab neighbors. The national liberation movement of the people of the Middle East, spearheaded by its native leaders (such as President Nasser, King Ibn Saud, of Saudi Arabia, and King Iman Ahmad, of Yemen) is constantly threatened by naked Jewish aggression. The clear duty of all Marxists and Communists in this situation is to help the Asian and African people crush the reactionary Jewish forces.

The second explanation I can think of for the intensified anti-Semitism in the Soviet Union today is the personally irrational attitude of Prime Minister Khrushchev. The Anti-Defamation League has stated that the primitive, vulgar anti-Semitic tone characteristic of Khrushchev's occasional interviews and outbursts on the subject of the Jews is unmistakable. This evaluation coincides with that of the most prominent Jewish member of the Canadian Communist Party, Mr. J. B. Salsberg, after a 2-hour interview with the Soviet Premier in August 1956.

According to Mr. Salsberg, Khrushchev first of all denied that there was anti-Semitism in the Soviet Union: and then went on to list a whole series of personal objections to Jews. He quoted the Soviet Prime Minister as saying that:

> Wherever a Jew settles, the first thing he does is build a synagogue. Of the thousands of Soviet citizens who have toured abroad, only three failed to return. All of them were Jews.
> * * * He [Khrushchev] agreed with Stalin that the Crimea, which had been depopulated at the war's end, should not be turned into a Jewish colonization center, because, in case of war, it would be turned into a base for attacking the U.S.S.R.

Anti-Semitism, the Swastika Epidemic, and Communism

"I was much disturbed by the above remarks," concluded Mr. Salsberg. "They reflect a backward prejudice against the Jewish group as a people. * * * Khrushchev's statements smack of White Russian chauvinism * * * his approach to the problem of Jewish nationality is an unforgiveable violation of social democracy. If Khrushchev's distrust of the Jewish people is warranted, then this is a terrible indictment, not of Soviet Jewry, but of Stalinist crimes and of distortions in the nationalities policy, in particular as it is applied to the Jewish people."

This is the Khrushchev who today accuses Konrad Adenauer of being another Hitler!

ANTI-SEMITISM, PATRIOTISM, AND CHRISTIANITY

Having set forth the facts about Soviet anti-Semitism, I now want to deal with anti-Semitism in this country. I have purposely observed this sequence because anti-Semitism in this country can, I believe, only be evaluated against the background of Communist anti-Semitism.

Thanks to our free press and thanks to the energetic attitude of the leaders of both political parties, active anti-Semitism is not a serious problem in our country. But I would warn against complacency. There is, let us be frank about it, a good deal of passive, or polite, anti-Semitism which expresses itself in various forms of discrimination and segregation.

Moreover, here and there, scattered across the country, there are little hate groups who make the Jews the chief target of their venom. More frequently than not, they have high-sounding names which describe them as "Christian" or "patriotic", when in reality they are both anti-Christian and anti-patriotic.

When Hitler was alive and the depression was still upon us, these groups were able to make some headway. Today they are isolated and without influence. But under certain circumstances, they could again become dangerous.

There is already some evidence that the KKK and other extremists in this country maintain contact with ex-Nazi grouplets scattered around the world. In terms of membership, this pro-Nazi international today has no more than nuisance value. But there is reason to believe that it commands substantial funds which leading Nazis smuggled out of Germany before the collapse of the Hitler regime, and that these Nazi

113

expatriates hate the Western democracies with undiminished passion and yearn for a revival of the Nazi-Soviet pact. In any case, this is a matter that could well stand investigation.

I believe we should keep our eye on these old professional merchants of hate.

I find much more reason for concern, however, in the fact that those involved in the swastika epidemic in our own country have been, for the most part, high school students and teenagers.

Since last Christmas, some 70 synagogues in the United States have been desecrated and a number of Jewish cemeteries have been vandalized. Some of the outrages were perpetrated by members of youthful neo-Nazi clubs, which had their fuhrers and flaunted the swastika emblem. A report from Kansas City this February 1, for example, said that 13 youths had been suspended from high school for membership in such neo-Nazi clubs. From the many arrests that have been made, however, it would appear that most of the swastika painters operated as individuals or in groups of two or three and were not members of any organization.

The actions of these young people bore many features of the standard psychological epidemics to which juveniles in every country are prone. But I would urge that we do not dismiss the matter with this easy analysis. A serious study should be made to determine the personal backgrounds of the young people involved, their political attitudes, if any, and the possible social and political consequences of this new type of epidemic.

Perhaps we, in America, too, must find ways of improving the education of our young people—yes, and of our adult population too. Somehow we must communicate to them the unspeakable evil which the swastika and the hammer and sickle both stand for. Somehow we must make them understand that anti-Semitism is anti-American; that it is today an instrument of Communism, as it was yesterday an instrument of Nazism, and those who ply it in this country, are unwittingly the tools of the Communist conspiracy.

Even more important, we must make them understand that

anti-Christianism goes with anti-Semitism, as godlessness goes with totalitarianism. It is no accident, in my opinion, that the two great godless movements of our time, nazism and communism, should both be vehemently anti-Semitic. But in checking through some of the writings of Karl Marx, I have been amazed to discover how similar his views on the relationship between Christianity and Judaism were to the views of the Nazi pagan philosophers.

The Nazis objected to Judaism because, in their eyes, it was the root monotheistic religion, because their creed of race and hate and war and brutality could not be reconciled with belief in God. They objected to Christianity because, in their eyes, it derived from Judaism, because its doctrine of universal love was as difficult to reconcile with their pagan beliefs.

Let me read to you what Karl Marx himself had to say on this same subject:

> Christianity sprang from Judaism. Christianity is the sublime thought of Judaism, Judaism is the everyday practical application of Christianity. But this application could become universal only after Christianity had been theoretically perfected as the religion of self-alienation of man, from himself and from nature.

By their statements both Marx and Hitler have made it clear that any movement which sets out to persecute Judaism inevitably winds up by rejecting and persecuting Christianity.

As free men who worship God, we cannot ignore the existence of anti-Semitism, even on a small scale, in this country or in other countries. We cannot ignore the desecration of a single synagogue, any more than we can ignore the taking of a single life.

Let us strive, therefore, to achieve a clearer understanding of the nature and origins of this evil, and let our leaders and our educators join in an effort to control and ultimately eliminate the virus in our own country.

Let us join in condemning every manifestation of anti-Semitism, wherever it may occur.

Let us give every assistance and encouragement to the Government of West Germany in the long and inevitably difficult struggle to eradicate the last vestiges of the Nazi evil.

Let us do all of these things. But in doing so, let us not lose our sense of proportion and priority. Let us not permit ourselves to be so distracted by the actions of a handful of juvenile delinquents and by the saturation propaganda of the Kremlin, that we take our eyes off the chief source of human injustice in the world today.

Let us raise our voices against the inhuman persecution of the Jews which is today practiced in the Soviet Union, and let us use our offices at every opportunity to persuade the Soviet leaders to grant equality of treatment to their Jewish subjects.

Let us protest, too, at every available opportunity, against the continued enslavement of the 100 million people of captive Europe, and against the vicious oppression of other minorities in the Soviet Union.

Under the Nazi regime many Christians and numberless Jews were united in a community of suffering. Under communism, the community of suffering is total. Thus, by a strange arrangement of circumstances, the godless totalitarians who have sought to destroy both Judaism and Christianity may have laid the foundation for an understanding that will grow best because it will have survived the worst.

Chapter VIII

FALLACIES OF THE NUCLEAR TEST BAN *

Mr. President, if I venture to speak today on the question of the nuclear test ban . . . I do so because of a gnawing conviction that the moratorium is wrong, that the Communists are not abiding by it, that it increases the danger of war rather than diminishing it, that it may ultimately cost us our freedom.

I now believe that we stand in mortal peril and that this peril is not many years removed.

The lack of understanding on the test ban issue cannot be explained in terms of its complexity. It is really not that complex. The scientific aspects of the problem can, I am convinced, Mr. President, be understood by any intelligent layman. To achieve comprehension, the basic requirement is the kind of understanding of politics and of the nature of communism and of the realities of power relationships that I believe most of us in this Chamber possess.

Why, then, is there so little understanding of the test ban issue? I can think of two reasons:

First, the facts have not been given to the public.

Second, our minds have been confused, our nerves dulled, our wills sapped, by what I consider the Kremlin's most spectacular triumph in the realm of propaganda and psychological conditioning.

We start from the premise that the whole complex of nuclear problems—including such matters as the question of nuclear weapons technology, the strategic and tactical use of nuclear weapons, the test ban, the moratorium—must be

---

* United States Senate, May 12, 1960.

viewed within the context of national purpose, as expressed by our foreign policy.

We have certain stated purposes on which there is broad bipartisan agreement. We are committed to the moral purposes that are stated with enduring eloquence in our great historic documents. We are committed to the defense of our own freedoms, and of the free world at large against Communist aggression. We are committed, sincerely, if vaguely and ineffectually, to the extension of freedom to the peoples now enslaved by Communism and to the principle of self-determination.

We are committed to the maintenance of peace, with justice, and without surrender. We do not believe in peace at any price. Benjamin Franklin once declared that those who believe they "can give up essential liberty to obtain a little temporary safety deserve neither liberty nor safety." There is as much truth in this in the age of thermonuclear weapons as there was at the time it was written by Franklin.

On these attitudes and purposes we agree. But there have been times in recent years when I have had the impression that the conduct of our foreign policy had somehow been separated from any guiding principles, that we were simply responding on a fire department basis to emergencies and crises created by the Kremlin.

I am even more profoundly convinced that the entire critical relationship between nuclear weapons and foreign policy has not been understood. The nuclear capabilities we have developed are sadly out of balance and at certain points are in conflict with the principles we espouse. They are, I fear, inadequate to cope with the spectrum of dangers that confront us. Our guileless approach to the moratorium is, in my opinion, a reflection of the same disjunction between our nuclear thinking and our national commitments.

All the purposes I have enumerated are interrelated. In order to maintain peace, in order to defend the free world, in order to embark on a positive foreign policy, in order to extend the frontiers of freedom, in order to keep faith with our forebears and our children, in order to reduce the danger of thermonuclear war to a minimum, in order to create a stable basis for peace, there are two prior conditions that must be met.

The first requirement, on which there is no dispute, is that we maintain a superiority in strategic nuclear weapons—that is, large-yield weapons of devastating power—so that the Soviets will never be tempted to seek a settlement of the cold war by means of a thermonuclear Pearl Harbor. We are committed to the avoidance of preventive war. If the Kremlin should strike first, only a portion of our original strength would get off the ground, and only a portion of this, in turn, would reach enemy targets. General Powers has expressed the opinion that a surprise Soviet missile attack could reduce our ability to retaliate to near-zero. This viewpoint has been challenged by other competent officers; but even the most optimistic estimates concede that a surprise strike by the Soviets might immediately eliminate 50 percent or more of our bombers and ICBM's. To serve as an effective deterrent to a surprise attack, therefore, our superiority must be nothing short of overwhelming.

Today, I am inclined to agree with the President that our retaliatory capability is sufficient to deter such an attack. Technological superiority, however, is something that must be constantly renewed. If the Soviets ever achieve superiority or if they beat us to a major breakthrough in the field of nuclear weaponry—for example, the anti-missile missile—a preemptive strike might become a serious possibility. We cannot ignore this possibility, the more so since Soviet military thinkers, and I shall cite evidence of this, have given such serious consideration to the concept of a preemptive strike.

Corollary requirement No. 1 would be the development of an anti-missile defense, the invigoration of our civil defense, and a mandatory shelter construction program. The greater our ability to survive a surprise attack and to retaliate, the less likelihood there is that such an attack will ever take place.

But our strategic deterrent by itself is not enough. Indeed, by itself it may be highly dangerous. There is much to be said for Thomas Murray's argument that we have placed altogether too one-sided an emphasis on multimegaton weapons, that our very capacity "to wreak unlimited nuclear violence inhibits us from the use of limited force which may be politically necessary." I am, in fact, inclined to believe that, with our exclusive reliance on nuclear retaliation, we have succeeded in frightening ourselves and our allies far more than we have frightened the Kremlin.

Obviously, if the Kremlin drops thermonuclear warheads on American cities, we will retaliate in kind; we would have no alternative. But if it is simply a matter of a limited challenge at Berlin or in the Mideast or in the Far East, can we, will we, respond to this by destroying millions of men, women, and children in Soviet cities? This is a terrible decision for any President to have to make, especially when he knows that minutes later a comparable number of American civilians will have perished in the ashes of our own cities.

Requirement No. 2, therefore, is the development of a system of tactical nuclear weapons capable of being used with discrimination against military targets both on the battlefield and in the rear. The possession of such weapons would enable the forces of freedom, in Europe and in Asia, to confront the vastly superior Communist manpower with firepower of "unacceptable" superiority. Only in this way can we offer deterrence to the increasingly serious threat of limited aggression.

"We arm to parley," Winston Churchill once said. The peace of the world can be considered secure only when we have met these two basic requirements, only when we have established deterrence at both the strategic and limited levels. At that point we could go to the conference table with the initiative firmly in our grasp. At that point we could truly embark on a positive foreign policy.

If our weapons requirements should be determined with reference to our national purposes and commitments, our policy on the question of nuclear testing should, in turn, be determined in the light of our weapons requirements. Instead, our once sound policy on the question of the test ban has now degenerated into nothing better than a frightened, unthought-out reaction to the international hysteria which the Kremlin has so cleverly fostered and exploited.

What makes it so difficult to cope with this hysteria is that all of us, whether we recognize it or not, have been afflicted by it, to a smaller or greater degree. There can be no question that the overwhelming majority of the decent citizens who favor a test ban believe in freedom and abhor the tyranny of communism. There can also be no question that the agitation for a complete cessation of tests has been the central item on the agenda of the world Communist movement for several years now. Of this there is ample documentary proof. Through the infinitely subtle propaganda apparatus which they command, through the thousands of channels of information to which they have access, the Communists have unquestionably succeeded in infiltrating this movement and in providing it with much of its guiding philosophy and stock of arguments.

There is nothing novel or really surprising about this situation. There has been a whole series of critical situations in which the Communists have succeeded in persuading the majority of the people in the non-Communist world to believe what the Kremlin wished them to believe. The widely held belief, for example, that the Chinese Communists were not really Communists, but simple agrarian reformers, helped to pave the way for the Communist takeover in China.

On the issue of the test ban, we are today the victims, at both governmental and private levels, of the same kind of befuddlement and psychological conditioning that led both public and Government to the wrong conclusions on the Chinese Communists, on the Greek insurrection, and other vital issues.

The general argument in favor of the test ban can be broken down into eight basic propositions, to which I shall hereafter refer as the eight fallacies of the test ban.

FALLACY NO. 1

Fallacy No. 1 is that a test ban agreement would serve to "open up" the Soviet Union, that the stationing of international inspectors at a number of fixed points would at least create a first chink in the armor of secrecy.

121

Soviet spokesmen have hinted that they might be willing to consider the establishment of a few fixed stations on their territory and a few on-site inspections. The distinguished Senator from Tennessee [Mr. GORE] pointed out, in his statement of March 2, that after 18 months of negotiations, the Soviets have yet to commit themselves to a single on-site inspection or to the establishment of a single station. All of our efforts to pin them down have failed.

On one occasion, as I have heard, Congressman HOLIFIELD cornered Mr. Semyon Tsarapkin, the chief Soviet delegate to the test ban conference, and demanded to know what quota of annual inspections the Kremlin was prepared to accept. Mr. Tsarapkin, according to the story, shrugged his shoulders and said: "A few." On another occasion Soviet Ambassador Zaroubin contemptuously said to Dr. Alvin Groves of Los Alamos, that the West could, if it wished, have all of its three inspections at the same time.

Personally, I consider it inconceivable that the Soviets will ever accede to the revised Bethe formula calling for 21 manned stations, 600 robot stations, and 300 on-site inspections per year. I consider it highly improbable that they will even accede to the original Geneva formula of 1958, which we now know to be absurdly inadequate, but which called for 21 manned stations on the territory of the Soviet Union, plus 20 to 30 on-site inspections. I am afraid that if they offer us anything remotely resembling the original Geneva formula—perhaps 50 percent of the formula, perhaps 25 percent—we will hail this as a great concession, sign a treaty on Soviet terms, and present this agreement as an assurance of "peace in our time."

It is utter nonsense to argue that such an arrangement would "open up" the Soviet Union. It can be taken for granted that the international inspectors would be confined to their stations and that most of these stations would be located in isolated areas. It can also be taken for granted that the inspectors would see nothing and would have minimal opportunities for contacts. If they engage in a handful of on-site inspections, they would do so in company of the Soviet members of their teams, who would exert themselves to the limit to frustrate their fellow inspectors, and would watch over them with eagle eyes.

I have the greatest doubt that 10,000 or 20,000 American tourists who will visit the Soviet Union next year will in any way help to "open it up." I would point out that the tourist traffic to the Soviet Union was just about as heavy in the mid-thirties, during the heyday of the Stalinist terror, as it is to-day. It opened up exactly nothing. The tourists saw what Stalin wanted them to see, and most of them returned to this country convinced that the stories of Bolshevik terror were greatly exaggerated.

In his article, "Beware Tourists to Russia," in the *Reader's Digest*, Eugene Lyons described the manner in which the Kremlin bemuses and befuddles the tourist innocents. But these impressionable ordinary tourists, I am convinced, are far more plausible instruments for "opening up" the Soviet Union than a handful of nuclear test ban inspectors at fixed stations and under constant surveillance.

FALLACY NO. 2

Fallacy No. 2 is the argument that we are now far ahead of the Soviet Union in nuclear weapons technology, that if the race should continue indefinitely the Soviets would probably surpass us, that a freeze on weapons testing would therefore be to our advantage.

This argument is based on a whole series of assumptions which, as I shall demonstrate later, are, at the worst, demonstrably false; at the best, highly questionable. Among other things, it assumes the following:

That we will be able to conclude a test ban agreement with the Soviets providing for an adequate and enforceable system of inspection.

That, despite any initial inadequacy, the system of inspection will ultimately be improved to the point where weapons tests of any significant magnitude will be detectable.

That, once detection has been established, there will be no serious difficulty in establishing verification.

That, if there is a voluntary moratorium on tests of less

than 20 kilotons magnitude, the Soviets will abide by this moratorium; that they will faithfully honor the provisions of the treaty and will not engage in clandestine tests, no matter how much the Kremlin may stand to gain from them.

Fallacy No. 2 has been advanced over and over again as a reason for entering into a formal test ban agreement. It is amazing to me that mature men could give serious consideration to an argument based on so flimsy a substructure of "ifs." Among other things, this argument, after assuming that the Soviets have the ability to surpass us technologically, even without cheating, does not consider what might happen to our technological lead if Khrushchev and company *should* cheat.

I believe we can take it as a maxim that, if there is something to be gained from it, the Communists will cheat. But let us be generous. Let us assume that there is a 50-50 possibility that Khrushchev and company would adhere to their word. Can the future security of the United States be based on a 50-50 possibility?

At the time the Soviets exploded their first A-bomb, it was estimated that we had something like a 4 to 5 year lead in nuclear technology and weaponry. By the time we embarked on the present moratorium in October 1958, this lead had unquestionably been cut down, according to informed estimates, to a figure of 3 or 4 years at best. If the Soviets have not been observing the honor moratorium, and I am certain in my own mind that they have not, we have already dissipated almost 2 years of our lead.

FALLACY NO. 3

Fallacy No. 3 is the fallacy of the ultimate technological plateau.

According to this argument, there is little point to the further development of our nuclear weapons because we already possess sufficient multimegaton weapons and weapons of other yields to destroy the Soviet Union several times over.

This argument ignores the fact that our stockpile of thermonuclear weapons leaves us helpless, unless we are prepared to resort to all-out nuclear war, to cope with some of the limited threats and challenges with which the Kremlin will confront us.

It ignores the fact that the NATO land forces can serve as an effective deterrent to such threats only if their manpower inferiority is offset by the possession of a broad and flexible system of tactical nuclear weapons.

It ignores the fact that research into the possibilities of antimissile defense is still in its infancy.

It ignores the fact that we require new multimegaton missile systems for coping with hardened missile sites and for other defensive purposes.

In short, it ignores the elementary fact that technology has no limits. There is no such thing as an ultimate technological plateau. On the contrary, with each new breakthrough, new and more fantastic developmental vistas seem to open up.

The hydrogen missiles we now possess and those that are scheduled for the next few years are not the ultimate weapons. Given a continuing developmental program, there will be a second and third and fourth generation of missiles and warheads.

The yield-to-weight and yield-to-diameter relationship will be improved so that the warheads can be miniaturized.

Missiles will be reduced in size and cost and greatly improved in accuracy. By enabling us to make many more missiles and much more effective and more mobile missiles at a greatly reduced cost, such a development would vastly strengthen our deterrence and would help to vindicate our peace policy.

The energy of fusion explosions will be tailored to produce a variety of effects which correspond to the nature of the intended targets.

Clean weapons of all yields will be produced, thus greatly increasing the utility of the atom for tactical, defensive, and strategic purposes.

Entire new weapons systems will come into being—weapons that seem as fantastic today as the atom bomb did in 1943 or the hydrogen bomb in 1945.

Such developments could have incalculable strategic consequences. If the Kremlin were to get there first on any major technological breakthrough in nuclear weaponry, my conviction is that we would, in short order, find ourselves confronted with a choice between annihilation or surrender. At the very least, this is a serious possibility.

I found Khrushchev's statement of January 14, 1960 ominous in terms of its emphasis on continuing technological progress. It am sure that this statement came to the attention of many of my colleagues, but I wish to recall it here nevertheless. In my opinion, it is a statement to be read and reread and pondered:

> Our armed forces have to a considerable extent been transferred over to missile-nuclear arms. These arms have been perfected and will continue to be perfected. The armament which we now have is formidable armament. The armament under development is even more perfect and more formidable. The armament which is being created and which is to be found in the folders of the scientists and designers is truly unbelievable armament.
>
> We state openly that in reducing the numbers of men in the armed forces we are not diminishing firepower. On the contrary, it has increased qualitatively several times.

Other Soviet spokesmen have gone further than Premier Khrushchev in stressing the importance of technological surprise and in hinting at the possibility of a preemptive attack. Marshal A. A. Grechko, in an article published in *Red Star* on February 23, 1960, emphasized the following points:

(a) Suddenness (or surprise) is crucial to success in modern war.

(b) Technological surprise may be equally crucial.

(c) The initial phase of the war will be of decisive importance.

(d) Soviet forces will employ nuclear weapons as their main armament.

Another Soviet officer, Marshal Nedelin, I note parenthetically, was last week appointed "Marshal of Soviet Rocketry."

What is the "truly unbelievable" armament of which Khrushchev spoke? Let me outline some of the possibilities on the technological horizon, possibilities that can only be realized by the renewal of testing both in space and underground.

First of all there is the matter of tactical weapons. The

126

so-called tactical rockets and cannon shells which we now possess are in reality medium-sized atomic bombs, with all the unpredictable danger of fallout. They are clumsy; they are potentially dangerous both to the user and to the civilian populace adjacent to the area of battle; they cannot be used with real discrimination. The military planners who have been working on the development of tactical nuclear weapons, have, as I understand it, been thinking of light, clean weapons with yields of from 1 to 100 tons, with a kiloton yield almost an outside figure. These weapons would be small enough to be fired from bazookas, from tanks, from weapons carriers, from light field guns, or in salvos from missile-launching trucks.

There is a limit beyond which weapons development cannot go without testing. Commenting on the semiannual AEC report, the *Washington Post* said on January 31, 1960:

> The AEC report said only that weapon research and development were continuing on weapons with greatly reduced fallout but special emphasis was being placed on small rugged weapons that could be assembled and made ready to fire in a matter of minutes. One already announced is the "Davy Crockett," a one-man bazooka-launched weapon. Although it is being produced for the Army, it has not been tested yet because of the moratorium. The Army is reported to be reluctant about ordering them in quantity before they have been proven.

The production of a clean, tactical, nuclear weapon would open the way to a whole series of technologically significant breakthroughs. By definition such a weapon would have to have a fusion warhead—that is, a heavy hydrogen or tritium warhead—which is not triggered by fissionable material or else triggered by only a minute quantity. Such an explosion would produce a small amount of carbon 14, but, compared to today's weapons, it would be 95 percent clean. The radioactive fallout would be negligible. This technique, once mastered, would be substantially applicable to warheads of all sizes, up to the multimegaton range.

It is the fissionable material in a thermonuclear bomb which makes it so extremely expensive to produce. The chemical components, chiefly heavy hydrogen and lithium, which are immediately responsible for the fusion explosion, are relatively cheap to manufacture. If a straight fusion weapon can be developed, and there is no doubt that it can be, this would open up the way to the production of thermonuclear weapons of all yields in vastly increased quantities and at much smaller cost.

Then there is the matter of the neutron bomb, to which there has already been some reference in the press. Such a bomb can theoretically be produced by tailoring the energy of a fusion explosion so that, instead of heat and blast, its primary product is a burst of neutrons. Such a burst would do negligible physical damage, but it would destroy all life in the target area. It would, in short, operate as a kind of death-ray.

I have heard that, in the light of present theoretical knowledge, the neutron bomb is no more questionable than the hydrogen bomb was 6 months before it was demonstrated that one could be built. Although there have been a few fragmentary references to the neutron bomb in the press, I was told, when I tried to obtain more information, that the matter was classified. When I pressed my physicist friend further, he threw up his hands in despair and said: "You must forgive me, I have never heard of a neutron."

I consider all the hush-hush that surrounds the neutron bomb to be a glaring instance of the official abuse of secrecy. To keep the facts of life on the nuclear age from the American people is foolish, and potentially disastrous. If there is a possibility that a neutron bomb can be built, if there appears to be any chance that the Soviets may succeed in building one before we do, then the American people have a right to the facts.

The current issue of *Foreign Affairs* contains a remarkable article on the question of the test ban by Dr. Freeman J. Dyson. Dr. Dyson quotes a paragraph from a report by the prominent Soviet physicist L. L. Artsimovitch, entitled "Research on Controlled Thermonuclear Reactions in the U.S.-S.R.," printed in December 1958:

It may also be possible to realize a pulsed thermonuclear reaction under conditions in which the high temperature is produced by a charge of conventional explosive (such as TNT or something more powerful) which surrounds a capsule containing heavy hydrogen. Without dwelling on the experimental details, we may note that conditions have been found under which the generation of neutrons in hydrogen reactions has been established reliably and reproducibly. In experiments carried out in 1952, there is no doubt that we have observed neutrons which are formed as a result of the heating of matter to extremely high temperatures.

From this, it is apparent that the Russians were experimenting with fission-free hydrogen devices as far back as 1952 and that, as a corollary of this, they have for years had some understanding of the possibilities of the neutron bomb.

Once upon a time there was no hydrogen bomb. But there were a few scientists, a tiny but brave minority, who said it could be made and who urged that we embark on a crash program of development, lest the Kremlin beat us to it. At that time we had a President, Harry Truman, who gave the facts to the people. Had he not done so, had he not enjoyed the public support that only comes from understanding, the production of the H-bomb might have been deferred beyond that fateful day in 1953 when the Soviets exploded their own first H-bomb.

I believe President Eisenhower owed a similar duty to the American people in the case of the neutron bomb. The President should have told the people what the scientists told him. Not to have done so was a dereliction that could only lead to the most dangerous kind of speculation.

Then there is the matter of the so-called Christofilos effect, first suggested by an amateur Greek physicist and subsequently confirmed in the Argus test shot. All we know at this moment is that, after the Argus shot, there was a temporary blackout in radio communications in the area due to the release of neutrons and rays at high altitude. These effects conceivably could have a revolutionary impact on modern war. They might be used by either side to interfere with the communications of the opposing side. It is not even precluded that a massive release of neutrons at high altitudes could be used to prevent missile attacks. The fact is that we do not understand the military potentialities of the Christofilos effect. Our national security demands that we learn more about these phenomena. But without tests, this is impossible.

Then there is the antimissile missile. The development of the antimissile missile by either side would have strategic implications comparable to the development of the A-bomb or H-bomb. We cannot afford to let the Kremlin get there first.

There are competent scientists and engineers, I know, who believe that, for all his genius, man will never be able to devise a missile capable of knocking down an incoming missile traveling at a speed of 15,000 miles per hour. But I am impressed by the fact that the corps of equally competent scientists and engineers who have worked on the antimissile system for the U. S. Army are profoundly convinced that both the problem of guidance and the problem of a suitable warhead for the Nike-Zeus can be solved. Indeed, they believe that their project is far enough along to warrant the advance procurement of vital components. This, in my opinion, is sufficient reason to order full speed ahead and to provide the necessary funding without stint. Perhaps their judgment will be proved wrong. Perhaps it will be proved right. But there is so much to be gained if they are right that, even at 10-to-1 odds, I would be in favor of risking the several hundred million dollars involved. Every day's delay may cost American lives if a showdown ever comes. It is not too much to suggest that delay in this area alone may cost us our freedom.

While we have been making considerable progress in the field of missile technology, we have been inclined to sit smugly on our stockpile of nuclear and thermonuclear warheads, apparently confident that, come what may, they are so fearsome that no aggressor dare challenge us. In the multimegaton field, it is not much of an exaggeration to say that we have been standing still, or almost standing still. The Soviets, I am convinced, have not been standing still. Somewhere along the line, if they run hard enough and push their clandestine tests hard enough, they may achieve a technological superiority in both strategic and defensive weapons that would make a surprise thermonuclear attack on the United States a distinct possibility.

According to expert testimony, the Soviet ICBM's are far superior in thrust to our own. This means that they can carry a much bigger cargo, so that, even with inferior technology, they have been able to arm them with warheads of substantially greater yield. According to these estimates, the Soviet ICBM's carry warheads of 5 megaton yields against the 2 megaton warheads with which our Atlas missiles are equipped.

The missile gap we confront is, by common consent, a matter for concern even as expressed in numbers of ICBM's. It becomes a matter for much greater concern when expressed in megatons. Whether we find this pleasant or not, the hard, inescapable fact remains that megatons constitute the basic currency necessary to purchase deterrence and perhaps necessary to purchase survival.

The word "megaton" has come to have an evil connotation because it is generally associated with the mass devastation of cities. But I would point out, in defense of this word, that the multimegaton weapon will almost certainly become the chief instrument for defending our own cities and our own lives against enemy attack. If we are ever attacked, an effective antimissile system alone may require thousands of multimegaton warheads; and we would need more thousands of high-yield weapons to strike back at the hardened missile sites of the enemy.

General Powers has declared that the Soviets now have the capability to wipe out virtually all of our retaliatory capacity with several hundred missiles. In reply to this, it has been argued that it would require an average of three 5-megaton missiles to knock out the average SAC base and ten 5-megaton missiles to knock out hardened missile sites. The deduction from this is that the Soviets will never be able to afford the thousands of missiles required to reduce our retaliatory capacity to what the military people call "acceptable level."

Is it not conceivable, however, that as a result of technological improvements, the Soviets, within the next several years, will be able to develop a missile system capable of delivering a more powerful warhead with greatly increased precision? In that case, 2 missiles instead of 10 might do an adequate job of destruction on a hardened missile site or on a SAC base. If, finally, such weapons could be made compact and cheap, the arithmetic of deterrence would have to be completely rewritten.

I ask you to imagine the consequences of a major technological breakthrough by the Kremlin in the fantastic, limitless horizon of nuclear weaponry. Suppose that at the next May Day parade in Moscow or at the opening of the next session of the Supreme Soviet, Prime Minister Khrushchev were to make the following statement:

Comrades, a year ago the glorious scientists of the Soviet Union solved the problem which is still baffling the scientists of the capitalist world. They produced a missile capable of knocking down an ICBM in flight. Today all the major approaches to the Soviet Union are guarded by batteries of anti-missile missiles.

Suppose, on the heels of such a statement, Khrushchev were to renew his Berlin ultimatum. What, then, would be the reaction of the free world?

We can suppose a lot more things. Suppose at the next May Day parade a division of Soviet troops marches by the reviewing stand with gun carriers, tanks, rocket launchers, and bazookas of clearly nuclear design.

Suppose that, while we concentrate on producing improved missile systems, Khrushchev one day announces that the neutron bomb has for the past 6 months been in mass production in the Soviet Union.

If any one of these things happened, we would be in immediate jeopardy. If the Soviets could time their announcements so that they hit the free world simultaneously, or salvo fashion, with the news of two or more major technological breakthroughs, then the effect would very probably be disastrous.

FALLACY NO. 4

Fallacy No. 4 is the fallacy of the "nth nation."

According to this argument, the world will be placed in serious jeopardy at the point where nuclear weapons come into the possession of the so-called "nth nation," the point, in other words, where control becomes impossible. It is therefore of overriding importance that we conclude an agreement, any kind of agreement, as rapidly as possible.

This argument is propounded in all earnestness by sincere pacifists, by the members of the Committee for Sane Nuclear

Policy, by many other people of both liberal and conservative opinion, by the Department of State, and by the British Foreign Office.

It is also propounded, with altogether different motivations, by the international Communist apparatus. The Kremlin's purpose in brandishing the menace of the "nth nation" is obvious enough: it is part of its effort to create a climate which will make it impossible for us to provide our NATO allies with nuclear weapons.

The NATO alliance is the chief target and immediate victim of the "nth nation" fallacy.

If NATO is today a sick and purposeless organization, wracked by defeatism, this, in my opinion, is due to two things: First, our one-sided reliance on massive retaliation; and second, our failure to convince our allies that we are prepared, if necessary, to fight a land war in Europe.

President Eisenhower has been indiscreet enough to inform the world that it would be pointless to try to fight such a war. But even more destructive on morale than his indiscretion has been our obstinate refusal to provide our NATO allies with the modern nuclear weapons they must have to be able to deter or resist an aggressive strike by the Red army. Who can blame our NATO allies if, lacking confidence both in our intentions and in their own military capabilities, they have fallen far short of the 40 divisions originally prescribed as essential for the defense of Western Europe? At his press conference of February 3, 1960, President Eisenhower said that he favored arming our NATO allies with nuclear weapons. When the Kremlin protested, the White House recoiled and announced that we had no intention of distributing nuclear arms to our NATO allies at this juncture. But this is a measure which we put off at our peril. It is a measure for today and not for tomorrow. It would do as much as, perhaps even more than, an airborne alert to increase our deterrent power over the coming critical period.

Despite their bluster, the Soviets will not be able to emulate us, because there is nothing they fear more than nuclear arms in the hands of the satellite armies. Would the Kremlin have dared to intervene in Hungary if the Hungarian Army had possessed nuclear weapons?

Since the provision of nuclear weapons to our NATO allies would, if anything, stabilize the situation and make peace more secure, and since the chances that the Soviets will share their nuclear weapons with their satellites are decidedly remote, the hypothetical danger of the "nth nation" is, I am convinced, a chimera—a chimera in the literal sense of being a mythical monster. I do not say that the theory will have no validity at some remote date in the future. But I do say that, in the context of the present, it has no significant validity, and that its only conceivable effect will be to keep NATO disarmed.

Somewhere along the line, Egypt or Israel or some other small nation may build a few nuclear weapons. We should certainly attempt to discourage this development, but I can see no ironclad way of preventing it, short of enforcing an "nth nation" ban on peaceful nuclear technology. But small nations will never become nuclear powers, and a word of caution from the only real nuclear powers would be more than enough to restrain them.

There remains the single question of Red China. In the case of China, the "nth nation" justification for accepting a test ban without adequate inspection, is doubly fallacious. It is the height of folly to believe that the conclusion of a treaty between the Big Four could persuade Peiping not to develop or test her own nuclear devices. No matter what we may do or say, Communist China, I am convinced, will explode some kind of device over the course of the next few years. It can be taken for granted that this will be the signal for an unprecedented campaign to bring Red China into the United Nations on the theory that this will make her more amenable to control. In fact, I think it highly conceivable that the Kremlin, by arrangement with Peiping, will soon explode such a device on Chinese territory in order to accelerate the panic.

The second part of the fallacy of the "nth nation" thesis, as applied to Red China, is that the explosion of a nuclear test or two by Mao Tse-tung would place the free world in mortal jeopardy. Given her poverty, her still massive backwardness, the enormous industrial and agricultural requirements of her 5-year plans, and the fantastic cost of nuclear weapons, Red China would be accomplishing miracles if she achieved nuclear power status 20 or 25 years hence. There are two schools of thought as to whether the West or the Soviets will have the most to fear from this distant prospect. In either event, there is absolutely nothing we can do to prevent or impede this development other than pressing unremittingly for international inspection based on complete "openness."

In the age of nuclear technology, nuclear weapons are inevitable. No great power will forever forego the right to nuclear weapons and forever resign itself to second-class status simply because the nuclear powers who were first on the scene have entered into an agreement to limit their club to a total membership of three.

We must free ourselves from the tyranny of the chimera of the nth nation.

The sharing of nuclear arms with our NATO allies will decrease the danger of war by putting some modern military muscle into NATO, by making NATO meaningful, by giving our allies confidence in NATO and confidence in our own intentions. It would simultaneously provide us with greatly increased leverage in pressing for "openness" in our proposals on disarmament and the test ban.

FALLACY NO. 5

The fifth fallacy is the fallacy that underground tests and tests at high altitude and in space, are detectable and verifiable.

Even the most ardent test ban advocates admit that under the best of circumstances, many tests could go undetected, and that, after detection, there would still be a formidable job of establishing proof. They argue, however, that it would be adequate to have a 1 in 5 or even a 1 in 25 chance of verification. A significant possibility of detection, according to this point of view, would be sufficient to deter any government from attempting a sneak violation of a test ban treaty.

In an age that is already notorious for its political folly, there has been no concept more fallacious than that of the enforceable ban. The hearings held by the Joint Committee on Atomic Energy from April 19 to 23, 1960, have, in my opinion, reduced the entire concept to a rubble of nonsense.

I believe the free world owes a great debt to the distinguished Senators and Representatives who organized and participated in these hearings. I wholeheartedly agree with Arthur Krock's statement in the *New York Times* of Sunday, April 4:

> The hearing ordered by the Joint Committee was an act of statesmanship, as well as service to its high responsibility for national security in the nuclear field.

The committee brought before it as impressive an array of scientific brains as had ever appeared in a congressional committee room. There were those who favored a test ban treaty, while admitting that it contained many elements of uncertainty. And there were those who were convinced that no system of inspection could be devised that offered anything better than a marginal hope of detecting and verifying a concealed test shot.

None of the scientists questioned the "big hole" theory, which was originally developed by Dr. Albert Latter of the Rand Corp. While the higher mathematics that go into the theory are beyond most of us, in essence the theory constitutes the kind of scientific commonsense that a nonscientific layman like myself can appreciate. Let me explain it in my own way: If one simply tamps an atomic charge into a hole in the ground and shoots it off, he will get a seismic signal that is roughly proportionate to the magnitude of the explosion. If, on the other hand, one explodes a test shot in the center of a large spherical cavity, the surrounding air muffles, or decouples, the explosion so that one gets a much smaller seismic signal. If the hole is made large enough, the seismic reading can be reduced by a factor of 300, which means that 300 tons would register as 1 ton.

By their joint calculations, Dr. Latter and Dr. Bethe have demonstrated that, in a spherical cavity 500 feet in diameter, a 20-kiloton device—that is, a device equal to 20,000 tons of TNT, which was the size of the Hiroshima bomb—would produce a seismic signal equal to that of 70 tons of TNT. Unless the seismograph were close in, this would produce no more than an imperceptible wriggle in a seismic reading.

The original Geneva agreement of 1958 had been based on the assumption that an international network of 180 stations, which would include 21 stations in the Soviet Union, would be adequate to detect tests of 5 kilotons. Later this was amended to read that the system would be adequate for detection of seismic readings of greater than 4.75. This would be, roughly, equivalent to the explosion of a 20-kiloton bomb.

I must say a 20-kiloton bomb could not have demolished the Geneva agreement more completely than did the "big hole" theory.

The debate that took place between the scientists representing the two points of view makes highly interesting reading.

Dr. Hans Bethe, Dr. Roberts, and some of the other scientists who favored compromise said that, while the "big hole" theory was unchallengeable as theory, it was questionable whether it would ever be translated into practice. Apart from the general agreement on the "big hole" theory, their opinions were challenged at virtually every other point by Dr. Edward Teller, Dr. Latter, Dr. Brown, and some of the other scientists who testified.

The first group said that a hole of 500 feet in diameter could only be excavated by running water through an underground salt deposit; that such an operation would cost $50 million, which would make it prohibitive in price; that salt deposits of the necessary cubic volume and deep enough underground could be found only in a very limited number of places; that such a cavity could not be excavated without detection of the human activity in the area and of the increased salinity in the adjacent waters and soils.

The second group pointed out that one salt dome of 500 feet cubic diameter already does exist in the United States; that limestone deposits, which are very widely distributed, also lend themselves to the construction of big holes; that a 500-foot hole could probably be built for much less than the estimated $50 million, but even $50 million was not a prohibitive sum when equated against the cost of a nuclear weapons program, and when it is assumed that the cavity could be used over and over again; that in a totalitarian state human activity was highly concealable; that any increase in salinity would dissipate rapidly.

Finally, they pointed out that the hole need not be 500 feet in diameter; this is the size of the hole needed to decouple a 20 kiloton explosion effectively. To take care of a 1 kiloton explosion, and at this level a considerable amount of really significant testing can be done, would require a big hole only one-twentieth the size. This would involve a very simple exercise in engineering and would reduce the cost to no more than several million dollars per hole.

They argued further, that, at the 1 kiloton level, it would be possible to conduct tests inside a specially constructed container, perhaps disguised as a factory.

Having argued at every point in support of the feasibility of an adequate detection system, Dr. Bethe went on to agree that the discovery of the decoupling technique made a more extensive detection network imperative. As I have pointed out previously, he proposed a system involving 21 manned stations, 600 robot seismic stations, and 300 on-site inspections per annum.

Dr. Bethe said that the installation of his proposed grid of seismic stations at 125 mile intervals would provide a 300 times greater sensitivity than the original Geneva network, which would compensate for a potential decoupling factor of 300. With the proposed network, therefore, it would still be possible to detect explosions of greater than 20 kilotons magnitude.

The scientists on the other side of the table challenged this argument on two scores. First, they said, it was naive to believe that the Kremlin, which has not yet agreed to the installation of a single station, could be talked into accepting

600 stations. Secondly, they pointed out that while Dr. Bethe's network might take care of a decoupling factor of 300, the technology of decoupling and of cheating in general was still in its infancy. It was suggested, for example, that a greatly increased decoupling factor could be obtained by surrounding the nuclear charge with several tons of graphite. When the charge went off, the graphite would be vaporized and the great heat required to produce vaporization would sap much of the energy of the explosion and reduce its seismic impact.

Dr. Roberts and others argued that it was theoretically possible to distinguish the seismic signal of an earthquake from that of a nuclear explosion and that the technique of obtaining and reading seismic signals might be improved by a program of research. Dr. Harold Brown of the Lawrence Radiation Laboratory stated that initially it had been believed that only a small percentage of the continental earthquakes which occur would produce seismic signals which did not clearly identify them as earthquakes.

On the basis of our experience in the Hardtack tests of 1958, however, Dr. Brown declared that, of the 5,000 or more continental earthquakes per year which produce seismic signals equivalent to a 1 kiloton explosion or greater, "only a few percent could be identified by the seismic signature method." This, he said, "left many thousands throughout the world which could then be suspected of being nuclear explosions of between 1 and 5 kilotons and about 100 which could be suspected of being nuclear explosions of 5 kilotons or more." Actually, I am told these statistics on earthquakes are conservative. There probably are tens of thousands. Even if we were to accept Dr. Bethe's estimate that 90 per cent of the earthquakes could be identified by their seismographic signal, it would still leave many hundreds and perhaps thousands of seismic disturbances that could not clearly be identified as such.

Dr. Brown and others pointed out that the earth is a noisy medium, that it is extremely difficult to filter out background noises produced by trains or trucks or other manmade disturbances, or by pressure changes in the atmosphere, or by waves beating on the shore. If the first upward motion on the seismograph, which might be expected from a nuclear explosion, is lost in the background noise, then the second motion on the chart, which is downward, would appear to be the first motion, and under these circumstances, the conclusion would be that the signal had been caused by an earthquake.

Dr. Brown pointed out that seismic signals could be confused or forged by simultaneously detonating large quantities of conventional explosives in some legitimate engineering enterprise which the Soviets might demonstrably open to public inspection.

Finally, the scientists pointed out that the Kremlin could achieve complete seismic concealment by setting up their test shots so that they would be triggered by seismic shocks of considerably greater magnitude. This would be an extremely simple arrangement, and there are enough natural earthquakes occurring each year to enable the Kremlin to run off such test shots to its heart's content. The debate went on and on and on, in this manner. I found the reading of the arguments on both sides fascinating. But I feel that the entire argument was rendered completely irrelevant by the two points on which the opposing sides agreed.

Point No. 1 is that even if the impossible did happen and the Kremlin agreed to 21 manned and 600 robot seismic stations plus 300 annual inspections, this would only provide us with the capability of detecting blasts of greater than 20 kilotons magnitude. Even with today's technology—and this technology will be improved—tests of far less than 20 kilotons magnitude could be extrapolated in designing improved weapons systems covering virtually the entire nuclear and thermonuclear spectrums.

Point No. 2 is that, even given the Bethe network, and even given the maximum conceivable improvement in methods of detection, there is a threshold below which no detection, let alone verification, would be possible. This threshold was estimated at approximately 1 kiloton. A kiloton blast, decoupled or reduced, by a factor of 300, becomes the equivalent of only 3 tons of TNT. What this signifies is that there will never be any method of detecting nuclear explosions in a range that covers virtually the entire projected spectrum of tactical nuclear weapons.

If these two points are true, what conceivable purpose is there to arguing about our ability to detect tests of greater than 20 kilotons magnitude?

It would be bad enough if this entire irrelevant argument had been confined to the hearing room of the Joint Committee on Atomic Energy. But it seems to me that the President and State Department have now bogged down in this grotesque and utterly irrelevant argument. And, in doing so, they have, unwittingly, helped the Kremlin to befuddle Western public opinion.

Perhaps I am obtuse or just plain unscientific, but for the life of me I see no point to a detection system which would cost several billion dollars to install and probably another billion dollars per year to operate, and which would still leave the Communists free to sneak test any device up to the size of a Hiroshima-type bomb.

But we have not yet come to the end of the nonsense. Dr. Bethe's proposed enlargement of the system would not in any way take care of test shots released over remote ocean waters, perhaps in the proximity of the Antarctic. With the Soviet Union and the United States both building missile submarines with nuclear propulsion, the vast stretches of the world's oceans are to be "inspected" by only 10 ship stations. What way would there be of preventing a Soviet submarine from surfacing in a remote area, firing a test shot, taking its observations, and then submerging for a long underwater trip back to its home station, We might detect such a shot; but how could we possibly prove, in the absence of a *corpus delicti* or a captured submarine, that it had been fired by the Kremlin? If we wanted to police the seas on a scale that would make inspection meaningful, it would probably cost additional billions of dollars per year.

If the discussion on detection capabilities was irrelevant, the debate on verification was doubly irrelevant. Verification would require the production of material evidence in the form of a radioactive core of rock.

Again I may be obtuse or unscientific, but what conceivable point is there to discussing the pros and cons of verification if one cannot even detect a test shot of less than 20 kilotons magnitude? There may be a flicker of hope that with thousands of stations, signals might be obtained indicating a test ban violation above a threshold of, let us say, several kilotons. But it is one thing to suspect a violation, and another thing to prove in a legally valid form that a violation has occurred. And, as I see the matter, the proof would have to have legal validity before we could cancel the treaty or ask for sanctions against the violator.

I should like, nevertheless, to summarize some of the testimony on verification that was given to the Joint Committee, because it all helps to demonstrate what a monstrously fallacious thing the so-called enforceable test ban is.

Although the scientists varied in their estimates, all of them agreed that verification was an exceedingly complex problem and that the mathematical odds were in favor of a determined and enterprising cheater. Several of the scientists estimated the odds against verification at 100,000 to 1.

The distinguished Senator from Tennessee has pointed out that in the case of the Rainier test shot, even though we knew the exact underground point at which the shot had been exploded, it required 3 months of drilling to come up with a radioactive core. But let me summarize for your amusement some of the complexities of the problem of verification as described to the Joint Committee.

Let us assume the inspection system is set up and a station at point X receives a seismic signal which cannot clearly be identified as an earthquake. Depending on the spacing of the stations, it would be necessary to carry out a minute examination of some 100 square miles to 500 square miles of Soviet territory. The first surveys would be aerial surveys utilizing all types and sizes of aircraft, ranging from helicopters to multi-engine, fixed-winged craft, and flying at survey altitudes ranging from 150 feet to 18,000 feet. The aerial reconnaissance would involve first, visual observation; second, photography; third, radiation, magnetic, electromagnetic, and infrared surveys.

Obviously, the first task of the aerial survey would be to determine whether or not the seismic event was an earthquake, or a nuclear explosion. A nuclear explosion might produce a fissure in the ground if it were not down deep enough; but this is a possibility we can rule out. There might be some metallic debris or other signs of human activity if the Communists were careless; but I believe that this, too, is a possibility we can rule out.

So, the aircraft flies over this suspected area. The inspectors find no signs of human activity, and their sensitive instruments pick up no surface evidence of an explosion. On the other hand, there is physical evidence that a genuine earthquake has occurred in this area. What do the inspectors do at this point? Do they call off the search and write off the seismic signal to a genuine earthquake? Or do they take the quite realistic stand that the earthquake may have been used as a shield for a test explosion? In the latter case, every suspicious seismic event would involve detailed inspection over a large area, by air, on the ground, underground, and underwater.

According to the most optimistic estimates, it would be possible, by means of such techniques, to narrow the area of suspicion down to one-half of 1 square mile and ultimately to a radius of 500 feet. Then drilling would commence. The smaller the test shot, the greater the difficulty of location. According to Dr. C. E. Violet, of the Lawrence Radiation Laboratory, the probability of locating radioactive debris from a 1.7-kiloton explosion would be approximately 1 in 100,000. To make the probability 1, or equal to unity, he said, one would have to drill 100,000 holes. A far more optimistic estimate was presented by Dr. Richard M. Foose, of Stanford Research Institute. Let us examine this "optimistic" estimate.

If the area of suspicion could be cut down to 500 feet in radius, it would require only 63 drill holes, in triangular grid pattern, to insure 100 percent completeness of search. The tables presented in connection with this "optimistic" estimate are "enough to make a cow laugh", to use a favorite expression of Comrade Khrushchev. The drilling of 63 holes would involve a total footage of 75,600 feet. This, I would point out, is the equivalent of three Mount Everests. At a cost of $5 per foot, exclusive of all mobilization costs, this would work out to $378,000. Working three shifts a day, it would require 1,008 man-days of drilling and this, mind you, simply to carry out one inspection of one undetermined seismic disturbance. If one were willing to settle for a 1-in-10 chance of verification, fewer holes would be necessary.

At this point, Representative Durham made the apt comment:

> If you had about 10 seismic disturbances and had to inspect them on the basis of what you told us here, you probably would have full employment in most of the country.

I am afraid that this employment would not be limited to our skilled and unskilled workers. To carry out 300 such on-site inspections per annum would probably require several entire graduating classes of seismologists, geologists, and of scientists and engineers in the critical field of nucleonics.

If the probability of detection is 1 in 1,000 and the probability of verification is 1 in 1,000—and these are far from being the most conservative estimates—then the combined probability of detection and verification is 1 in 1 million. If the combined probability figure were a thousand times smaller than this, it would still be preposterous. It would be bad enough if it were simply a matter of absurdity. But, as I have pointed out previously, and as I want to emphasize again, these estimates of probability become utterly irrelevant when you consider that they apply to tests of greater than 20 kilotons magnitude, that below this level, no detection would be possible.

How ridiculous can we get?

As for tests in the lower reaches of space or in outer space, all the evidence points to the conclusion that the Soviets would be able to conduct such tests with impunity, even with devices of considerable size. As everyone knows, our Argus shot went completely undetected.

Let us assume that the Geneva network is installed in the Soviet Union and that a clandestine 100-kiloton test shot is fired at an altitude of several hundred miles somewhere in the northernmost reaches of Siberia on the fringe of the Arctic Ocean. Light-measuring instruments, if stationed close enough, might detect the explosion. But if the shot were fired against the background of a brilliant display of the aurora borealis, how could we ever prove that the transitory flicker registered by our light instruments was not actually caused by a sudden brilliant burst of the aurora? There might be electromagnetic disturbances similar to those which caused the temporary communications blackout after the Argus shot. But if the shot were fired at a period of considerable sunspot activity, how could we ever prove that the sunspots had really not been responsible? No matter how great our suspicions might be, in the absence of radioactive debris there would be no way of clinching our case against the cheater.

It is time that we put an end to all this sorry exercise in futility and irrelevance.

It is high time—it is past time—that we presented the facts to the American people.

It is time that we woke up to the fact that these protracted negotiations are part of the conflict strategy of the Soviet rulers, that they have used these negotiations first, to impose a moratorium on nuclear weapons testing by the United States; second, to intensify the international propaganda in favor of a total test ban, without inspection or with inadequate inspection; third, to create a condition of international hysteria which would restrict or prevent the possibility of effective Western reaction to aggression.

It is time we realize that the extension of the moratorium is a deadly serious business, that a single, major, technological breakthrough by the Soviet scientists who have produced the A-bomb, the H-bomb, and the sputnik, may confront us with a choice between enslavement and annihilation.

On February 11, 1960, President Eisenhower submitted to

the Soviet Government a four-point plan for ending the deadlock in the nuclear test ban negotiations. His proposal called for an immediate ban, under assured controls, of all nuclear weapons tests in the atmosphere and in the ocean, of space tests up to altitudes where effective controls can function, and of underground tests above a seismic magnitude of 4.75.

It also called for a joint program of research and experimentation, and offered to extend the ban systematically to remaining areas underground as adequate control measures were devised.

I favor the proposal of an immediate, complete, and unconditional ban on the several categories of tests that result in atmospheric contamination. Such an agreement could have gone into effect without delay since such tests are easily monitored, whereas the detection of even very large underground tests, of tests in space, and of tests over remote ocean areas, requires the establishment of extensive monitoring facilities.

By and large, however, President Eisenhower's plan was a good one. It was a simple, straightforward proposal on an issue of vital importance to the whole of mankind. I agree with him that, had the Soviets accepted this proposal, it might ultimately have paved the way for a much broader agreement on disarmament.

But, instead of accepting our proposal, the Kremlin responded with a diplomatic ploy. It announced that it was prepared to "accept" the President's proposal to ban all major tests of nuclear weapons if the West would sign a pledge not to conduct any nuclear tests, big or small, for a number of years to be decided by negotiations. A period of 4 years was suggested. Among other things, it specifically "accepted" the President's proposal that during the period of the moratorium, a joint program of research would be carried out for the purpose of improving detection capabilities.

At the time it was made, the Soviet counterproposal was hailed as a concession to our point of view. For the life of me, I cannot understand why. In my opinion, their counterproposal constituted an act of international blackmail, and we should have called it this. It was as though the Kremlin were pointing a pistol at the head of mankind and saying to us: "We refuse not to contaminate the atmosphere, unless you agree to a moratorium on undetectable underground tests, which do not contaminate the atmosphere, but which might conceivably add to your defensive capabilities."

The Soviet counteroffer conceded nothing. It was merely a rehash of the old Soviet position, substituting the concept of a voluntary moratorium for that of a formal ban on small underground tests. But instead of exposing it for the fraud it was, the President suggested that the Soviet offer was indicative of a sincere desire to come to terms: and Ambassador Wadsworth issued a joint communique with the Soviet and British representatives which carried the strong implication that the Kremlin had accepted the American proposal with certain minor modifications.

The distinguished Senator from New Mexico [Mr. Anderson] deserves the thanks of all of us for immediately denouncing the Soviet offer as a "phony" and for the incisive analysis which he presented to the Senate on March 22. We are equally in the debt of the Senator from Tennessee [Mr. Gore] for the dignified but forthright manner in which he raised the matter of the joint communique and explained to Ambassador Wadsworth that, in signing it, he had made an unwitting contribution to the Soviet propaganda campaign.

But Senator Anderson's eloquent warning fell on deaf ears. On March 22, 1960, the very day on which he spoke in the Senate, there took place a meeting of the so-called Committee of Principals: Secretary of State Christian Herter, Allen Dulles, George E. Kistiakowsky, the President's science adviser, Atomic Energy Commissioner McCone, and Deputy Defense Secretary Douglas, sitting in for Secretary Gates. According to an article by Mr. Chalmers Roberts in the *Reporter* for April 27, the Committee of Principals, with only Commissioner McCone opposing, decided in favor of conditional acceptance of the Soviet counterproposal.

According to Mr. Roberts, the joint communique issued by President Eisenhower and Prime Minister Macmillan on March 29, 1960, from Camp David was based largely on the agreement reached by the Committee of Principals on March 22. In the Camp David communique, the two heads of government said that they had agreed that, once remaining issues had been resolved and a treaty signed, "they would be ready to institute a voluntary moratorium of agreed duration on nuclear weapons tests below that threshold—4.75 on the seismic instruments—to be accomplished by unilateral declaration of each of the three powers."

This statement contained two vital concessions to the Soviet point of view. By implication, it extended the scope of the proposed test ban treaty to cover undetectable tests in space. In this respect, and in consenting to a moratorium on undetectable underground test shots, we abandoned the cardinal principle of enforceable inspection which has thus far guided us in our negotiations on disarmament and the test ban. In my opinion, it constituted the single most catastrophic retreat since the inception of the test ban negotiations.

I agree wholeheartedly with Mr. Arthur Krock's statement in the *New York Times* of March 31, 1960:

The response of the President and the British Prime Minister to Soviet Russia's latest nuclear disarmament proposal gave Premier Khrushchev what he wanted.

Because of the softness and lack of understanding which the administration had displayed on the test ban issue, this has become the area of greatest danger at the forthcoming summit conference. But I feel that the hearings recently held by the Joint Committee on Atomic Energy provided the Administration with every justification for reconsidering its position. In the light of this testimony, I consider it mandatory that we free our hands to resume tests that are not subject to detection and do not contaminate the atmosphere—at the very least to resume small underground tests.*

---

* *Author's note:* At the time this speech was made, the best available scientific information was to the effect that our nuclear weapons development program could be adequately served by underground tests and tests in space. This evaluation, in turn, was conditioned by the prevalent belief that the moratorium on testing, in one form or another, was bound to be extended. On this one point, I have had to revise my position in the light of the massive series of atmospheric tests conducted by the Soviet Union in September and October of last year, and in the light of new

I do not think the Administration need feel in the least embarrassed over revising its stand at this point. The original moratorium was based on the belief of competent scientific advisers that an adequate system of detection and verification could be devised. On the basis of the most recent scientific testimony, it is now apparent that the chances of developing such a system are exceedingly slim; certainly it is not something that can be counted on within the next decade.

In theory, despite our recent concessions, we still adhere to the position that any agreement on testing must be based on a truly enforceable system of inspection. We would be acting in consonance both with this principle and with recent scientific evidence if we now reverted to the President's eminently sensible proposal of February 11, 1960.

I believe that the fate of our country and the fate of the entire free world community may hinge upon our early resumption of underground nuclear testing. Every day of delay cuts down our nuclear technological lead over the Soviets. It is not inconceivable that, as a result of our voluntary 2-year moratorium, they have already caught up with us and surpassed us at a number of points.

FALLACY NO. 6

Fallacy No. 6 is that the cessation of nuclear tests will, *ipso facto*, result in a relaxation of the dangerous tensions that have grown up in the world. This fallacy we can dispose of in a few minutes because that is all it deserves.

The Conference of International Experts on Nuclear Test Detection took place in Geneva in the summer of 1958. While the conference was still in progress, and after it became apparent that the West was yielding and that a joint statement on agreed findings would be issued, the Quemoy-Matsu crisis erupted.

---

scientific evidence that important aspects of our nuclear weapons development program were critically dependent on atmospheric testing.

I am convinced, however, that the development of cleaner warheads will limit the fallout from our atmospheric tests to a level that does exceedingly little, if any, damage to public health.

On October 31, 1958, the United States exploded its last nuclear test shot and announced to the world that it was embarking on a voluntary 1-year moratorium, while the possibilities of a test ban were being further explored with the Soviet Union. Simultaneously, the Soviet Government embarked, or announced that it was embarking, on a reciprocal moratorium.

Exactly 4 weeks later, on November 27, 1958, Khrushchev promulgated his famous Berlin ultimatum. The 18 months that have elapsed since the ultimatum was issued have witnessed a whole series of missile-rattling perorations by Mr. Khrushchev, the bloody riots in the Panama Canal Zone, the establishment of a quasi-Communist regime in Cuba, and stepped up activity by the Communist Parties throughout the free world.

This is the relaxation of tensions which we purchased with our voluntary moratorium on nuclear tests! I do not consider this sequence of events accidental. I am not surprised by them. It is only natural that the Communists should have been emboldened by their success in bludgeoning us into a nuclear test policy, the folly of which was eloquently described by both President Eisenhower and Secretary of State Dulles in statements made as late as the end of 1957.

My prediction is that, if we now formalize the moratorium by entering into a test ban treaty with inadequate inspection, the Kremlin will again be emboldened, and will become more demanding, not less demanding.

FALLACY NO. 7

Fallacy No. 7 is the oft-repeated statement that in the course of the Geneva negotiations the Russians have conceded far more points than has the West, that they have shown a genuine desire to reach agreement, that the two sides have already arrived at an agreement on all but 4 or 5 of the 17 articles of the treaty, and that an agreement on an enforceable test ban is, in fact, just around the corner.

It is entirely true that the Soviets have made concessions on a number of points, even on many points. But these concessions have always been on points of secondary importance. On the really basic question like the number of on-site inspections per annum, they have shown themselves absolutely adamant.

Let me give one example of the "great" concessions the Soviets have made. When the "big hole" theory was first presented to them at Geneva by Dr. Bethe, the Soviet delegates denied its validity. The "big hole" theory, however, is something that can be demonstrated mathematically: it has also been verified in recent tests conducted with conventional explosives. After a period of resistance, the Soviet delegation finally abandoned its opposition to the "big hole" theory, but without specifically accepting it. This was just as if they had agreed not to argue against the proposition that two plus two equals four—but without specifically agreeing that it does.

Dr. Bethe and some of our columnists hailed this as one of the most significant of the Russian concessions and as another indication of their genuine desire to compromise. I am not a scientist but I have had some experience with facts. Consequently, I find Dr. Bethe's logic here very difficult to follow.

Compared with the altogether minor concessions which the Soviets have made on a number of points, the West has made three concessions of fundamental importance.

Our first major concession, was our agreement, in violation of everything we had previously said, to consider the questions of nuclear testing in isolation from the general problem of disarmament.

The second major Western concession was our agreement to extend the test ban treaty to cover undetectable tests in outer space. This, again, constituted a violation of our fundamental position that there should be no disarmament of any kind without enforceable inspection.

Our third major concession, and in my opinion potentially the most disastrous, was our submission to the Russian demand that the conclusion of the treaty be accompanied by a voluntary moratorium or, to be exact, by the extension of the already existing voluntary moratorium on undetectable underground tests.

It is true, too, that agreement has been reached on some 12 or 13 articles of the 17-article treaty. But the articles on which no agreement has yet been reached constitute the heart of the treaty. Let me quote the comment of the *Washington Post* on April 20, 1960:

> In its present form, the incomplete treaty is like an automobile with a chassis, wheels, transmission, body, dual controls, upholstery, and trim. Missing from it is the engine, electrical sytem, and fuel.

Finally, it may also be true that a test ban treaty is just around the corner. But, if a test ban treaty does come into being, in the light of present attitudes and of the Camp David pronouncement I believe we can safely predict that it will not be the kind of test ban agreement about which we were talking one year ago. It will not, in short, be a test ban agreement in which our national interests are protected by a system of enforceable inspection.

FALLACY NO. 8

The eighth fallacy is the thesis, exceedingly popular after the first Geneva conference, that the question of a test ban can easily be resolved if we simply turn the problem over to the scientists on both sides.

According to this fallacy, the scientists at Geneva, who came together unencumbered by political prejudice, had no difficulty in arriving at a meeting of the minds. The conference was conducted in an atmosphere of openness and cordiality; and there emerged from it an honest agreement on the guiding scientific principles for a test ban agreement.

The true story of what happened at the Geneva conference is very far from the romantic idyll which was presented to the press of the world.

In checking through the documents pertaining to the conference, the first thing that strikes one is the almost indecent haste with which we rushed to get to Geneva. Here was a projected conference of extraordinary complexity, in a field where there was virtually no body of experience to serve as a guide. But the delegation to the conference, consisting of 3 senior scientists and some 20 technical advisers, was thrown together, briefed, and dispatched to Geneva all within a period of a few weeks.

The picture of idyllic apolitical relations which were supposed to have existed at the conference, was badly punctured by the recent testimony of the American scientists to the Joint Congressional Committee on Atomic Energy. Let me quote a few items from these hearings.

Dr. Wolfgang H. Panofsky, High Energy Physics Laboratory, Stanford University, told the committee:

After the report of the 1958 conference of experts was filed with the governments of the three countries, all of them (including the United States) formally accepted the report. As a result, the U.S.S.R. delegations like to refer to the report as a formal agreement on technical facts rather than as a technical working paper. In so doing, they propose that the experts' report is an unchangeable point of departure for the political negotiators. On the other hand, the United Kingdom and United States delegations have assumed that the technical facts should be brought up to date to reflect changes in our knowledge.

Dr. Harold Brown, Deputy Director of the Livermore Weapons Laboratories, made this commentary on the behavior of the Soviet scientists.

On a number of occasions, I have seen them [the Russian scientists] accept something in private scientifically, or at least appear to accept it scientifically, and then come back for the record with quite a different attitude. There is always a technical explanation. Sometimes it holds almost no water. Sometimes it is quite fallacious. Other times there is some basis to what they say.

Dr. Brown went on to say:

No conference of experts' report can logically be criticized for not taking adequate account of the self-evident fact that a violator of a treaty or a moratorium on nuclear weapons tests must be expected to take full advantage of whatever methods he can find to reduce the probability of detection.

One can say, looking back, that perhaps not enough attention was paid to them (the difficulties of detection) particularly in such items as the possibility of very large decoupling, the difficulties of on-site inspection, and the possibilities of shielding explosions in space.

I cannot conclude my comments on the fallacy of the scientific idyll at Geneva without some reference to Dr. Hans Bethe, the chief adviser on nuclear testing to the President's Scientific Advisory Committee.

Dr. Bethe is one of the greatest living theoretical physicists, and, as a man of science I have nothing but respect for him. He has the good and the bad qualities of the theoretical physicist. He is by reputation stubborn in his convictions, but willing to listen to demonstrable evidence when he is proven wrong. Unfortunately, Dr. Bethe's predictions in the field of science have frequently been wrong, and his predictions in the fields of technology, military science, and politics have fared even worse.

In the immediate postwar period he frequently declared that the Soviets would not get the atomic bomb for decades. Before the H-bomb, he took the stand that it could not be made and should not be made. And when we developed the hydrogen bomb, he was just as emphatic in his declaration that the Soviets would never discover the secret for themselves. Before the big hole theory was developed by Dr. Albert Latter, Dr. Bethe had declared that decoupling was impracticable. After Latter had developed his theory, Dr. Bethe was big enough to examine and confirm the validity of the theory. In the light of this new knowledge, Dr. Bethe was also realistic enough to propose a substantial enlargement of the original Geneva detection network. But, in proposing it, he came up with the proposition that it was possible to construct completely tamperproof instruments and communication lines for his network. Experts with whom I have discussed the matter tell me that to this date no such thing as a completely tamperproof mechanical device has yet been produced. Nor did Dr. Bethe offer any suggestions.

On the basis of such a record of error on vital matters, what value should we place on the political sagacity of Dr. Hans Bethe?

At this hour of peril, how much reliance can the Nation place on the ability of the President's chief test ban expert to forecast accurately the course of future events in science or in politics?

CAN OUR NUCLEAR PARALYSIS BE TERMINATED?

On May 7* the President stated that we will resume underground nuclear testing, presumably by the end of the year.

---

* All of these dates, it should be remembered, relate to 1960.

This declaration was hailed by many as a welcome reversal of policy. But his statement leaves much unanswered and even more undone.

It commits us to limit the new test series to nonmilitary devices, when the crying need is for underground tests of new warheads and new devices designed to provide our land forces with tactical nuclear weapons and our defenses with antimissile capabilities.

It still leaves us committed to the offer made in the Camp David communique of May 29. This called for (1) a treaty banning not only detectable tests in the atmosphere, underwater, underground, and at high altitudes, but also banning undetectable tests in space; and (2) a moratorium on undetectable underground tests while a research program on improved methods of detection was carried forward.

It ignores the fact that with each new extension of the moratorium—no matter what we may say about our intentions at the end of the stated period—it becomes psychologically more difficult to renew testing.

In the war of propaganda, the Communists have used the test ban issue to place the West on the defensive, and to create a condition of international hysteria which would restrict or prevent the possibility of Western reaction to Communist aggression. They have been able to place us on the defensive for the simple reason that we have not given the facts to the American people and the people of the free world. The President's statement of May 7 still does nothing to give them the facts.

The President's statement still leaves us without a positive program that would enable us to carry the propaganda offensive to the Communists.

The President's offer of March 29 already conceded far more than should have been conceded. His statement of May 7 strongly suggests the conclusion that at the forthcoming summit conference it will be used as a bargaining device, and that our offer of March 29 may now be regarded only as an opening position which will be further compromised.

In the light of Khrushchev's recent conduct, in the light of the Berlin ultimatum, in the light of the situation in Cuba, and the many other evidences of aggression and subversion, what possible justification can there be for a continuation of the moratorium on underground tests, with or without a treaty banning tests in detectable media?

For my own part, as I have stated previously, I believe it can be taken as a virtual certainty that the Kremlin has not been observing a corresponding moratorium, and that it will not do so if a treaty is signed.

If the Administration does not accept this point of view, is it prepared to assure the American public that the Kremlin, its opposition to inspection notwithstanding, has honored the moratorium and will continue to do so? And if it cannot offer this assurance, on what grounds does it justify the extension of the moratorium?

By our exclusive reliance on the doctrine of massive retaliation; by our failure to concentrate on the development of clean tactical nuclear weapons as the chief means of off-setting the Communist superiority in manpower; by our failure to arm our NATO allies with the nuclear arms that are available; by our voluntary 2-year moratorium on tests, which, I am positive, have not been reciprocally observed by the Communists; by our failure to accord the antimissile missile the priority it deserves; by our failure to explore the potentialities of the neutron bomb and of the so-called Christofilos effect; by our failure to pursue the further development of nuclear weapons with all the energies at our command; by our recent abandonment of the principle that all disarmament measures, including a test ban, must be based on a system of enforceable inspection—by all these catastrophic errors in judgment, we have placed the free world in mortal peril.

That is why I am worried.

* * *

The Pulitzer prize-winning novel, "Advise and Consent," pictures an America of a few years hence, an America in which demagogues can inflame huge gatherings and bring them to their feet cheering with the slogan, "I would rather crawl to Moscow on my hands and knees than be killed by an atomic bomb."

Is this to be the image of America tomorrow? God forbid it. For should this book prove prophetic, it will mean that our people have rejected the choice between liberty and death made by Patrick Henry and the Founding Fathers, the choice which drew the cheers of America and of free men everywhere from 1775 down to the recent past.

It would mean the victory of the apostles of nuclear surrender. It would signify our total moral and spiritual capitulation.

It would mean that free America has chosen a slavery which is worse than death.

STATEMENT ISSUED SUBSEQUENT TO THE RESUMPTION OF NUCLEAR TESTING BY THE SOVIET UNION.

Washington, November 1, 1961.

In the two months that have elapsed since Khrushchev announced that the Soviet Union was about to resume atmospheric testing of nuclear weapons, the Kremlin has exploded 26 bombs, culminating in the explosion this Monday of Khrushchev's 50 megaton monster—the biggest and dirtiest nuclear explosion in history.

The Kremlin's defiance of world opinion is disturbing. But I am even more disturbed by the laggard tempo of our own test series. To date, we have exploded three underground devices, all of them of minor size. I had taken it for granted, as I know many people did, that, we had prepared for the contingency of the breakdown of the Geneva test ban talks by making all essential technical preparations for the resumption of tests. But when these talks finally did collapse after many months of Soviet intransigence, and when the Soviets began shooting off multimegaton weapons in the atmosphere as daily events, it developed that we had made no serious preparations for this contingency.

The awesome series of Soviet tests demands that we step up our own test program on a crash basis.

We must, in particular, bend every possible effort to convert the neutron bomb from a theoretical certainty to a practical reality. The neutron bomb would not only be a far more effective battlefield weapon than any now available to us; it would provide us with the most effective anti-missile warhead nuclear technology is today capable of producing.

As I have had occasion to point out in the past, our scientists had carried the preliminary theoretical work on the neutron bomb as far as it could go without testing. The late Thomas E. Murray, former Atomic Energy Commissioner, in an article written just before he died, implied that this weapon could have been tested last year had it not been for the moratorium, and had we pursued its development energetically.

We must not beguile ourselves with the thought that we possess enough weapons to destroy the Soviet Union many times over. The maintenance of the so-called balance of terror rests far more on nuclear technology than on the mere size of nuclear stockpiles. More than one expert in the field has pointed out that our vaunted nuclear superiority could be invalidated overnight if the Soviets were to score a major technological breakthrough—a breakthrough, for example, to the anti-missile missile, which the Soviets now claim to have developed.

We are in a race for survival. We do not need any 50 megaton terror explosions. But we must run as hard and as fast as we can.

Chapter IX

THE LESSONS OF THE CUBAN DISASTER*

Mr. President, I believe that President Kennedy's speech before the Society of Newspaper Editors, last Thursday, marked a turning point in our history and a turning point in the course of world affairs. It signifies that the humiliating period of retreats and defeats is now at an end. We accept the fact that we are locked in mortal combat with an implacable adversary. We are prepared to stand and fight wherever it may be necessary. We are prepared to fight together with our allies; but, if necessary, we will go it alone.

Ever since the close of World War II, under both Democratic and Republican administrations, we have been beguiled and bedeviled and pushed around and defeated by the forces of international communism. We had overwhelming military and political power in our hands, but we had neither the understanding nor the will to use it. Our good faith was absolute; our innocence was boundless; our blunders were seemingly endless.

While we have sought after coexistence and grasped eagerly at each new Soviet blandishment, the Communists have been able to take over one position after another in the free world. Today, we stand with our backs to the wall. There is no room for further retreat, because further retreat will threaten us with final disaster.

Now the President of the United States has warned the American people that we face a relentless struggle in every corner of the globe that goes far beyond the clash of armies or even nuclear armaments. He has warned them that conven-

---

* United States Senate, April 24, 1961.

tional and nuclear arms are only a shield, behind which the Communists operate by means of subversion, infiltration, and other underhand tactics; that in this way they occupy vulnerable areas, one by one, in a manner which makes armed intervention difficult or impossible for the free world. He has warned that our national security may be lost piece by piece, country by country, without the firing of missiles or the clash of arms.

In response to this challenge, the President has called for an intensification of our efforts in every field, and in many ways more difficult than war. He has accepted the struggle in which we are engaged as a struggle for the very survival of our way of life; and he has told the American people that we must take up the challenge, regardless of the cost and regardless of the peril.

If we as a nation are now prepared to stand, it is obvious that the first place where we must stand is Cuba. We cannot tolerate 90 miles from our shores a Soviet Socialist Republic, modeled slavishly after the Kremlin's own brand of tyranny, armed by the Kremlin, commanded by the Kremlin, and openly dedicated to the establishment of a Soviet Latin America.

We cannot tolerate it, nor can our Latin American neighbors tolerate it.

I find it difficult to understand the strange paralysis of understanding and of will that seems to have infected so many of our good friends in Latin America. The word "intervention" seems to have befuddled their senses, so that they stand hypnotized and inactive in the face of imminent destruction.

I do not think there is a single word in the English vocabularly that has generated more confusion than the word "intervention."

Thus, the United States now finds itself accused of "intervention" by the Soviet Union, which pretended that it was simply helping the popular will to assert itself when it sent 5,000 Red Army tanks into Budapest to crush the Hungarian revolution.

It finds itself accused of "intervention" by Prime Minister Nehru, who apparently could not make up his mind that the massacre of 50,000 Hungarians by the Red Army constituted intervention.

It finds itself accused of "intervention" by liberal European newspapers, some of which have charged that the United States has tried to do unsuccessfully in Cuba what the Soviet Union was able to do successfully in Hungary.

It finds itself accused of "intervention" at the United Nations by the delegations of many of the recently created African and Asian nations, who have been led to believe that the United States is endeavoring to establish some kind of imperialist empire in Latin America, and who equate all intervention with imperialism.

It finds itself accused of "intervention" by Latin American political leaders, whose heads would be the first to roll if Castro succeeds in exporting revolution to their own countries.

And even in our own country, there has been much confused talk about the American "intervention" in Cuba, as though we had done something wicked, something of which we should be ashamed, something that we cannot possibly explain to our friends in the United Nations.

World opinion in general, outside the Communist bloc, has been so bemused by the word "intervention" in relation to the Cuban situation that it has lost all sight of the basic moral and human issues.

The word "intervention" by itself is intrinsically neither good nor evil. Intervention can serve the cause of evil, and it can also serve the cause of justice. The entire stucture of civilized law is, in fact, based on the concept that, when an individual engages in wrongdoing, it is essential in the interest of moral order that society intervene against him, sometimes to restrain, sometimes to set right, sometimes to punish.

The Communists have intervened, are intervening today, and will continue to intervene in every situation where they can serve their own evil ends.

Sometimes they have intervened by direct and massive military action, as in Korea, Hungary and Tibet.

Sometimes they have intervened through quisling minorities, operating under the protection of Red Army bayonets.

This was how they seized power in Poland, Czechoslovakia, Bulgaria and Hungary.

Sometimes they have intervened by fostering, training, equipping and directing guerrilla and terrorist movements.

In this way, they almost succeeded in seizing power in Greece, they threatened and seriously retarded the postwar recovery of the Philippines, Burma, and Malaya, they conquered the greater part of Vietnam, and are now threatening the democratic republic of South Vietnam. And it is in this way, and with logistical support from the Soviet Union, that they have today occupied large parts of the Kingdom of Laos and now threaten its total subjugation.

Sometimes the Communists have intervened by stealth and fraud, posing as anything but Communists, so that they could seize the leadership of reform movements and install themselves in power before dropping their masks. This was the pattern in Guatemala and it was the pattern again in Cuba.

The Communists have never apologized for intervening. Indeed, they use threats of intervention openly as an instrument of foreign policy.

At the time of the Suez crisis, they threatened to raise an international brigade to fight at the side of Nasser, and Khrushchev brandished his nuclear weapons in repeated public statements. In the case of Cuba, he has again brandished his nuclear missiles vociferously and arrogantly.

When, therefore, Nikita Khrushchev talks about intervention as some heinous crime, committed only by depraved capitalistic nations, this should be enough to make the "cows of Kazakhstan" laugh.

But it is what Soviet intervention stands for, rather than intervention *per se,* that makes their intervention, whatever form it may take, a crime against mankind and against freedom.

The installation of a Communist regime in any country, whether by revolutionary action, or by stealth, or by military occupation, is a crime against humanity for the simple reason that communism is inherently evil. It is evil because in those countries where it has taken power, it has cost the lives of scores of millions of people; because it is militantly opposed to belief in God; because its totalitarian government violates all of man's God-given rights; because it subjects man to the cruelest slavery in history; because, while traditional autocracies can be overthrown by popular revolt, communism has perfected the techniques of repression to the point where successful popular revolt is virtually impossible.

If American arms had intervened in the battle of the Cochinos beachhead on the same scale as Soviet arms intervened, the outcome of this battle, I am sure, would have been different, and the Castro dictatorship would now have become an evil memory of the past.

Had we intervened effectively, there would today be every reason for rejoicing. The trouble was that our intervention was deficient in planning and determination and scope. This, I believe, was our error; this was the lesson to be learned.

I do not suggest that we should have sent in the Marines to put down the Castro dictatorship. This would have been completely unnecessary. The majority of the Cuban people have come to realize that the Castro regime is not an indigenous reform movement, but a quisling tyranny created by the Kremlin as a base for the subversion of Latin America.

The 100,000 Cuban refugees who have escaped to American soil attest to the intense hatred of the Cuban people for this regime of oppression and misery and national treason. The thousands of Cuban patriots who are fighting in the mountains, in open defiance of Castro's firing squads, also attest to this.

No regimes in history have created as much popular hatred and revulsion as have the Communist regimes in every country where they have been installed.

The press has made much of the fact that no popular uprising occurred to greet the invasion by the brave band of some 1,400 patriots that went ashore on the beach at Cochinos. Many newspapers have concluded from this that the estimates of popular discontent in Cuba were greatly exaggerated.

In my own opinion, it proves no such thing. In the first place, we have now learned that, the instant the invasion began, the Castro regime instituted a reign of terror without parallel in this hemisphere. According to newspaper accounts, within a matter of 48 hours, 50,000 people had been rounded up. Think of it! Fifty thousand people in a country of 6,000-000. This was as though a Communist dictatorship had rounded up 1,500,000 people in the United States and placed them in concentration camps.

In the second place, I believe it is only natural for people living under so cruel a dictatorship to wait for two or three days, to see how things are going before they decide to risk their own lives.

From the many contacts I have had with Cuban exiles, I am convinced that, had the battle of the beachhead been decided against Castro, a national uprising would have taken place despite the mass terror and mass executions.

In short, I disagree with the pessimistic, defeatist attitude of those who now say that the invasion was premature. True, it lacked coordination. True, there was bungling. True, more could have been done to soften up the Castro regime in advance. But the chief weakness, as I see it, was the fact that on the eve of the invasion we had not yet faced up to the problem that President Kennedy posed and answered so resolutely.

The first battle was bound to be of critical importance. Yet we had not decided what we were prepared to do and just how far we were prepared to help if the freedom fighters ran into difficulty.

According to the accounts which have reached the press, the battle of the Cochinos beachhead was really decided when Castro threw into the fight Soviet tanks and jet fighter planes. About the presence of Soviet jet aircraft over the beachhead there is still some doubt. But there is no doubt about the role played by Soviet tanks and other Soviet weapons. Nor is there any doubt about the fact that Cuban Communist pilots are in Czechoslovakia today, receiving training in Soviet fighter aircraft.

In my opinion, had we equalized the position on the Cochinos beachhead by providing the freedom fighters with close air support, there might be a different story to tell today.

I say that we should have done so, and that we should be prepared to do so.

We can no longer tolerate a situation in which a quisling totalitarian regime, directed at the subversion of the entire Western hemisphere, is able to maintain its hold over the Cuban people because of the massive quantities of arms placed in its hands by the Kremlin.

The time is long past due for a firm announcement that we will tolerate no further shipments of Soviet arms to the Western hemisphere. I believe we should advise both Mr. Khrushchev and Mr. Castro that we will tolerate no Soviet military aircraft in Caribbean skies.

I believe that if in the next round of battle we are prepared to give the Cuban freedom fighters the air support necessary to obliterate Communist air power in Cuba, the Cuban freedom fighters will take care of the rest.

By saying these things, I do not mean to ignore or underestimate the bungling which unquestionably took place on our side. The point I wish to make is that this bungling was of secondary importance. The first attempt to liberate Cuba from the Castro tyranny failed for the simple reason that we had yet to make the stern resolve that this fight must not be permitted to fail.

There is an enormous paradox inherent in the superiority of the Free World over the Communist World in the essential elements of strength, and the consistent record of defeat of the Free World by communism.

The material resources of the Free World in skilled manpower, wealth, arms and machinery are unquestionably greater; our political system demonstrably better; our intellectual resources incontestably superior; our moral and ethical values incomparably higher.

Why, then, do we consistently lose?

Are these defeats due to uncontrollable forces with which the statesmen of the West cannot cope and for which they cannot be held responsible? Or are they the result of specific, recognizable failures, failure of this policy or that source of information, failures of particular men and particular agencies?

The Communists believe that inevitable forces of history are determining the cold war in their favor.

There are philosophers and historians who, while they may dispute the Communist interpretation of the outcome of inevitable forces, nonetheless believe that the decisions of men are determined by the operation of vast forces beyond their control.

But we who uphold freedom believe that men determine events; that men can, by the exercise of their reason, by their free choice, change themselves, change their community, change their country, and change the course of the world struggle.

We must believe, therefore, that sufficient foresight and proper reading of clear communist intentions by Western statesmen could have saved Eastern Europe; that proper evaluation and determined action could have saved China; that boldness at the critical hour could have saved Indochina; that a determined will to win could have saved North Korea; that simple common sense could have saved us from the present Cuban fiasco.

Wrong decisions result in defeat; right decisions result in victory. We of the Free World have consistently lost because we have made a whole series of wrong decisions, based on faulty philosophy and poor information. That is our trouble.

It is senseless to say, in a spirit of misplaced sportsmanship or in a gush of superficial unity, "Let's not look back; let's not be Monday morning quarterbacks; let's not blame individuals for what has happened. Let's hope that the future will be better and move forward with the same philosophy, the same policies, the same team."

I believe that only new policies and new attitudes can reverse the decline of the West. Unless, after such a fiasco as our three-year Cuban policy, we find out and nail down which recommendations, which misinformation, which decisions, which attitudes, which particular men brought us down to defeat, we will gain nothing from our reverses and will only proceed to new and greater disasters.

It is in this spirit that I wish to examine certain aspects of the American policy failure that brought Fidel Castro to power in Cuba.

It has become customary to blame Castro's emergence on the poverty of the Cuban peasant masses, on the abuses of the Batista dictatorship, on American identification with the Batista dictatorship, on everything but our own lack of understanding and our own misconceived policy.

I agree that there was poverty in Cuba, that there was a need for social reform, that the Batista dictatorship had become unpopular, that until near the end we did not take the necessary measures to indicate that we did not approve of its excesses. But all of this still doesn't explain Castro's rise to power.

I am convinced that the situation could have been saved had we embarked upon an intelligent and energetic policy as late as 1958 or even 1959. An examination of our policy during this last period will reveal, at the very least, a consistent wrongheadedness which is nothing short of frightening.

If Batista had fallen and had been replaced by a democratic, and therefore pro-Western, government, there would have been every reason to rejoice. But the fact is that when Batista fell, his regime was replaced by an infinitely more evil dictatorship, and a dictatorship to boot, controlled from the Kremlin and dedicated to the subversion of Latin America.

I say that there was nothing inevitable about this.

There was opposition to the Batista dictatorship, especially in the cities. But this did not mean that the Cuban people were pro-Castro. At no time did Castro have more than 2,000 men under him in the Sierra Maestra mountains. Although they engaged in sabotage, Castro's "barbudos" fought no important engagements and had no serious military significance.

The real opposition to Batista was based on the middle class and the student body and the Catholic Church in the cities. This opposition was pro-democratic, overwhelmingly anti-

Communist, and only vaguely sympathetic to Castro, because he appeared to be moving in the same direction. It has been estimated that the urban opposition to Batista suffered 11,000 casualties compared with the 1,000 casualties suffered by Castro's forces from the beginning to the end of their insurrection. But this urban opposition movement lacked leadership, lacked unity, lacked publicity and, above all, it lacked American encouragement.

If the State Department was really convinced that the Batista regime had so lost the support of the people that its downfall had to be accelerated, why was no effort made to encourage the formation of a democratic middle of the road movement as an alternative to Castro? Surely it would have required very little encouragement to foster such a movement!

Why did we not take the initiative in urging elections under the supervision of the OAS? And why did we turn a deaf ear to Batista in 1958 when he seemed disposed to consider such elections?

Why was there no alert to the danger that if Batista were toppled while Castro, with his scattering of followers, commanded the only united and cohesive opposition movement, the consequence, the clearly inevitable consequence, would be the emergence of a Communist dictatorship in the heart of the Caribbean?

Why did we close our eyes to the operation of Castro agents on American soil, to the shipments of arms that went out from Florida to Castro and to the constant departure of reinforcements for the Sierra Maestra guerrillas?

These are questions that require answers. I think the answer to this is that our State Department was inclined to look upon the Castro movement as an agrarian reform movement, as it was once inclined to look upon the Chinese Communists as agrarian reformers. And so we decided to put all of our eggs in the Castro basket, to force Batista out so that Castro could take over, and hope for the best.

The Subcommittee on Internal Security has taken testimony indicating that this was so from three former United States Ambassadors: Ambassador Arthur Gardner, Ambassador Earl

E. T. Smith, and Ambassador William Pawley.[2] According to them, the State Department either ignored or appeared not disposed to believe their repeated warnings that most of Castro's chief lieutenants, and probably Fidel Castro himself, were Moscow Communists. Raul Castro, Che Guevara, and some of Castro's other top henchmen had received training in Moscow; this was commonly known. Fidel himself had played a leading role in the Bogota riots of 1949, which cost the lives of 1000 people, and he had been publicly denounced at the time by the Colombia radio as a foreign Communist agitator.

For a long time there was a lot of wishful thinking to the effect that Fidel Castro was probably not a Communist because there was no proof that he carried a Communist membership card and the Communists sometimes appeared to have differences with him. What a tenuous assumption on which to base American foreign policy!

Fidel Castro may not carry a Communist membership card to this day. But for all practical purposes he is a Communist. No one, I think, would now challenge this statement.[3]

This was as true of Fidel Castro yesterday as it is today. He was known to be pro-Soviet, and anti-American. His own brother and others of his chief lieutenants were graduates of Moscow. And finally, there was his role in the Bogota riots. Latin American students, by tradition, have a penchant for joining revolutionary movements in their own countries. But it is not part of their national tradition to travel to other countries for the purpose of instigating murderous riots. The pattern here is almost conclusively suggestive of Communist affiliation. Certainly, the Colombian police had no doubt on this score.

The question must be asked: Why was the information about the Communist direction of the Castro movement not given to the people of the United States and of Cuba before

[2] Since this speech was made, testimony has been taken from Ambassador Robert Hill and Ambassador Whiting Willauer, further confirming the testimony given by Ambassadors Gardner, Smith, and Pawley.

[3] In December 1961 Fidel Castro put an end to all doubts by publicly announcing that he had always been a Marxist-Leninist.

Castro seized power? Why were the American people permitted, if not encouraged, to believe, for a period of more than a year, that the Castro movement, although it might contain certain Communists, was essentially an agrarian reform movement?

I am certain that Secretary Herter did not wilfully suppress information of such critical importance. But if the State Department had this information and it was not passed on to the Secretary of State, or if it was passed on in a diluted manner, or if Secretary Herter was "protected" from his ambassadors, then it is important to know who in the Department was responsible for this delinquency.

I have said that our Cuban policy disaster may be traced back to the same fallacious political policy that has led us to disaster after disaster in the postwar period.

We have suffered from an almost obsessional attitude toward all the failings on our side, toward every aberration from Simon-pure democracy in our own society and on the part of our allies.

I believe that this exaggerated, ultraliberal preoccupation with the failings on our side, has induced a tendency to minimize the failings and evils that exist on the other side. The proponents of this philosophy have felt that there exists on both sides good and evil, the same human frailty, the same capacity for human failing, the same desire for peace and understanding. Coexistence, therefore, is possible and it must be sought after even at the cost of further compromises.

This tendency to believe the best of communism while believing the worst about ourselves and the Free World has wrought massive and irreparable damage since the close of World War II.

In the case of China, there were our desk-position policy-makers who hated Chiang Kai-shek so much that they were happy to see him defeated and to help precipitate his defeat, even though the obvious consequence was the establishment of a Communist regime in China.

In the case of Korea, American influence only last year exerted itself to force Syngman Rhee out of power, ostensibly because his regime was autocratic and inefficient. In doing so, we did not stop to ask what the consequence of this would be. In my opinion, the successor governments have suffered from the same characteristic Asian autocracy and inefficiency, but they have lacked Syngman Rhee's iron determination to stand up against communism.

In the case of Cuba, as I had pointed out, we were guilty of the same error, when we accelerated Batista's downfall at a time when no democratic alternative had been prepared, and when his downfall could only lead to a Castro government.

What I find particularly perplexing is that many of those who protest against the autocratic features of the Syngman Rhee regime or the Chiang Kai-shek regime, are prepared to swallow autocracy and dictatorship wholesale if they have a "progressive" label pinned on them.

The regime of Kwame Nkrumah in Ghana is infinitely more dictatorial and oppressive, for example, than the Syngman Rhee regime was at its worst. But it is not criticized, presumably because it speaks in the name of "social reform" and "anti-imperialism." The Toure regime in Guinea has already assumed many of the trappings of Soviet totalitarianism. But we are urged to avoid abuse in dealing with Guinea and to seek to win Toure over to our side.

It is time to take inventory of our position. We can no longer afford the luxury of toppling friendly anti-Communist regimes simply because they do not adhere to the norms of democracy that civilized society has taken centuries to evolve.

In World War II, to save ourselves from the evils of Nazism, we entered into a military alliance with Soviet totalitarianism, which was equally as evil. As Churchill put the matter: "If a lion were about to devour me, and a crocodile came along and started biting off the lion's foot, I should welcome this assistance, even though I have no particular fondness for crocodiles."

It is time that we start building our alliances as best as we can, never endorsing dictatorship, using our influence and example in the interest of greater freedom, but seeking military agreements as frank arrangements of convenience, as we did in World War II.

The President of the United States has spoken on the menace of Castroism, and in words not easily misunderstood. The nation is with him, indeed the entire Free World will rally to his support.

Chapter X

SOUTHEAST ASIA: THE DANGERS OF APPEASEMENT

I consider it an honor to be present at this historic Conference of the Asian People's Anti-Communist League.

You meet at a moment of peril and crisis.

We are all, I know, downhearted by recent developments in
Cuba and in Laos. We are fearful and worried over the growing Communist guerrilla action in South Vietnam, over the
growing threat to the free nations of Southeast Asia. We are
all concerned, too, over the propaganda implications of the
Kremlin's one-sided triumph in space.

On the basis of our postwar record, I could not blame you
for believing that the American giant has been asleep. This
indeed, was the theme of a recent article in *Reader's Digest*
by that great Asian and world statesman, General Carlos P.
Romulo. "Wake Up America!" was the title of his article.

I believe there is symbolic significance in the fact that this
article, calling upon America to raise itself from its slumber,
was written by an Asian. It is in Asia that the Communists
have scored their greatest victories since the close of World
War II. It is in Asia, too, that the armed forces of communism
and of freedom have clashed most frequently. In China, in
Korea, in Vietnam, in Tibet, in Malaya, in the Philippines
and on the northern frontiers of India, hundreds of thousands
of Asian patriots have given their lives in the battle for freedom.

---

* Manila, The Philippines, May 3, 1961.

And while the whole Free World is threatened by the advancing Communist tide, it is Asia that is most immediately threatened. Your countries stand on the front line. Here in Asia there is no more room for retreat and there is precious little margin for error. The fate of freedom the world over, in my opinion, may very well be decided in the Far East in the bitter battles that now loom on the horizon.

The West would do well to heed the warnings of the Asian peoples, not only because of their present peril, but also because of their hard-won experience in the battle against communism. There have been defeats in the Far East, tragic defeats. But there have also been great victories.

I cannot help recalling that it was here in the Philippines under the leadership of the immortal Ramon Magsaysay, that freedom won one of its most significant victories over the subterranean forces of communism.

The most important item of news which I can convey to you today is that America is now awake. I believe that the moment of awakening can be dated from President Kennedy's historic speech on Cuba before the American Society of Newspaper Editors.

In this speech, the President of the United States warned the American people that "we face a relentless struggle in every corner of the globe that goes far beyond the clash of armies or even nuclear armaments." He warned them that conventional and nuclear arms are only a shield, behind which the Communists operate by means of subversion, infiltration and other underhanded tactics, that in this way they occupy vulnerable areas one by one in a manner which makes armed intervention difficult or impossible for the Free World. He warned that our national security may be lost piece by piece, country by country, without the firing of missiles or the clash of arms.

In response to this challenge, the President has called upon the American people for an intensification of our efforts in every field, "and in many ways more difficult than war." He has accepted the struggle in which we are engaged as a struggle for the very survival of our way of life, and he has told the American people we must take up the challenge "regardless of the cost and regardless of the peril."

What President Kennedy's statement signifies is that the period of blunder and slumber, of retreats and defeats, is now at an end. We have recognized the nature of our adversary, we have accepted the fact of mortal combat, we realize that we stand with our backs to the wall. And we are prepared to fight.

Democracies by their very nature are slow-moving and easy-going. They are prone to believe the best of other people, prone to take the easy way out, prone to grasp at every blandishment that offers hope of peace and coexistence. But as Hitler and the Japanese war lords learned to their dismay, free nations and free men, once aroused, have the strength of giants.

For my own part, I am confident about the future because I believe that we have now emerged from the innocence and gullibility and half-sleep that have paved the way for so many defeats in the postwar period.

I venture this prophecy, I offer this encouragement, even though I am distressed, as I know you are, over the trend of events in Laos. In Laos again we have been the victims of Communist perfidy and deception.

It was no accident that the Laos crisis was precipitated *after* the American elections, when the old Administration was on its way out and the new Administration had yet to take over.

It was no accident that the Kremlin had made all the logistical preparations for a massive airlift of war materials to the Laotian and Vietnamese Communist forces.

It was no accident that the British and French Governments were encouraged to believe that a cease fire was just around the corner if we agreed to accept a neutral coalition government and the reactivation of the so-called tripartite commission.

It was no accident that while the Kremlin continued to dangle the carrot of an imminent cease fire in front of anxious Western noses, the Communists forces continued to attack and Soviet planes continued to supply them.

All of this was true to the pattern of Soviet conflict strategy.

But once we had committed ourselves to the course of patience and negotiation and compromise, it was difficult to extricate ourselves.

The outcome should have been clearly predictable. The Communists have advanced under cover of negotiations, so that they now occupy the three northern provinces of Laos as well as the strategic Plain des Jarres.

If the question of Laos is now placed on the table of a fourteen nation diplomatic conference, the Communists will be entering the negotiations in a position of formidable strength.

They will not evacuate the territory they have occupied in the course of the current hostilities: this, I believe, we can take for granted.

They will not disarm their forces.

If an agreement is made calling for the cessation of arms shipments to both sides, we are in for a repetition of the sorry experiences we have already had in Korea and Vietnam. We will observe the agreement. The Communists will violate it wholesale. And the tripartite "neutral" commission will, at the best, be helpless, at the worst will prove itself "neutral" on the side of the Communists.

If a coalition government is established, it can be taken for granted that it will be headed by Prince Souvanna Phouma, fresh from his triumphant reception in Moscow, and that the Communists will be given a number of key ministries in this government.

Someone, I cannot remember who, has expressed the hope that Laos will be able to survive such a coalition government, just as Finland survived the coalition government that was forced on her by the Kremlin at the end of World War II. I am afraid I cannot place much stock in this analogy.

From everything that I have heard about them, the Laotian people are kindly, hospitable and lovable. But they are not Finns, nor do they have the very special qualities which enabled the Finns to survive the ordeal of coalition government and to get rid of their Communist Minister of the Interior and Communist Minister of Defense, while countries like Czechoslovakia succumbed to similar coalitions.

The Finns are one of the toughest people in Europe, one of the toughest peoples I dare say in the entire world. They have a tremendous sense of unity, unlimited physical courage, and a political sophistication accumulated during decades of resistance to their Bolshevik neighbor. Had they not possessed all of these qualities in unique degree, the Finns would not be free men today. And even with these qualities, for a period of years after World War II it seemed that the lights would go out in Finland.

By all means, let us hope for miracles and let us work for miracles. But let us not be foolish enough to derive comfort from the establishment of a coalition government in Laos by hoping for a repetition of the Finnish experience.

If the Kremlin pushes its luck in Laos too hard, almost anything could happen. I am convinced that the present American Administration will not sit idly by while the Communist armies complete the conquest of the country.

If hostilities in Laos are terminated by an agreement on Soviet terms, the future there is dark, but it is not completely hopeless.

When the Laotian people learn the meaning of communism, they will hate it, I am certain, as intensely as do the people of China and the people of Vietnam and every other people that has experienced its scourge on their backs.

If the Free World will now firmly resolve that there will be no further concessions to communism in the Far East and no further retreats before it; that it will not tolerate the piece by piece guerrilla subversion of South Vietnam and Thailand; that it will as actively support the freedom fighters in the Communist-dominated territories as the Communists support their guerrilla detachments in free territories—if we make this resolve and adhere to it, then, even with a coalition government, the fate of Laos may not be sealed.

If it is not presumptuous of me to do so, I have a recommendation I would like to place before you.

What happens in Laos is of immediate concern to every Asian country, and not merely to the Laotians. If the Communists take complete power in Laos, then Thailand, South

177

Vietnam and Cambodia, and after them Malaya, Singapore and Burma will be immediately imperiled.

The Asian peoples understand this and, because they understand it, the Philippines and Pakistan urged SEATO to take military action, if necessary, in Laos, and they offered contingents of military forces for such action. But the British and the French recommended delay and negotiations, and it was their counsel that prevailed.

As an American, I was unhappy to learn that we had decided to go along with the Anglo-French position. After all, the purpose of SEATO is to help the peoples of free Asia defend themselves against communism. If SEATO remains as inactive or as slow to react in future crises as it has in the Laos crisis, then it will, instead, be serving as a barrier to effective self-defense by the Asian peoples. That is why, however things now develop, there must be no repetition of Laos.

For my own part, I would not blame the Asian members of SEATO if they felt bitter and disillusioned over SEATO's laggard reaction in the Laos crisis. I would not even blame them if they felt that Western indifference in this instance was simply a manifestation of West's general indifference to the fate of the Asian peoples. I can assure you, however, that this is not so. It was, instead, a manifestation of the Munich psychosis, a recurrent sickness of Western society that does not discriminate between Caucasians and Orientals, but which is characterized, fortunately, by abrupt termination.

When Prime Minister Chamberlain returned from Munich, he justified the surrender of the Sudetenland to Hitler with the words "Czechoslovakia is a far away land about which we know little."

The Munich psychosis did not begin with Prime Minister Chamberlain and it did not end with him. Too often in our own times, there has been a tendency on the part of the democratic leaders to believe that they could purchase their own security or somehow make their nations more secure, by trafficking in the security and freedom of other nations.

I have described this as a psychosis because in my opinion it represents an effort at complete escape from both our moral tradition and political reality. How many historical catastrophes does it take to prove that softness and appeasement foster aggression, insecurity and war?

I believe that SEATO is essential to the defense of Asia. I have absolutely no doubt that the Western members of SEATO will, in the final analysis, honor their commitment to defend Asian freedom. But perhaps the Asian peoples can help SEATO by their example.

The period of allied retreat in Europe prior to World War II came to an end with the invasion of Poland. If the Communists push their luck too hard in Laos, Laos may well turn out to be the Poland of Asia. But even if it should turn out to be an Asian Munich, I would remind the Communist despots that Munich was the final allied concession, that the very next act of Nazi aggression resulted in World War II.

I would urge the free nations of Asia, while cooperating with the West, not to rely slavishly on it. If it comes to a major war with the Sino-Soviet bloc, we shall have to fight together. But before it comes to such a war, I am afraid that there will be a series of situations, similar to Laos, where the security of entire areas of Asia are decided in battles of limited scope.

I feel that in these situations a lead can be given by the anti-Communist nations of Asia, acting in concert.

I believe it would stir the imagination of free peoples everywhere if the governments of the Philippines and Thailand and of non-SEATO countries like South Vietnam, Malaya, Nationalist China and South Korea, announced to the world that they were prepared to permit the recruitment of volunteers in their countries to help defend Laos or South Vietnam or Thailand or any other area that may be threatened by Communist aggression.

I believe it would be a wonderful thing if, armed with this permission, the Asian People's Anti-Communist League would then appeal for volunteers for an "Asian Freedom Legion" and for funds to help equip these volunteers.

I am convinced that there are scores of thousands of dedicated anti-Communists in Asia who would be ready to volunteer for such service even if the Legion could offer only token payment.

I am convinced that such a demonstration of free Asian unity, of the ability to work together and the will to fight together, would inspire even the peoples of the neutralist countries and would command the unstinted respect of the West.

I am convinced that such an initiative, even on a limited scale, might be of decisive importance in situations like Laos.

I am convinced that this new demonstration of united Asian resistance to communism would inspire not only the admiration but the active support of the entire Free World.

From everything I have read, I believe that the Asian peoples are not only militantly anti-Communist but that they have an affirmative faith in the ultimate triumph of freedom. They do not accept the Communist tyrannies in China, in North Korea and North Vietnam as permanent. They believe that regimes which so debase the human being and which inspire such passionate hatred, cannot endure too long.

In this respect I believe that the Asian peoples have shown more wisdom, more morality, and more political realism than many of us in the West. In the West, I regret to say, there is far too great a tendency to accept the Communist rule in Europe and Asia as something permanent, something to which we must reconcile ourselves, something with which we must strive to achieve coexistence.

This quest for coexistence, where coexistence is not possible, represents an abandonment of the first of all moral and religious precepts: "Thou shalt love thy neighbor as thyself." Whether they realize it or not, those who argue in favor of an entente with the Kremlin, are urging that, for the sake of preserving our own precious skins, we forget about the agony of the hundreds of millions of people enslaved by communism.

I say that we cannot forget about their agony.

I say that if we declare peace with the tyrants, morally we are declaring war on their victims.

I say that we cannot defend freedom if we limit it to mean only our freedom.

Southeast Asia: The Dangers of Appeasement

I believe that in the long run we will protect ourselves best and defend freedom best if, together with Thomas Jefferson, we "swear upon the altar of Almighty God, eternal hostility to every form of tyranny over the minds of men."

To accept Communist rule in any country as permanent or unassailable is as wrong politically as it is morally. If the Communists always attack, and the Free World always defends; if the Communists are able to extricate themselves from every defeat by means of a Korean armistice; if every Free World victory is regarded as temporary while every Communist victory is regarded as irreversible—if these attitudes which have heretofore characterized Western policy persist for many more years, then I consider it inevitable that we, in our lifetime, will live under communism.

If we refuse to accept communism as inevitable and refuse to regard Communist victories as irreversible, then certain political conclusions automatically flow from this position.

If the Communists mount guerrilla operations in South Vietnam and South Korea in an effort to undermine the elected governments of these countries, then I say that South Vietnam and South Korea should be encouraged and assisted in mounting guerilla operations for freedom in those portions of their countries now occupied by quisling regimes.

Guerilla warfare, skillfully used, can be a potent weapon. Even with the best trained anti-guerrilla fighters, it requires five or ten defending soldiers to cope with a single guerrilla. Why should the Communists be permitted to retain a monopoly on this weapon? Why should we not encourage the spirit of resistance behind the bamboo curtain by creating diversions, and by sabotage and by ambushes and by undermining the Communist economy in every possible way?

Let there be no mistake: guerrilla war *is* war and, like every other war, it must be carried to the enemy.

The total commitment to freedom also points to certain definite conclusions in the case of Quemoy and Matsu. If you have this commitment, then it is morally wrong to surrender other people to slavery, just as it is morally wrong to kill or to enslave.

And if one truly believes in liberation from Communist tyranny, then it is politically and militarily the height of folly to surrender positions which inconvenience the Communist enemy, which help to keep alive the hope of freedom on the mainland, and which would, in Communist hands, be used as stepping stones for further aggression.

The total commitment to freedom also points unmistakably to the stand we must take on the perennial question of recognizing Red China and admitting Red China to the United Nations.

I say that we must take no measure that in any way enhances the prestige of the tyranny that now governs mainland China, we must do nothing to indicate that we accept or endorse it or regard it as permanent, we must strive to see that it enjoys the disrepute it deserves, we must do everything in our power to call its permanence into question and to challenge its authority to speak in the name of the Chinese people.

In short, I believe that many of the matters that we find so complex really have simple answers if we once recommit ourselves to first moral principles.

I cannot say that the views I have expressed here are, on every single issue, the views of the American Administration. But I can assure you that in President John F. Kennedy the Free World has found a leader of rare mettle: a leader who speaks quietly, but who will not be intimidated by Khrushchev's bluster; a leader whose whole being is dedicated to peace but who will not shrink from the test of war; a leader who meant every word when he said in his inauguration speech: "Let every nation know, whether it wishes us well or ill, that we shall pay any price, bear any burden, meet any hardship, support any friend, oppose any foe, to assure the survival and success of liberty."

If Nikita Khrushchev or if Mao Tse Tung think that they can play a cat and mouse game with President Kennedy, let them beware. For they will learn that, in this moment of peril, through the normal processes of democracy, the Free World has found a champion who is more than a match for the absolute dictators spawned by the cannibalistic processes of Communist society.

Of one other thing I am certain. Man of the 21st century will not be a brainwashed Communist robot, in a glorified international commune, told what to read and what to think and what to do and what to eat, and how much time he may spend with his family. Let Khrushchev and Mao Tse Tung prate about communism being the wave of the future. But I know, as certainly as I know anything, that the future of mankind lies with freedom.

The greatness of the Declaration of Independence is that it strikes a responsive chord in the hearts of all men, everywhere and for all time. "We hold these truths to be self evident: that all men are created equal, that they are endowed by their creator with certain inalienable rights, that among these rights are life, liberty and the pursuit of happiness." . . . What man of good will can hear these lines without believing them, and without feeling that they correspond to something he has always believed?

The eternal will to freedom is something that no dictator will ever succeed in suppressing. That is why, forty-four years after the Russian Revolution, the rulers of the Soviet Union must still maintain themselves in power by means of a totalitarian dictatorship. That is why communism is doomed.

That is why we must never lose faith in the righteousness of our struggle or in its ultimate outcome.

Chapter XI

THE BERLIN WALL:
THE IMPERATIVE NEED FOR ACTION*

On Tuesday the three allied commanders in Berlin filed a protest with the Soviet commandant against the East German action in sealing the frontier which separates East Berlin from West Berlin.

Having just come from Berlin, I confess that I was gravely disappointed by our failure to react in any way for three whole days to this flagrant violation of treaties and of human rights.

This is a contingency that could easily have been foreseen. It is a contingency which, in fact, has been the subject of frequent discussion in the press of the Free World. I have taken it for granted, as, I assume, many other people did, that the Western allies, after all their discussions, had a plan prepared to meet this contingency. Our failure to react for three days, however, proves, or at least suggests, two things that can only serve to encourage the Kremlin to further provocations. It suggests, first, that we had no plan ready to meet this contingency. And, second, it suggests that the NATO alliance is incapable of an immediate, united, affirmative response to Soviet actions on Berlin.

I was just as gravely disappointed by the tone of the protest when it finally did come. To say that it was totally inadequate would be an understatement. The protest, in my opinion, was so weak, so toothless, so completely incommensurate with the crime that had been committed that it was nothing short of dangerous.

---

* United States Senate, August 18, 1961.

The Berlin Wall: The Imperative Need for Action

Wednesday's *New York Herald Tribune* reports that West Berlin officials were "dismayed" and "amazed" at the weakness of the allied note "and that the West Berlin population was disheartened." It spoke of a "crisis of confidence" between the three million West Berliners and the Western allies.

Newspapers reported indignant mass demonstrations in West Berlin. The demonstrators, according to the *Herald Tribune,* carried banners which read:

"Are we being betrayed by the West?"

"We are indignant over the lack of action. Is it all only promises?"

"Paper protests do not stop tanks."

"Ninety hours without action. Doesn't the West know what to do?"

"We demand toughness."

"Kennedy to Berlin."

"We demand an economic boycott."

The distinguished *New York Herald Tribune* correspondent, Gaston Coblentz, made this comment on the note: "The message appeared likely to help convince Soviet Premier Nikita S. Khrushchev that he is on the right track in contending that Western declarations of willingness to fight for Berlin are a 'fairy tale'."

Mr. President, we have been warned on every side that the Berlin crisis may lead to war. I am convinced that it will not lead to war if we can persuade Prime Minister Khrushchev that we mean business when we say that we will fight, if necessary, to defend the freedom of Berlin.

On the other hand, there is a very serious chance of war by miscalculation if Khrushchev believes that the West will back down again, as it has in the past, that it is not irrevocably committed to the defense of Berlin.

Perhaps the most disturbing thing I learned during my recent visit to Europe is that Khrushchev apparently does not take our declarations on Berlin seriously. He is convinced that the United States is divided, that the NATO alliance is divided, that the West talks big but acts little.

I report this to the Senate on the very highest authority.

It is from this standpoint that the Allied note on Berlin is particularly dangerous.

Every time we fail to live up to our commitments, every time we limit ourselves to oral protest when the situation calls imperatively for action, every time we give the impression of weakness or hesitation, we fortify Khrushchev's beliefs that the West will "chicken out" if he pushes things to the brink of a showdown.

Unfortunately, since the terrible days of the Hungarian Revolution, we have given Khrushchev far too many reasons for believing that we are incapable of decisive action.

The Hungarian Revolution was without question the greatest opportunity the West has had to force the Kremlin back to its pre-war frontiers and to reestablish a stable political balance in Europe. The satellite empire was seething with discontent. Poland and East Germany, in particular, stood on the very brink of explosion. The Red Army units stationed in Hungary had, in the first phase of the fighting, given indications of massive disaffection. Thousands of them, in fact, had gone over to the side of the Hungarian Freedom Fighters with their weapons. The Kremlin itself, as Khrushchev has publicly admitted, was aware of the gravity of the crisis and was divided on the course to be followed.

But instead of taking action to support the heroic Freedom Fighters of Hungary, we limited ourselves to pious declarations of sympathy.

We took no action to make it clear to the world that we accepted the Government of Imre Nagy as the legitimate government of Hungary.

We took no action to force the seating of Nagy's newly appointed delegates to the United Nations.

We did not, as we should have done, insist on the immediate dispatch to Hungary of a corps of United Nations observers.

We did not warn the Kremlin that any new attempt to intervene in Hungary would have the gravest repercussions.

We did not take diplomatic advantage of this situation, as we might have done, by urging negotiations on self-determination for the Captive Peoples of Europe in exchange for concessions from the West.

It would have been bad enough if we had been completely inactive. But our guilt went further than this. In almost so many words, President Eisenhower assured the Kremlin that we looked upon Eastern Europe as its legitimate sphere of influence and that we had no intention of intervening.

The result was that those voices in the Kremlin which urged caution were overruled by the Khrushchev faction, which urged military action. The Soviet troops, which had been withdrawn from Hungary after their first inglorious defeat by the Hungarian Freedom Fighters, were sent pouring back into Hungary in a surprise attack, supported by a force of five thousand tanks.

And while the Hungarian people fought against the massed Soviet tanks with rifles and homemade grenades and their bare fists, and while twenty thousand of them perished in the streets of Budapest alone, we still did nothing.

I can think of no more dismal moment in our entire history. I believe that Bishop James Pike spoke for a considerable part of the American people when he said in a sermon in New York: "The blood of the Hungarian people is on our hands."

This was an instance where historical retribution was quick to follow. For the fact is that we are paying for our inaction in Hungary in the present Berlin crisis. There would, I venture to say, have been no Berlin crisis at all, had we followed the course of resoluteness in Hungary.

In the Berlin crisis we are paying, too, for our inaction in Laos. In the early days of the Laos crisis, Khrushchev apparently was still uncertain about our reaction. He felt his way gingerly because he apparently believed that we might take the action we had committed ourselves to take through our membership in SEATO and through our repeated declarations that we would defend Laos.

187

The first Soviet planes that flew into Laos brought only benzene. We did nothing.

The next group of planes that flew in brought small arms munitions. Still we did nothing.

The next group of planes brought artillery and artillery ammunition; and still we did nothing.

Finally, when they were convinced that we would take no action no matter how great the provocation, the Soviet airlift to Laos brought in Communist military personnel. At this point they knew that Laos was theirs for the taking.

Our failure to back up the Cuban Freedom Fighters was inevitably construed by Khrushchev as another evidence of weakness and indecision. Khrushchev must have compared our inaction in this case with the action he himself would certainly have taken had he been confronted with a situation in reverse on his own frontier.

The nuclear test ban moratorium is another instance where we have been long on words and short on action.

On December 29, 1959, President Eisenhower announced that, in view of the lack of progress at Geneva, the United States would not renew the moratorium but would reserve the right to resume testing, with proper notice to the international community. Since that time, we have declared on at least three or four occasions that we would make a final effort to reach an agreement at Geneva and that, if this effort failed, we would have no alternative but to resume testing.

This was the position taken by both candidates in the election of last year.

Instead of giving ground at Geneva, the Soviets have withdrawn concessions to which they previously agreed and now insist on a complete power of veto through a three-man directorate. On this they are so obdurate that there is next to no hope they will budge from it.

But in the face of the hardening Soviet insistence on the veto, in the face of the mounting scale of their threats and aggression and subversion, we still shrink from the decisive act of resuming testing. We stand there like a mouse, petrified by a serpent that is about to devour it.

The Berlin Wall: The Imperative Need for Action

If war should erupt over Berlin, it will be a war of miscalculation, a war that neither we nor the Soviets want. But, to a far greater extent than we realize, such a war would be the consequence of our failure to act in Hungary and Laos and Cuba, of our failure to act on the nuclear test ban moratorium, and, more immediately, of our failure to take any action in response to Khrushchev's monstrous action in Berlin.

I am convinced that we will not back down on Berlin. I know that this conviction is shared by Chancellor Adenauer and the leaders of the West German Government. I have every reason to believe that it is also shared by our other NATO allies.

This is all to the good. But it is not enough. It is just as important to convince Khrushchev that we mean business as it is to convince our allies. And it is here that we have failed.

Mr. President, in the months that remain to us before the Berlin crisis comes to a head, it is essential that we do everything in our power to convince Prime Minister Khrushchev that we mean it when we say that we are prepared to fight over Berlin, to convince him that we have the capacity for decision and the capacity for action, if need be.

The flabbiness of our protest over the sealing off of East Berlin, the serious delay in issuing it, the total avoidance of action, will have precisely the contrary effect.

Mr. President, to illustrate my point, I ask unanimous consent to insert into the Record at this point the brief text of the allied protest note of August 15th:

COMMANDANTS' PROTEST

Berlin, Aug. 15 (Reuters)—Following is the text of a note sent today by the United States, British and French commandants in Berlin to the Soviet commandant:

During the night of Aug. 12-13 the East German authorities put into effect illegal measures designed to turn the boundaries between the West sectors of Berlin and the Soviet sector into an arbitrary barrier to movement of German citizens resident in East Berlin and East Germany.

Not since the imposition of the Berlin blockade has

there been such a flagrant violation of the four-power agreements concerning Berlin. The agreement of June 20, 1949, in which the U.S.S.R. pledged itself to facilitate freedom of movement within Berlin and between Berlin and the rest of Germany, has also been violated.

In disregard of these agreements and of the wishes of the population of this city, for the welfare of which the four powers are jointly responsible, freedom of circulation throughout Berlin has been severely curtailed.

Traffic between the East sector and the Western sectors of Berlin has been disrupted by the cutting of S-bahn (elevated) and U-bahn (subway) service, the tearing up of streets, the erection of road blocks and the stringing of barbed wire.

In carrying out these illegal actions, military and paramilitary units, which were formed in violation of four power agreements and whose very presence in East Berlin is illegal, turned the Soviet sector of Berlin into an armed camp.

Moreover, the East German authorities have now prohibited the many inhabitants of East Berlin and East Germany who were employed in West Berlin from continuing to pursue their occupations in West Berlin. They have thus denied to the working population under their control the elementary right of free choice of place of employment.

It is obvious that the East German authorities have taken these repressive measures because the people under their control, deeply perturbed by the threats on Berlin recently launched by Communist leaders, were fleeing in large numbers to the West.

We must protest against the illegal measures introduced on Aug. 13 and hold you responsible for the carrying out of the relevant agreements.

Gaston Coblentz, in his article in the *Herald Tribune*, quoted a typical Berlin reaction as follows:

"Well, the first five paragraphs tell the Communists what they already know—that they have sealed off East Berlin. The last paragraph says rather politely that they really should not have done it."

I am in complete agreement with this evaluation.

There are those who say that we *can* take no action, and others who say that we *should* take no action in reply to this new Communist provocation, because any action we took would increase the tensions and increase the danger of war.

But there are many measures we can take and should take which would in no way increase the danger of a military confrontation.

The first group of measures are in the realm of propaganda and information.

Wednesday's *New York Times* carried an account of the massive effort the Kremlin is making to win the neutrals over to its side on the Berlin issue. But if there was ever a situation that the Free World could utilize to underscore the difference between democracy and communism, between freedom and slavery, it is the situation that exists in divided Berlin.

When I was in Berlin, I asked whether USIA had ever made a documentary film on the refugee influx and the Marienfelde reception center. I was told that they had had such a film in mind for some time but that it had not yet been made. Now it is too late to make this film, because the refugee influx has been reduced to a mere trickle.

But the world must be told, with all the energy and emphasis at our command, about what is going on in Berlin.

I believe that we should immediately, *within a matter of days*, organize a massive airlift of newspapermen and journalists from all over the world to beleaguered Berlin, so that Latin Americans and Africans and Asians can see with their own eyes the difference between freedom and communism within the confines of a single city, so that they can see the barbed wire and the tanks and all the instruments of terror which the Communists must use to prevent their people from seeking freedom, so that they can speak to the scores of refugees still in Berlin and get from them the story of Communist tyranny.

I believe we should offer these trips to Berlin to correspondents of all the non-Communist countries, on an expenses paid basis, telling them that they will be free to go where they will and speak to whom they will in West Berlin, and encouraging them to seek entry into East Berlin so that they can report first-hand on both sides.

There were several thousand correspondents present in Paris when Khrushchev blatantly disrupted the Summit Conference and delivered his tirade against President Eisenhower. Let us see to it that there are at least an equal number of correspondents on hand in Berlin as eyewitnesses to the greatest crime Khrushchev has committed since his bloody suppression of the Hungarian Revolution.

The second group of measures are of an economic nature. While we do not want to shoot off all our ammunition in reply to this initial challenge, there are important economic measures we could take immediately that would still leave us with plenty of economic measures in reserve.

As a first measure I believe that, acting in concert with our Western allies, we should immediately suspend all shipments of machine tools and chemical processing equipment to the entire Soviet bloc. This would account for approximately fifty per cent of their imports from the West.

The Soviets have had a few spectacular technological successes which have been highly publicized in the West. But, despite these successes, a careful reading of the Soviet press reveals that their machine tool industry suffers from a chronic inability to produce high precision equipment. This fact was established, with careful documentation, by the Subcommittee on Internal Security, in hearings that resulted in the cancellation of a license for the export of high precision miniature ball bearing machines to the Soviet Union.

To help overcome this difficulty, the Soviets are avidly shopping for such equipment in this country, in England, in France, in Italy, in West Germany, wherever they can get it. And, with the exception of a few very special items, we obligingly make all of this equipment available to them.

This is the most dangerous kind of folly. Since the Soviets threaten us with war, since there is a very serious chance that their threats and aggression may actually result in war, I propose that we terminate this folly forthwith by suspending all shipments of machine tools and chemical processing equipment until the Soviets cease to threaten the peace and consent to a durable settlement in Europe based on the essential principle of self-determination.

By doing so, we would be hitting the Kremlin where it hurts most. We would be giving them a convincing demonstration of our capacity for action. We would greatly enhance our bargaining position in future negotiations. And we would be endowing our statements of intent on the Berlin crisis with the essential quality of credibility.

The East German quisling regime has threatened to impose a blockade on West Berlin if economic sanctions are taken against it. I think we should warn the miserable puppets of the Pankow Government and their masters in the Kremlin that if any such measure is taken, we shall respond to this with a total embargo on all trade to the Soviet bloc.

There are also graduated measures that we can take in the realm of diplomacy. The Kremlin has endeavored to endow the forceable division of Berlin with the appearance of East European approval. It has done this by calling together all its quisling regimes of the Warsaw Pact and ordering them to sign a joint proclamation supporting the action of the East German authorities.

The satellite regimes, as everyone knows, are completely without popular support. While they are dependent on the Kremlin, they are very concerned about American recognition because, in the eyes of their people, this recognition gives them a thousand times more status than Soviet recognition.

As a warning to the satellite regimes, I should like to propose that, while not withdrawing recognition at this point, we recall our ambassadors to these countries for an indefinite period. And we should let them know that, if they engage in further provocative actions under the bidding of the Kremlin, we reserve the right to take further diplomatic sanctions.

I am convinced that this action would make a profound impression on the people of West Germany, on the peoples of the satellite countries, and even on the quisling politicians who must endeavor to strike a balance between the demands of the Kremlin and the limits of popular endurance.

Finally, I believe we should take action through the United Nations.

One way or another, the issue is bound to come before the United Nations. Since this is so, I think it is better that we should take the initiative rather than leave it to either the neutralist or communist bloc.

I am completely opposed to the proposal that the entire matter of Berlin be referred to the United Nations for settlement. If we did this, we should be abdicating the rights which are ours by virtue of conquest and by virtue of the previous Four Power agreements on Berlin. We should be setting a precedent which would automatically bring into question all of the rights acquired under other treaties, the moment any signatory to any treaty decided that he wanted it abrogated or else rewritten in his favor. It would be an abdication of sovereignty over the conduct of our foreign affairs.

If the issue of Berlin is raised at the United Nations, it should be raised on the grounds that it constitutes a threat to the peace of the world.

We should, in connection with raising the matter, prepare a White Paper setting forth the essential facts about the Berlin situation since the close of World War II. We should ask the General Assembly to look into the Kremlin's violations of the right of self-determination for the German people, to look into its action in artificially fostering a crisis which threatens the peace of the world, to look into its arbitrary and brutal action in cutting the city of Berlin in half, and to look into the causes of the mass exodus of refugees from the East Zone.

Finally, I believe that if the forthcoming meeting between Ambassador Dean and Ambassador Tsarapkin produces nothing better than the same old Soviet insistence on the right to veto, we should announce forthwith that we are planning to conduct underground nuclear tests, and we should set forth our reasons to the world in a White Paper that details the history of the test ban negotiations, the record of Soviet intransigence, the record of our own very great concessions in an effort to achieve agreement, and the record of Soviet perfidy and violated agreements.

This again would be action, as opposed to talk. Because of the confusion that we have helped build up on the question of the test ban, we might lose something in terms of the esteem of the uncommitted countries. But what we might lose would be insignificant compared with the psychological impact this would have on the Kremlin.

To recapitulate my proposals, I believe there are five actions we can take to persuade the Kremlin that we do have the will and the capacity for decisive action.

First, I propose that we organize a massive airlift to Berlin of thousands of journalists and correspondents from all over the world. We might call this the "Truth Airlift".

Second, I propose that we immediately suspend shipment of all machine tools and chemical processing equipment to the Soviet bloc, and warn them that further aggression will result in further economic sanctions.

Third, I propose that we recall our Ambassadors from the satellite countries for an indefinite period, and warn them that further complicity in the Kremlin's aggression will result in further diplomatic sanctions.

Fourth, I propose that we raise the issue in the United Nations, and demand that a special commission be set up to examine into the question of self-determination for the German people and the reasons for the mass influx of refugees from East Germany.

Fifth, I propose that we resume testing forthwith if the impending meeting between Ambassadors Dean and Tsarapkin fails to budge the Kremlin from its insistence on the veto.

There are bound to be negotiations with the Kremlin. If we fail to take action of any kind, if we confine ourselves to verbal protests over each Soviet provocation, we shall go to the conference table gravely handicapped, because we shall have no *quid pro quo* to offer in demanding that the Soviets retreat from all those actions they have taken that are in violation of the occupation statute and the Four Power agreement on Berlin. From such a conference we shall inevitably emerge the loser.

But worse still, if we fail to take action, we greatly increase the chances of war by miscalculation.

I believe the proposals I have presented here are realistic.

I believe they would in no way increase the danger of a military clash.

I believe that, taken in concert, they would persuade the Kremlin that we mean business about Berlin, and that the democracies are not effete and incapable of action.

I believe that, in the long run, a course of action such as I have outlined is the one sure way to defend Berlin and the one sure way to preserve the peace.

Mr. President, we cannot escape the fact that Khrushchev judges us not by our words but by our actions.

We must draw the necessary conclusions from this. Because history, too, will judge us by our deeds rather than by our words.

Chapter XII

BRITISH GUIANA HEADS TOWARDS COMMUNISM*

On July 17, 1961, I warned the Senate that Dr. Cheddi Jagan and his Communist-dominated People's Progressive Party would probably win in the British Guiana elections scheduled for August 21, 1961, that such a victory would give the Kremlin its first beachhead on the South American continent, and that a combination of Castro and Jagan would bring us to the brink of catastrophe throughout Latin America.

I pointed out that whereas the international Communist movement was doing everything to insure the victory of Jagan, we were doing nothing, not even through the broadcasting facilities available to us, to place the true facts about the Jagan movement before the people of British Guiana and to encourage and assist the opposition.

Since the triumph of Jagan in the election some questions have been raised on the floor of the Senate and in the American press about the propriety and political wisdom of describing Dr. Jagan as a Communist and treating him as one.

It has been stated that the surest way to push Guiana into the Communist orbit would be to describe the newly elected government as Communist, without any proof. Thus the *New York Times* of August 23 commented editorially:

Dr. Jagan has been labeled by some high American officials and some Senators as a Communist, or the equivalent of one. If this were to prove the official U.S. Government attitude, Dr. Jagan and his government would certainly be in the communistic camp alongside of Cuba very soon. If British Guiana is handled by the United States with some understanding, sophistication, and sympathy, there is every reason to hope it will become a desirable member of the inter-American system.

* United States Senate, August 31, 1961.

I do not believe one should make the charge of communism lightly. It is a very serious charge, and, falsely made, it is true that it can alienate people.

But must one have a man's Communist Party membership card or a whole batch of Communist Party membership cards before describing a man as Communist or a movement as Communist dominated? This kind of proof, as everyone knows, or should know by this time, is virtually impossible to obtain.

It is, however, important to know who is a Communist and who is not a Communist, because if we are not able to make this central distinction, we can have no foreign policy worthy of the name. In making this determination, I believe we must be fastidious in gathering our evidence; but once the evidence is in, we must apply certain elementary rules of common sense.

If an animal looks like a duck, walks like a duck, swims like a duck, quacks like a duck, and lives habitually with ducks, I believe that every rational person would be prepared to agree that the animal in question is a duck.

Cheddi Jagan talks like a Communist. He behaves like a Communist. He has played a leading role in Communist front organizations. He has consorted with international Communist leaders. He has distributed official Communist literature. He has sided with the Kremlin in every conflict of policy with the free world. He has hailed Communist victories in Cuba and in China and has himself been hailed and supported by the Communist propaganda apparatus. Yet, in the face of this record, there are still people who insist on believing that perhaps Jagan is not a Communist, perhaps he is just a European-style social democrat or an agrarian reformer.

To those who now state that there is no proof, or ask that we wait until the proof is in, I say that the proof has been in for a long time.

I recommend to all of those who have any doubts about the Communist affiiliations of Cheddi Jagan and Communist domination of his movement, that they read the White Paper published by the British Government in October 1953, after it had been compelled to suspend the constitution and depose the first government of which Cheddi Jagan was the head. I also urge them to read the report of the British Guiana Constitutional Commission in 1954. I urge them to examine the personal record of Cheddi Jagan, of his wife, Janet, who has been described as the director of the Communist terrorist apparatus in British Guiana, and of his chief lieutenants.

If they take the pains to do so, I am sure we shall hear no more pleas that we wait "until the proof is in."

Let me quote some of the most relevant items from the British White Paper and from the report of the British Guiana Constitutional Commission.

In paragraph 101, the report of the British Guiana Constitutional Commission stated:

On the evidence as a whole, we have no doubt that there was a very powerful Communist influence within the P.P.P.

That is Jagan's party—

At the time of the elections at least six of the party's most prominent leaders—specifically Dr. Jagan (leader of the legislative group), Mrs. Jagan (general secretary and editor of Thunder), Mr. Sydney King (assistant secretary), Mr. Rory Westmaas (junior vice chairman), Mr. B. H. Benn (executive committee member and secretary of the Pioneer Youth League) and Mr. Martin Carter (executive committee member)—accepted unreservedly the "classical" Communist doctrines of Marx and Lenin; were enthusiastic supporters of the policies and practices of modern Communist movements; and were contemptuous of European social democratic parties, including the British Labour Party."

This report was issued under a British Labor Government, and with the scrupulous regard for the facts that is characteristic of British investigatory procedures.

And yet, in the face of that, the *New York Times* editorial to which I referred quoted Jagan as stating that his movement is dedicated to "the ideal of socialism." "Pending evidence to the contrary," said the *New York Times,* "the United States has everything to gain by taking Dr. Jagan's pronouncements at their face value."

It is difficult to understand how such a position could be taken in the face of the facts and findings presented by a British Labor Government Commission.

The British White Paper of 1953 devoted a substantial section to the ties of the People's Progressive Party with international Communist organizations. I now quote several paragraphs:

Leaders of the party have been closely associated with international Communist organizations for many years. Mrs. Jagan was a member of the Young Communist League in the United States before 1943 and Mr. R. Westmaas frequently attended Communist meetings in Great Britain before returning to British Guiana in November 1952. At least 10 members of the party have made trips behind the Iron Curtain during the past 2 years and these trips have increased in frequency since the party came into power. Such party members who visited the United Kingdom had frequent contacts with Communists here.

In official broadcasts Ministers gave evidence of their attachment to Communist ideas. Dr. Jagan announced he believed that socialism, having replaced capitalism, would "itself evolve into the higher Communist stage of society." In an official broadcast the Minister for Education said his intention was to remove churches from their present participation in the educational system of the country and to revise the curriculum and textbooks of schools "to give them the true Guianese Socialist and realistic outlook."

The party and, in particular, Mr. R. Westmaas, one of its vice presidents, have promoted the formation of a Communist political youth organization, the Pioneer Youth League, affiliated to the Communist-controlled World Federation of Democratic Youth (WFDY) and World Peace Council (WPC). All Ministers have been present at one time or another at league meetings where propaganda of the WFDY and WPC was distributed. On August 16, 1953, a Youth Congress, to which oversea delegates were invited by the Minister for Works, was held to coincide with the Communist World Youth Festival at Bucharest.

The British White Paper charged, among other things, that "the PPP Ministers insisted on the removal of the ban on the entry of certain well-known West Indian Communists into British Guiana," that "they introduced a bill to repeal the Undesirable Publications Ordinance, thus removing the power of the Governor in Council to exclude subversive literature," that they had attempted to oust established, non-Communist trade unions by legislative action, that Communist literature had been brought into the country by Dr. Jagan and had been seized by customs, that the PPP had attempted to gain control of the public service and had "encouraged junior officers to act as informers," that they had undermined the loyalty of the police, and had planned to organize a so-called "people's police."

Dr. Jagan was quoted as saying on May 3, 1953: "Comrades,

in the past, when we asked for bread, we were given bullets, and those who fired at workers were honored by the masters. But when the PPP gets into power, the same bullets which were fired upon the poor people will be fired on our oppressors. We shall organize a police force; it will be known as the people's police."

The White Paper pointed out that the organ of the People's Progressive Party had followed the lead of the Communist-controlled Warsaw Peace Congress of November 1950.

It pointed out that Dr. Jagan in the summer of 1951 had attended "The Third World Festival of Youth and Students for Peace" and had at that time broadcast an attack on British imperialism over Radio Prague.

It pointed out that in 1951 Dr. Jagan attended the general council meeting of the Communist-controlled World Federation of Trade Unions, and had called upon this instrument of Communist subversion to establish a special colonial department to assist trade unions in colonial countries.

It pointed out that when the police raided PPP headquarters, they found photographic documents and captions supporting the charges that the Americans had waged bacteriological warfare in Korea.

It charged that there was a well-developed cell system organized by the People's Progressive Party, with a "hard core of some 400 or 500 members who are ready to do violence."

The complete Communist domination of the People's Progressive Party was exposed and denounced by one of the few prominent non-Communist leaders of the party, Mr. Forbes Burnham, who broke with Jagan in 1955 and formed his own party, the People's National Congress.

The report of the British Guiana Constitutional Commission published a list of representative literature distributed by the People's Progressive Party. Let me read a few of these edifying titles:

"The Right of Nations to Self-Determination," by V. I. Lenin.

"Patriotism and Internationalism," by S. Titarenko.

"The Labor Movement in Great Britain," issued by the British Communist Party.

"They Were Killed Because They Were Negroes," published by the West Indies Committee of the British Communist Party.

Cheddi Jagan has remained a faithful minion of the world Communist conspiracy to this day. Within the past year, he has hailed Castro as a "liberator" and has been hailed by Castro. He has banned the distribution in British Guiana of a USIA publication entitled "What Can a Man Believe," contrasting life in free countries with life in totalitarian countries. Jagan's Minister of Natural Resources, the Honorable H. B. Benn, stated only a few months ago, "It is easier to stop tomorrow than to stop communism."

I could go on and on with this recital of the record. But surely in the light of the record I have already presented, no reasonable person could doubt that Cheddi Jagan and Janet Jagan and their Ministers are Communists, that their movement is Communist dominated, that it does take its orders from the Kremlin.

It has been argued that if we truly believe in the principle of self-determination, we could not in good faith have intervened in any way in the British Guiana elections; that if the British Guiana people want a Jagan government, they are entitled to have a Jagan government.

But I say that it is not self-determination when the Jagan movement campaigns with the unlimited financial means of the world Communist movement at its disposal, while the opposition parties are refused contributions by British and American concerns doing business in British Guiana, for fear that this would antagonize Cheddi Jagan.

It is not self-determination when Moscow, Peiping, and Havana inundate British Guiana with propaganda favorable to Jagan, while the Voice of America and BBC do nothing to expose the true nature of the Jagan movement or the true nature of communism, or to give support and encouragement to the opposition.

It is not self-determination when the World Bank, with American approval, weights the election in Jagan's favor by granting him a loan of $1¼ million just before the election, thus enabling Jagan to pretend to his people that he knows how to deal with the Americans and that the American Government is prepared to support him. This, in my opinion, is a scandal that cries out for explanation.

It is not self-determination when the Jagan party deceives the people of British Guiana by concealing its Communist identity from them and parades, as Castro did, in the guise of a reform and independence movement.

It is not self-determination when the people of any country vote for reform and democracy, but get, instead, a Communist dictatorship from which there is no way of extricating themselves.

On the contrary, such fraud constitutes a flagrant perversion of the right of self-determination which all men who believe in freedom should expose, rather than defend.

The Washington *Post,* in an optimistic editorial, appealed against any attempt to interfere with the right of the British Guiana people to self-determination, and held forth the hope that after they had had experience with the Jagan regime, the people of British Guiana would take back their endorsement at the polls, just as the people of Kerala voted the Communists out of office. Whether this optimistic parallel holds any water depends in the final analysis on our British allies and on ourselves.

Kerala was never an independent state. It was a state in the sense that Connecticut is a State. Even under an elected Communist government, it remained constitutionally subordinate to the State of India, without the power to levy armies or other powers reserved to sovereign governments. Even then, before the Communists could be voted out of power, it was necessary for New Delhi to impose martial law in Kerala and put an end to the excesses with which the Communists had been terrorizing the population.

Within 2 years, if Britain does not intervene, British Guiana is scheduled to become fully independent. Meanwhile, at least theoretically, Britain reserves the right to intervene in an emergency.

Will Britain use this right if Jagan proceeds to Castroize British Guiana, to set up a one-party dictatorship, to confiscate foreign enterprises, and to create a people's police and a people's militia as instruments of control?

Will it use this right if there is evidence, as I fear there will be, that British Guiana under Jagan is being used for the infiltration and subversion of Brazil, Colombia, Venezuela, Dutch Guiana, and other Latin American countries?

The United States and Great Britain must accept the fact that the Caribbean area has become a major theater of Communist political and military operations; and we must make plans, in concert, to deal with this danger.

If we do not do so quickly, if we continue to drift and hope for the best, as we have done in regard to Cuba, then, as certainly as day follows night and defeat follows inaction and folly, we shall, within the next several years, see the Caribbean Sea converted into a Communist lake, and communism triumphant through large parts of the Latin American mainland.

As I said previously, I have been deeply disturbed by the fact that the World Bank granted Jagan a loan of $1,250,000 only six weeks before the election. Everyone knew that the election was about to take place in British Guiana. Everyone knew, or should have known, the essential facts about Jagan's record, including his long and clearly demonstrable record of Communist activities. But despite these things, Jagan came to Washington late in June, the World Bank granted the loan which British Guiana had requested, and Jagan was, by implication, given complete credit for negotiating the loan by being permitted to sign personally for it.

I know it will be said that the World Bank is an international organization and we cannot expect to direct or control it in all of its actions. But the United States is a rather large stockholder in the World Bank, a stockholder, in fact, to the extent of 33 per-cent. In addition, the President of the Bank and several other top officers are American citizens.

In an effort to find out how the loan to Jagan had come about, I asked to speak to one of the American officials of the World Bank. I said to this official: "Did the World Bank give any consideration to Jagan's background and character before

British Guiana Heads Towards Communism

granting the loan? Every banker I know considers that the most important element in connection with a loan is the character, the reputation, and the integrity of the one who applies for the loan; they are more important than his credit rating or his property holdings. Did your bank ask those questions about Jagan? Did anyone tell you he is a Communist and has been running with Communists?"

He replied, "Yes, the question has been raised."

But I have not yet been able to find out what was said in this connection.

This situation must be extremely disturbing to the American people. It must shock them to realize that such a thing was allowed to happen at this critical hour in world developments.

I was told that the application for the loan had been pending 2 years. So I asked, "Why was there such great haste, just 6 weeks before the election? If the application had been pending for 2 years, could you not have waited until the people of British Guiana had had a chance to reach their decision? Could you not have waited another 6 weeks?" But I did not get a very good answer to that question, either.

I hope that what I have said has not in any way suggested an "I told you so" attitude. It is no solace at all to be proved right when our national security is at stake, and when the cost of being proved right runs so high. But we shall never survive the terrible trials that lie ahead of us unless we first of all expose to ourselves and find the explanations for all the blunders and errors—errors of commission and errors of omission—of which we have been guilty.

What I find particularly frightening about the situation in British Guiana is that we have been aware since 1953 that this was a political crisis area, where the Communists might conceivably come to power.

But we did nothing.

In the name of economy, we even withdrew a few labor attaches who, according to accounts, had been doing an effective job of counseling the anti-Communist trade unions.

Worse than this, as I have pointed out, we fortified Jagan's

205

position by providing him with technical assistance and by approving the World Bank loan of $1¼ million, which was personally signed for by Jagan himself. I have been told by Americans who were in British Guiana at the time that, had we wanted to help Jagan win, we could have taken no more effective measure than the granting of this loan in the weeks immediately preceding the election. Indeed, when we consider that Jagan won by only a few seats,[2] I do not think it is too much to suggest that this loan made the difference between victory and defeat for the forces of communism in British Guiana.

---

[2] Jagan's victory was, in fact, a minority victory. Although his party won a majority of the seats in the legislature, it received only 42.63 per cent of the total vote cast. In several constituencies, the Jagan candidates won by the most marginal majorities. This was, in short, a situation where the entire outcome of the election could have been reversed by a few thousand votes. It is also noteworthy that Jagan did *not* campaign on a Communist program, that his support came almost exclusively from the East Indian community, and that he was able to win this support only by conducting a campaign along strictly racial lines.

The following table of statistics presents the central facts about the composition of British Guiana's population and the outcome of the recent elections.

BRITISH GUIANA

Area:	83,000 sq. miles
Population:	575,270
Population by Ethnic Groups:	
Indian	279,460
African	190,380
Mixed	66,180
Amerindian	22,860
Portuguese	7,610
Other European	5,230
Chinese	3,550
Total Electorate:	246,125
Total Votes Cast in 1961 Election:	220,114 (89.4%)
Votes Cast in Favour of:	
People's Progressive Party	93,075 — 20 seats (42.63%)
People's National Congress	89,501 — 11 seats (40.99%)
United Force	35,771 — 4 seats (16.38%)

Now, despite Jagan's record, despite the sorry experience with being nice to Castro and with aid to Tito and to Poland, we find that there is talk of keeping Jagan from going Communist by making bigger and better loans to him.

There is an alternative to folly; there is an alternative to inaction. I believe that the record of our tragic failure in British Guiana is still another argument for the establishment of a Freedom Academy[3] where methods of combating communism can be studied and devised and where we can train cold war experts for the side of freedom.

---

[3] A bill calling for the establishment of a Freedom Academy was passed by the Senate before it adjourned in July 1960. It was not, however, passed by the House. The measure was reintroduced both in the House and in the Senate when Congress reconvened in January 1960. As this goes to print, the bill is still in committee.

Chapter XIII

SHOULD WE RECOGNIZE RED CHINA?*

We meet in this City of New York tonight at a time when something is happening across town which may determine the survival or the death of the United Nations. And I speak not merely of the imperfect UN that we have known, but of the ideal that we have hoped for.

Two crises threaten the United Nations: the first is an organizational threat, the Troika proposal of the Communists, which would rob it of its practical *capacity* to act; the second is an organic threat, posed by the contemplated admission of Red China, which would rob the United Nations of what is left of its moral *authority* to act and would call into doubt its very reason for existence.

The moral crisis may well be the more dangerous of the two. True, the United Nations has admitted Communist regimes before, to its great discredit and shame. But at least it had the excuse of false illusions and of hopes that these regimes were prepared to live amicably in the family of nations.

Such is not the case with Red China.

There is no question about the nature of Red China in the eyes of any who seek the truth. It is a government which, by its words and by its deeds, openly and constantly violates every basic principle for which the United Nations stands.

There can be no avoidance of the issue on grounds of ignorance. The argument against Red China has been intensely and successfully waged for a decade and if the UN votes to admit

---

* Carnegie Hall, New York, September 21, 1961.

Red China now, it can only mark a conscious, deliberate desire to do so.

If Red China is admitted, it will mean that control of the United Nations has passed from the hands of the strong who are concerned with an honorable peace based upon justice, to the hands of the weak who are concerned principally with saving their own skins and augmenting their own influence, no matter how they must abase themselves or debase the United Nations.

The reasons against the admission of Red China are more powerful today than they have ever been, because the nature of Red China is better known than it has ever been.

Its aggression against the UN has now been repeated in Vietnam, in Tibet, in Laos, in India and in Burma.

Its contempt of the UN has now been emphasized by continued violations of the Korean armistice.

Its subversion of its neighbors has now been intensified and expanded to nations all over the world, including those in our own hemisphere.

Its pronouncements in support of military aggression to achieve its ends have now been raised to the level of dogma.

Its persecution of its own people has now been made even more horrible since is has been systematized into the dreaded commune system which regiments every minute of every day, carries exploitation and dehumanization to the furthest limit possible, and strikes horror into the hearts of all who have the capacity to feel horror at the destruction of the human personality.

Its criminal acts have now increased to the point where it has even gone into the dreaded and abhorred business of peddling narcotics. Here is a government which many solemnly propose to seat in the United Nations, a government which has made a state industry out of producing opium and other narcotics and peddling these drugs to criminal elements all around the world at an annual profit of several hundred million dollars!

The intent of the Communist nations to rule or ruin the

United Nations, which has always been apparent to those with eyes to see, is now unavoidably apparent to everyone.

And so, if the predictions of most analysts are correct, the organization which embarked at San Francisco in 1945 with such noble hopes, is now prepared, consciously and deliberately, to embrace the most evil regime in history at a time when its Communist allies are openly seeking, in the most climactic and obvious manner, to destroy its very existence.

If the UN goes over this precipice, I do not believe anything can save it.

It shall by its own act forfeit the respect and confidence of honest men everywhere.

It shall by its own will swallow the poison which shall destroy its heart and soul and leave only an empty shell.

The arguments against admission of Red China are so basic and compelling that it seems unnecessary and even frivolous to take up the shopworn litany of shabby cliches advanced in favor of admission. Yet, perhaps the larger part of mankind, in public affairs anyway, lives and acts by frivolous arguments, and they must therefore be answered.

It is contended, for instance, as though it were relevant, that we cannot ignore one-quarter of the human race. This is a peculiar argument to come from those who do ignore one-quarter of the human race in the most cruel way possible, by consigning and abandoning them to perpetual slavery.

Certainly we cannot ignore them. We should think about them and plan for their welfare every day of our lives. But our thoughts and efforts should be directed toward their betterment, their liberation, not toward a shameful action that will in a sense legitimize their enslavers and raise them to the status of a lawful government and an accepted member of the family of legitimate governments.

It is said that we cannot ignore the government that rules 600 million people, that we need listening posts, that we need to pay more attention to Peking for our own good.

Certainly we must pay more attention. More important, we should be ceaselessly devoting our time and energy to ways and means of combating this dread enemy. The Chinese Communists should never be off our minds. The Free World should have a million listening posts in Red China. We should know everything they do, and everything they plan to do.

But this is not a job for embassies and UN discussions. It is a task for intelligence agents, for thousands of dedicated students of communism who are at the same time apostles of freedom.

It is maintained by India's Ambassador to the United Nations, for instance, that since a Communist regime is in actual control of the Mainland it is, therefore, the "rightful representative" entitled to sit in the UN.

What a principle of representation this is!

Because the Red regime has succeeded in murdering 30 million of its people and destroying the minds of those who resist it, because it has choked off all dissent and all exchange of ideas, because it has organized a reign of terror and intimidation which has enabled it to maintain its grasp for a decade, we are told by India and others that these actions have somehow legitimized its rule and that the fact of naked power and control is all that is important in deciding representation.

If the UN adopts this principle, it will repudiate the ideals upon which it was founded; and having rejected its origin and reason for existence, it will have doomed itself.

Then there is the argument that by bringing them into the United Nations, the UN can subject the Chinese Reds to its "good influence" and thereby bring about their reform. If ever there was an illustration of the Biblical injunction "Pride goeth before a fall," it is here.

For sixteen years the Soviet Union has been subjected to the "good influence" and persuasive powers of the United Nations. At no time throughout that period has it ever consciously conceded any point to the UN which inhibited its plan to subjugate the world. And I wonder if those who prattle idly about bringing good influence to bear upon Communist regimes paused at all to reexamine their thinking at the sight of Khrushchev pounding his shoe on his desk last year; or if the present deliberate effort of the Communist bloc to destroy the effectiveness of the United Nations gives them any pause for reflection upon the fruits of their good influence.

The presence of Communists in the United Nations has done nothing to reform them. But their presence has effectively sabotaged the UN and now threatens to disrupt it completely.

Finally, our own past folly of recognizing Communist regimes is used against us. People say to us: "You have already admitted Russia, you have already recognized the satellite regimes, why balk now at admitting one more? If Russia is good enough to sit in the UN, why isn't China?"

Unfortunately, this argument is usually answered by some legalistic evasion or by the explanation that Russia's admittance was essential to the founding of the UN, or something of that sort.

What we *should* say is that we were wrong to ever admit Russia; that we were wrong to ever admit any Communist regime; and that having been wrong a dozen times, we do not propose to be wrong the thirteenth time.

We may say that, so far as this admittance question goes, the United Nations has but one flag still flying, one lone flag of honor and of decency, the flag of resistance to Red China and all the unspeakable evil it represents. The UN has swallowed a lot but it has refused to swallow Red China.

That flag, floating as it does above the debris of broken hopes and spineless compromises, is in my judgment the last hope, the last chance for a United Nations that stands for something eternal and significant in human history.

If we pull down that flag by voting to admit this worst of all criminal regimes, we have merely turned the United Nations into a sort of arena where thieves and murderers meet on equal terms with the legitimate representatives of the free nations of the world.

No honor can attach to such an organization. No moral authority can reside in its pronouncements. No lasting good can come from its deliberations.

No nation has done more for the United Nations than ours. We have made a home for it here on our own shores. We have financed it. We have repeatedly subordinated our national interest to its wishes. We have compromised our principles in deference to it.

The United States is the greatest friend the UN has, and the UN cannot survive without the enthusiastic support of our country. But this organization is now apparently on the verge of taking a step which is clearly repugnant and odious to the American people, to the Congress of the United States which has expressed its opposition in a series of unanimous resolutions, and to the Administration policy which has prevailed under three Presidents.

If they must have Red China, so be it. But if they take this fateful step, our relationship to the United Nations can never again be the same.

While we can yet prevent this catastrophe, let us do all we can, just as we are doing tonight.

But the United Nations should be told that if Red China is admitted, it is not only the United States that has lost a contest, it is the UN that has lost its life.

We might linger uncomfortably in its ranks, but we could no longer look to it for guidance, or submit our vital interests to its handling.

We will have to look elsewhere for that Parliament of Man which will seek peace along the only path in which it can successfully be sought, the path of honor, the path of justice, the path of principle.

Chapter XIV

THE CONTINUING DANGER IN THE CONGO*

Before Congress adjourned last September, I took the Floor several times to express misgivings about the course of events in the Congo and about our policy or lack of policy in this critically important area of the world.

I was troubled over the dangerous degree of leftist influence in the coalition government which was established at the so-called Louvanium Conference in early August of last year.

I was troubled by the evidence that, while we were footing the bill for the lion's share of the UN operation in the Congo, we had very little to say about UN policy in the Congo; that this policy was in fact controlled by the Afro-Asian bloc and, in particular, by Nehru's unspeakable Minister of Defense, Krishna Menon, a man who has justly come to be regarded as the personification of crypto-communism.

I was disturbed, above all, by the UN military action of last September, and by the grave implications of this action for the future of the UN and for the future of the Western alliance.

Toward the end of last November, as my colleagues know, I visited the Congo, where I had extensive conversations with Prime Minister Adoula, President Tshombe, and members of their respective governments. Since there has been a good deal of misinformation about the purpose of my visit and about what transpired during the course of my visit, I think it might be useful, first of all, to set the record straight.

There have been some reports in the press to the effect that

---

* United States Senate, January 25, 1962.

I had gone to the Congo against the opposition of the Department of State; that I had encouraged President Tshombe to hold out for complete independence; and that I had told him that American policy in the Congo was misdirected because there were Communists in the Department of State.

The real truth is that a major part of my purpose in going to the Congo was to try to explore the possibilities of a Tshombe-Adoula agreement in informal discussions with the two leaders.

I left for the Congo on November 21. On Monday morning, November 20, President Kennedy asked me to come to his office. We talked about the Congo situation for almost an hour. The President expressed the hope that I could help to arrange a meeting between Tshombe and Adoula.

I told the President that I would make every effort to bring about such a meeting. And the record shows that I did precisely that.

As a final commentary on the misrepresentations that have appeared in the press, I want to read the text of the letter I received on January 10 from Secretary of State Rusk.

Dear Senator Dodd:

Reference is made to our recent telephone conversation and to your subsequent telegram of January 4, pointing out certain statements made in a newspaper column to the effect that the Administration had opposed your recent visit to the Katanga, and that an official of the Department had reported that you had made certain remarks with respect to communist infiltration in the Department of State to Mr. Tshombe.

I am happy to set the record straight with respect to both of these matters. The Administration did not oppose your visit. We feel that your efforts to assist in bringing about the meeting between Mr. Tshombe and Mr. Adoula, which led to the Kitona Agreement, were beneficial. We have found no evidence that a Department official reported that you had discussed with Mr. Tshombe the question of communism in the State Department. Indeed, our

Embassy in Leopoldville reports that US representatives who were with you during your conversations state clearly that you did not mention this question.

I hope very much that this letter will clarify the questions that have been raised.

Sincerely yours,

/s/   Dean Rusk

At a later date, I plan to report to my colleagues in greater detail on what I saw and learned in the Congo. As of this moment, I feel that a frank and detailed presentation may have an adverse effect on the delicately poised political situation in the Congo and on the critical discussions which are still going on between the Central Government in Leopoldville and the Government of Katanga.

It is because of this that I have taken the stand that the hearings now proceeding under the separate auspices of the Senate Subcommittee on Internal Security and of the Subcommittee on Africa of the Foreign Relations Committee, should be held in Executive Sessions.

But I believe there are certain aspects of the situation in the Congo which cry out for immediate consideration and understanding. It is to these aspects that I plan to address myself briefly today.

There has been a tendency to justify the UN military action against Katanga on the grounds that this action produced the Kitona agreement, that the Kitona agreement has laid the foundation for Congolese unity, that it has undermined the extremists and fortified the moderates in the Central Government.

Gizenga and Gizengaism, we are told, are now dangers of the past.

It is my profound wish that the prospects were really so cheerful and so uncomplicated.

There are, as I see it, four primary dangers in this Pollyanna approach to the Congo crisis.

The first danger is that we will be lulled into a false sense of security concerning the extremist elements in the Leopold-ville government.

The action against Gizenga is to be welcomed. But even if Gizenga is eliminated, this will not, by a long shot, terminate the danger of communism in the Congo.

Pro-Soviet extremism in the Congo has always been a many-headed monster; and Gizenga is only one of many potentially dangerous elements in the Leopoldville coalition. He is not a member of Lumumba's party but heads his own smaller party, the African Solidarity Party. As Vice-President under Lumumba, he automatically laid claim to Lumumba's mantle when Lumumba died.

There have been other claimants to the mantle of Lumumba. Most notable of these is Christophe Gbenye, Minister of the Interior under Lumumba, later Minister of the Interior under Gizenga in Stanleyville, and again Minister of the Interior in the Leopoldville government today.

Gbenye, who is even more responsible than Lumumba for the reign of terror in Leopoldville in the summer of 1960, told me proudly that he considers himself the legitimate heir to Lumumba as leader of the National Congolese Movement. Gbenye is a force to be reckoned with since he controls the largest single group of deputies in the Parliament, and the largest single group inside the Congo's gargantuan cabinet of 44 members.

When I was in Leopoldville, I was told that sharp personal differences had developed between Gbenye and Gizenga. Apparently, Gbenye was determined to assert his undisputed claim to Number One position in the radical nationalist movement.

The vote of 67-10 against Gizenga in the Congolese Parliament does not signify a total victory for the forces of moderation. On the contrary, what it signifies is that the Lumumbaist bloc, under Gbenye's leadership, voted solidly to take action against Gizenga.

Gbenye told me in the course of our conversation that he was not a Communist and that he went to church regularly. I am prepared to be open-minded about anyone and it is entirely possible that I was misinformed in stating that he had been trained in Prague. I told Gbenye that I accepted his statement that he had not been to Prague.

On the other hand, while I was in Leopoldville, I learned that Gbenye's newspaper, *Uhuru*, still pursued a persistently pro-Soviet and anti-American line; and I also learned that he had set up an unauthorized secret police force responsible to him personally, because the official sureté was under the control of Mobutu's father-in-law, Victor Nendaka, a confirmed anti-Communist.

During the December fighting in Katanga, I was further disturbed to learn that Gbenye had announced the dismissal of Nendaka and that this action had been countermanded thanks only to a threat of military action by General Mobutu.

When I first spoke in the Senate, I pointed out that according to the Moscow *New Times*, 23 out of 44 members of the Cabinet could be considered followers of Lumumba.

The Senator from Minnesota challenged this assertion. He said that only 14 out of 44 members of the Cabinet could be clearly established as Lumumbaists.

In reply, I said I found that this estimate was alarming enough, especially in the light of the fact that the Lumumbaists had secured for themselves the two central positions which Communists and their allies always seek in coalition governments: the Ministry of the Interior and the Ministry of Justice.

When I was in Leopoldville, I was told that the extremists had gained considerably in strength since the coalition government had been established, that the balance was now very precarious, and that Adoula would find it very difficult to survive if he did not, in one way or another, solve the problem of the Katanga secession. Adoula's position may be somewhat more secure today. I hope it is. But, despite the welcome victory over Gizenga, left wing extremism will remain a real and potent and highly dangerous force in the Congo for a long time to come.

Nor can we ignore the fact that the Communist bloc embassies, which were driven out by General Mobutu, have now opened up shop again in Leopoldville.

To anyone who knows anything about Communist tactics, it stands to reason that these embassies will endeavor to expand their influence by working through sympathizers and dupes, both in the Parliament and in the Cabinet.

In issuing this warning, I do not mean to cast doubt upon or belittle the personality of Prime Minister Adoula. I must say that my impression of Adoula surpassed my expectations. I found him an exceedingly able, thoughtful, and dedicated man, and I am convinced, from certain of his statements, that he is strongly anti-Communist.

I was also very favorably impressed by General Mobutu and President Kasavubu.

But there are dangerous men as well as good men in the Leopoldville coalition; and this is something we cannot afford to close our eyes to.

The second danger inherent in any blindly optimistic attitude is that we will take no measures to curb the extremists in the Leopoldville government in their desire to destroy Tshombe completely.

The Kitona agreement can provide the basis for an agreement that has the voluntary assent of both sides.

But this will only happen if the further discussions between the Central Government and the Katanga Government are pursued in the spirit of good will and mutual concession.

If, on the contrary, the extremists in Leopoldville insist on interpreting the Kitona agreement as a document of uncondiional surrender, if they regard it as a kind of first step in a "Carthaginian peace" which culminates in total destruction, then the consequences are unpredictable.

Perhaps such an unconditional surrender could be enforced if we were willing to keep a UN army of occupation in Katanga for the next ten years or twenty years.

But short of this, wisdom and charity dictate that we should strive for an agreement that has validity and durability precisely because it reflects a genuine mutuality of interest.

It is my belief that such an agreement can be achieved. It is my belief, for that matter, that such an agreement could have been achieved without all the bloodshed and violence and hatred engendered by the UN action.

But the consummation of an agreement based on true assent will require far greater willingness than the Adoula Government has thus far displayed to compromise.

It will require that we direct our pressure and influence toward both sides with equal energy, instead of exerting pressure on Tshombe only.

It will require that we unbend from our own rigidly negative attitude toward Tshombe and offer him a few concrete manifestations of our own good will.

Above all, it will require that we attempt to avoid the substitution of a Gbenye-Adoula coalition directed against Tshombe for the previous Gizenga-Adoula coalition which, by its very nature, was also directed against Tshombe.

The third danger in the Congo situation relates to the second.

Because it has concentrated 9,000 of its 15,000 troops as an army of occupation in Katanga, the UN has not been able to do an adequate job of maintaining public order in the rest of the Congo.

Worse than this, there is now serious evidence that the UN, in its desire to exercise political pressure on Tshombe, has encouraged and facilitated the movement of Gizengaist troops into north Katanga.

In doing so, the UN has brought the chaos and bloodshed of the north Congo into areas where there was complete public order so long as they were administered by the Tshombe Government.

In the Congo, everything depends upon public order and upon the maintenance of race relations.

The mayhem and rape and pillaging that accompanied the Army mutiny in July of 1960 resulted in the exodus of almost 50% of the white technicians and administrators from the country.

Most of the Congolese army have remained in a permanent state of mutiny since that time, looting stores and banks and terrorizing the populace, both black and white. With the exception of a few disciplined units, the National Congolese Army has been the chief source of national insecurity in the Congo and the prime promoter of chaos.

The scale of the chaos in the northern Congo is already terrifying enough.

In the cities, the UN has been able to maintain order and a semblance of social organization.

But in the jungle villages which make up most of the Congo, the bush hospitals and dispensaries and agricultural stations are closed and the doctors and missionaries have left. The jungle village has gone back eighty years to the control of the witch doctors and sorcerers.

Tin production is down to 50% of prewar level; cotton production down to 30%; rice production down to 25%. And with each new massacre or racist incident, there is another exodus of white technicians and doctors and advisors—and the economy and social order of the Congo spiral down another turn, in the direction of complete chaos and an eventual Communist take-over.

In the northern Congo, the UN has unquestionably done some good in maintaining public order. But it has never acted to disarm the bandit army units, nor has it, until very recent days, taken any action against units owing allegiance to Antoine Gizenga.

It even failed to take action against the Gizengaist troops responsible for the massacre of the Italian airmen at Kindu.

The last few days has brought several indications that the UN, at long last, is beginning to give some attention to the bandit army units that have been terrorizing north Katanga. But prior to this there was evidence that the UN forces in the Congo had provided transportation and connived with the Gizenga units that have in recent months invaded Katanga.

The situation is a complicated one because all of these units, at least theoretically, belong to the National Congolese Army and are under the control of the Leopoldville government.

The Leopoldville Government, in fact, has appointed Vice Premier Jason Sendwe as administrator for the liberated areas in north Katanga.

Whenever news has arrived of the occupation of another town by units of the so-called National Congolese Army, the Leopoldville Government has been prone to accept responsibility for the "liberation." But whenever news has arrived of atrocities committed by these units, no time has been lost in making it clear that the units responsible for these atrocities were under Gizenga's personal influence.

The north Katanga town of Albertville was captured by units of the National Congolese Army in mid-November.

Tshombe charged publicly that the UN had disarmed his units there and had provided transportation for the invading forces. The *London Daily Telegraph* carried a detailed account of how the UN transported the National Congolese Army troops.

These charges the UN denied.

But the fact is that the two UN officials, Dr. Conor Cruise O'Brien and George Ivan Smith, had flown to Albertville and were on hand to greet the "liberating" army when it arrived.

Twenty-four hours later, the so-called army of liberation was rampaging through the streets, attacking whites, pillaging and raping. A large part of the white population fled from Albertville as a result of these terrorist acts.

Under the Tshombe administration, Albertville was a peaceful prosperous city, where white people lived in harmony with blacks.

Today, I have been told, it is an economic desert, where race relations have been poisoned for many years to come by the terrible events that took place under Dr. Conor Cruise O'Brien's "liberation."

While I was in Leopoldville, I received, through the Embassy, a telegram from the Indian UN commander in Albertville, which read, almost verbatim: "I invite you to visit Albertville so you may see with your own eyes how effectively the UN forces are maintaining public order there while the National Congolese Army continues its advance into northern Katanga."

The consequences of the advance of the National Congolese Army into northern Katanga, as we all know now, was the terrible massacre of 20 Catholic missionaries in the town of Congola, and the probable massacre of another five missionaries and their assistants in the town of Sola.

That the UN has provided transportation for at least some of the invading Gizengaist forces is now a matter of public admission. A long dispatch in the *Washington Post* on January 14 contained this significant paragraph: "Diplomatic sources today revealed a closely guarded secret: that it was United Nations aircraft which transported Gizenga's forces to north Katanga two weeks ago in response to his request. The UN apparently wisely calculated that, with only the rump of his army left in Stanleyville, Gizenga would be vulnerable to Adoula pressure."

I wonder how the massacred missionaries of Congola would feel about this purported stratagem. I also wonder whose decision it was to move more Gizenga troops into north Katanga six weeks after the animal quality of these troops had been revealed by the rape of Albertville and by the terrible massacre of the 13 Italian airmen at Kindu.

The events that have taken place since the military "liberation" of northern Katanga got underway in mid-November, raise several important questions.

That the UN has welcomed and encouraged the invasion as an instrument of pressure on Tshombe is a matter of record. That the Central Government claimed responsibility for the "liberation" at several different points is also a matter of record.

But was the invasion ordered by Antoine Gizenga in his capacity as Vice Premier? Or was it ordered by General Victor Lundula, who, as Commander-in-Chief of the Gizenga forces under the Stanleyville regime, is still supposed to be in command of the Stanleyville units that have been moving into northern Katanga and Kivu provinces? This question is all the more important because the newspapers are now publicly discussing the possibility that General Lundula may be appointed Minister of Defense in the Adoula government.

The final question I should like to ask is whether the State Department had foreknowledge of the plan to move more

National Congolese Army troops under Gizengaist influence into northern Katanga. And if it did have foreknowledge, did it oppose the projected movement in the light of the unhappy experiences at Albertville and Kindu?

If it did oppose the movement, then I say that we are at least indirectly guilty for the terrible massacres that have been perpetrated by these troops in Congola, Sola, and other centers.

The fourth danger inherent in the Pollyanna interpretation of Gizenga's decline, is that the UN action in Katanga, because it *appears* to have succeeded, will be construed as a precedent for the future. Nothing, to my mind, could be more dangerous.

If the Katanga intervention is accepted as a precedent, it will sanctify the abdication of our foreign policy to the United Nations; it will open the way to UN intervention in the internal affairs of member nations; and it may commit us to supporting a whole series of wars that are favored by the Afro-Asian bloc and the Soviets.

If we had the virtue of consistency, the stand we have taken on Katanga would have led us to propose that the United Nations should be authorized to intervene militarily, upon the request of any central government, to prevent the secession of any national minority or grouping. Had such a principle been incorporated into the UN Charter or adopted as a general resolution, the UN would have been involved in half a dozen wars in recent years. It would have intervened to prevent the separation of Pakistan from India, of Sudan from Egypt, of Syria from the UAR, of Senegal from the Mali Federation, and of Mauritania from Morocco.

How preposterous our position in Katanga really is, becomes apparent the moment you attempt to convert this position into a general principle. And, if our position in Katanga does not flow from any general principle, then it remains to be explained why we have decided to make an exception in the case of Katanga.

Morally, Katanga had every right to secede, given the deep-rooted ethnic and cultural differences between the tribes of Katanga and those of the northern Congo, and given the incredible chaos and the serious Communist infiltration which exists in the North. From the standpoint of political realism, however, Katangese secession would certainly be inadvisable because it is true that a completely independent Katanga could not survive if the rest of the Congo went Communist. On this point I am in basic agreement with the State Department.

For that matter, Tshombe himself has not really demanded complete secession. He has instead advocated a loose confederation, with the Central Government controlling currency, customs, foreign affairs, the army and other essential instruments of national policy, but with a very large measure of autonomy in other fields reserved to the member governments.

But, as desirable as Congolese unity may be, I remain opposed to the UN military action against the so-called Katanga secession. The mere fact that a political solution may be desirable does not lead, *ipso facto*, as some of our State Department logicians have argued, to the conclusion that the UN must be authorized to use military force to achieve such a solution.

I am opposed to the socially and morally unjust discrimination against American negroes which still exists in most of our states. But I would resist with all my powers any effort on the part of the UN to terminate this state of affairs by sending Ghurka and Ethiopian troops into Little Rock or Washington or Hartford. This is the internal business of the United States; and any attempt to give the UN authority over the internal affairs of this nation or other nations would, as I see it, spell its doom.

That is why I am so concerned over the UN action in the Congo. Because, despite all the pious statements to the contrary, it unquestionably did constitute intervention in the affairs of the Congo in an attempt to impose by miliary force a political solution advocated by the Afro-Asian nations, the Communist bloc, and, regrettably, by the United States.

There are those who regard the UN's action in the Katanga with joy, hailing it as proof that the UN is at last beginning to function in its proper role as a "parliament of man." I wonder if they have ever though through the implications of this position.

If we permit the Katanga action to be regarded as a precedent, we may soon find ourselves supplying and footing the bill for UN military actions all over the world that have been duly authorized by a Communist bloc-Afro-Asian coalition in the General Assembly.

Mr. President, in the interest of the Congo, in the interest of the UN, the UN operation in the Congo must return to the path of legality and propriety. It must return to its primary functions, which are the maintenance of public order, the maintenance of social services, the safeguarding of human life, and the conciliation of disputes.

There are other grave lessons to be learned from the tragedy of the Congo.

Perhaps the chief lesson to be learned is that when we abdicate control of our foreign policy to the uncertain mercies of the UN, we get our friends into a mess, we get ourselves into a mess, and we get the UN into a mess.

I believe that to a large extent the errors of which we have been guilty have stemmed from misinformation and lack of information. I have been amazed, for example, to discover how fastidiously the State Department has ignored the information submitted by American missionaries of various denominations who have until recently worked in the Congo or are still working there today.

I met some 30 or 40 of these missionaries while I was in the Congo. To my thinking, missionaries are an important and proper source of information, especially in a primitive country. Not merely are they honest, dedicated men without any political axe to grind, but their vocation gives them a unique opportunity to live with the people, to learn their language, and to understand their psychology. To my thinking, in fact, a man like the Methodist missionary, Howard Brinton, who has spent most of his 43 years in the Congo and who speaks 3 native languages like a native, has an infinitely greater understanding of the Congo than a State Department desk officer who may have spent one year somewhere in Africa.

I hope that the Senate Foreign Relations Committee, in the course of its current hearings on the Congo, will not neglect to take the testimony of men like Howard Brinton and Bishop Booth and the many other wonderful American missionaries I met in the Congo. I am certain that Congress will be interested in their evaluation of the situation in Katanga and of the terrible damage which the UN action has done to the delicate fabric of social order and race relations.

I note in passing that we once disregarded the advice of American missionaries in China, who tried to tell us the simple truth that the Chinese Communists were not really agrarian reformers. Instead, it was fashionable at the time to ascribe all such alarmist statements to the so-called "China Lobby." By the time we had rubbed this sand out of our eyes, China had gone Communist. I recall this precedent by way of replying to those who have in recent months raised the spectre of a "Kantaga Lobby."

I shall have more to say about the lessons of the Congo experience at a later date. But meanwhile I should like to say that I have no fear for the future of the Congo, on two conditions.

The first condition is that we no longer passively abdicate the conduct of our foreign policy in the Congo to Krishna Menon and his Afro-Asian cohorts in the UN.

The second condition is that we pursue a policy dedicated to unifying and strengthening the precious forces of moderation in the Congo.

We must build this unity around the indispensable figures of Prime Minister Adoula and President Tshombe, whom I consider two of the greatest statesmen free Africa has yet produced.

There are those who hold up the bogie of a possible confrontation between the Free World and the Communist World in the Congo if we reduce the UN role there. To them I say that if we are not prepared to confront the Communists in an area so remote from the centers of Soviet power, then we will not be prepared to confront them anywhere.

Once we decide that the Congo will remain free, it will remain free.

Chapter XV

POWER IN SPACE AND PEACE ON EARTH*

We live in an era when the survival of freedom depends on many things.

It depends on the supremacy of our economy and on its continued vitality.

It depends on our military strength in being, both conventional and nuclear.

It depends on our statesmanship, and on our ability to comprehend an enemy more cunning and more determined than any adversary we have had to face in our long history.

It depends on our courage and on our steadfast adherence to those principles that gave this nation birth and have thus far, in every major conflict, inspired it to victory.

It depends also on our ability to push ahead, far faster than our adversary, toward the fantastic new horizons which modern technology has brought into view.

The past 17 years have witnessed the creation of the atom bomb, the hydrogen bomb, the intercontinental ballistic missile, the 100 megaton warhead, and the manned satellite.

In the wings, almost ready to be brought on stage, stands the neutron bomb, a kind of death-ray weapon that could be used with devastating effect on the battlefield.

And at a distance of no more than five or ten years, stands the effective conquest of space by man. Let us hope that it will be for purposes of peace only. But we cannot ignore the possibility that space may also be used for the purposes of war.

The dawning of the space age was dramatically confirmed

---

* Washington, D. C., March 1, 1962.

by two events of the past week. These events, also, make it essential that we re-examine our national effort in space.

The first event was John Glenn's historic three orbit flight around the world in the Friendship 7 capsule.

The second event was Khrushchev's proposal that the Soviet Union and the United States embark on a series of co-operative space enterprises.

John Glenn's flight was one of the proudest and most jubilant moments in our nation's history, and justly so.

It succeeded in persuading a free world that had begun to fear the Soviets were forever ahead of us in the space race, that American technology would soon establish its pre-eminence in this field, as it has in every other field.

The whole world applauded John Glenn's accomplishment.

They applauded the flight as one of mankind's great triumphs in the never-ending struggle to extend the frontiers of knowledge.

They applauded, too, because Project Mercury was conducted according to the rules of openness which honest men everywhere believe must prevail if there is to be any hope of peace on earth.

In commending John Glenn on his flight, President Kennedy said that "in this new space ocean we must be second to none." I am sure we all agree with this.

There is, however, a danger in the aftermath to the John Glenn flight. The danger is that we will all feel so proud and so good about it, and about the recent successes of our satellite program, that we will be inclined to assume that all is well in space.

I believe we would be honoring John Glenn in the most effective way of all if we used his flight as the starting point for a re-examination of our entire effort in space.

First, we must ask ourselves whether we are doing as much as we might be doing.

And, second, we must also ask ourselves whether the basic orientation and structure of our space program is what it ought to be; whether we have perhaps not placed too much emphasis on the peaceful, scientific exploration of space, and too little emphasis on the development of military space power.

We are a peace-loving nation, peace-loving almost to the point of self-effacement and folly. This redounds to our moral credit. But we are up against a foe who, unfortunately, is singularly unimpressed by morality or moral credit.

When we had a monopoly on nuclear technology, we offered, through the Baruch Plan, to place all of our technology and our entire stockpile at the disposal of an international atomic authority, if other nations did likewise. This offer was certainly one of the most far-visioned and generous in history. But it was rejected out-of-hand by the Soviets.

It was rejected by them because they understood, far better than we understand, the weaknesses of Western democracy; because they were confident that we would not push ahead with all our energies, that our pace could be further slackened by skillfully plied propaganda, and that the time was not too far distant when they could outstrip us in the realm of nuclear technology.

And while we dawdled along with no sense of urgency, the Soviets forged ahead on many fronts. Despite our very great nuclear headstart, we beat them by only a hair's breadth to the hydrogen bomb. We dawdled for a few more years; and then, in rapid succession, the Soviets beat us to the ICBM, beat us to Sputnik, beat us to the moon shot, and were the first to put a man into space. In recent months, through their perfidious unilateral termination of the nuclear testing moratorium, the Soviets have shot ahead of us in important areas of nuclear technology. Among other things, they have exploded a 58 megaton bomb, and have demonstrated the almost certain capability to equip operational missiles with 100 megaton warheads.

These have been devastating humiliations for a nation whose primacy in the field of technology had been taken for granted by the entire world. The Kremlin has exploited these successes in a massive propaganda campaign designed to persuade people of the superiority of the Communist system. But far more ominous than their psychological warfare implications were the military implications of these successive humiliations.

We are, at last, mounting a space effort which may permit us to overtake the Soviets and put an end to the humiliations of recent years. In its overall scale, this effort is truly massive. We have thus far put up 67 satellites, against the 14 satellites which the Kremlin has hurled into space. In most aspects of space science, our program has already far surpassed the Soviet space program.

But we must ask ourselves whether the Soviets have been placing as much emphasis on their scientific space effort as we have on ours; whether all the secrecy surrounding the Soviet space program has to do with pure scientific research, or whether this secrecy is not intended to conceal a massive Soviet technological effort designed to establish the Kremlin's unchallenged military control over the space environment surrounding the earth.

All the evidence, in fact, indicates that the Soviets have been placing their prime emphasis on the development of manned spacecraft. Vostok II, in which cosmonaut Titov circled the earth for 24 hours last August, was a five ton vehicle capable of accommodating two or three men, or of carrying a sizeable nuclear payload. The Soviets claimed, in addition, that Titov had been able to pilot Vostok II to an earth landing.

In terms of the development of a maneuverable spacecraft and of giant boosters to hurl them into space, I have been told that the Soviets are at least 18 months ahead of us. This is a frightening thought.

No less an authority than General Bernard A. Schriever, the top military man in the U.S. missile program, has foreseen the possibility that the Soviets may beat us to the development of true military vehicles for space use and has warned against it. General Schriever has insisted that we must place more emphasis on manned spacecraft and space platforms, that we must develop a capability to rendezvous with, inspect, and, if necessary, destroy unidentified satellites.

"If we cannot deal with such satellites," General Schriever warned, "the ability of this nation to exist and to preserve its essential values will be severely compromised or non-existent."

He cited our failures to follow-up on our early starts in aviation and rocketry as "examples to indicate the danger that lies in inadequate planning for the future. Now we may find ourselves in a similar position in regard to space."

General Curtis LeMay, the Commander of our Strategic Air Command, has issued a similar warning. "The first nation to develop a manned space vehicle with complete mission flexibility," said the General, "could possibly dominate the space above the atmosphere."

But despite the warnings of our military men, our space effort, as it is now structured, is dedicated primarily to the peaceful pursuits of science. Of the $50 billion that is scheduled to be spent in the current decade, only some $15 billion will go for direct military applications.

As President Kennedy pointed out in his reply to Khrushchev, we have from the beginning steadfastly advocated the ideal that space should be a domain of peace, barred to weapons of war. We have urged the creation of an international space agency through which the great nations of the world could pool their technologies and their efforts, in the common interest of mankind.

In an historic demonstration of our own dedication to the ideals which we proclaimed, we established a civilian space agency, the National Aeronautics and Space Administration, to assume direct responsibility for our major national effort in space.

But, unfortunately, the open-handed attitude of this country toward the sharing of scientific information and techniques has been met with customary perverseness by the Kremlin.

The Kremlin is always willing to take whatever information we have to offer. It eagerly accepts every invitation to exhibits of American space technology and to the public launchings of American space vehicles. But the Kremlin has divulged virtually no information in return, while every vehicle thus far launched in its space program has been launched in secrecy, without forewarning and without foreign observers.

When Congress passed the National Aeronautics and Space Act in July 1958, it declared that, as far as the United States was concerned, "activities in space should be devoted to peaceful purposes for the benefit of mankind."

At the same time, however, Congress recognized that we are up against an adversary whose attitude is not governed by humanitarian or pacifist considerations. It realized that what *"should* be devoted to peaceful purposes," may not, in fact, be dedicated to such lofty ends.

Congress, therefore, made a clear-cut division in the assignment of responsibility. All matters pertaining to the exploration or peaceful uses of outer space were to be handled by the civilian agency, NASA. Those activities associated with the development of weapons systems and the defense of the United States were assigned to the Department of Defense.

The Legislative branch was wise enough to realize that such a division of authority was bound to result in interdepartmental disputes—in competition for personnel, in conflicting estimates of priorities, in rival claims of jurisdiction. It, therefore, provided that conflicts as to the assignment of responsibilities between NASA and Defense were to be resolved by the President, with the advice and assistance of a group known as the National Aeronautics and Space Council.

The Space Council is under the able chairmanship of Vice President Lyndon Johnson. No more fortunate selection could have been made for this position. I know from firsthand experience how much dedication and time and thought the Vice President has given to problems of space.

The other members of the Space Council include: the Secretary of State, the Secretary of Defense, the Administrator of NASA, and the Chairman of the Atomic Energy Commission. The armed services are not directly represented on this all-powerful body.

Today, scarcely three years after the passage of our space act, a careful reading of the press will reveal to anyone that there is a serious division within our national space program with regard to its basic orientation.

NASA's primary dedication to the cause of science and

space exploration has led it to the conclusion that we must get to the moon ahead of the Soviets as a matter of national prestige. The overriding importance which they attach to this project is indicated by the fact that they have allocated the staggering sum of $25 billion for this one project.

The moon project is of the greatest importance. It will mark man's first serious venture into space from earth's immediate environment. It will extend man's scientific knowledge almost as much as it will his physical reach. The ultimate scientific benefits, direct and indirect, are beyond calculation.

Our military space experts are, however, convinced that we must, in the first place, think in terms of the national security of the United States rather than in terms of scientific prestige and pure scientific accomplishment. They, therefore, favor an all-out program to devise and perfect defensive and offensive space systems for the protection of the Free World. Their prime concern is with control of the earth's immediate space environment rather than with probes into outer space.

Few of us can even begin to imagine the fantastic weapons systems that the future will bring. But that there will be weapons systems in space is a fact on which virtually every military space expert is agreed.

General LeMay, speaking in Detroit last October, expressed confidence that eventually there will be developed "a manned vehicle that can take off from existing runways, go into orbit, maneuver into a 'parking orbit,' de-orbit, maneuver while re-entering the earth's atmosphere, and land at an airbase in the conventional manner."

It is something to think about that our entire ICBM warning system might overnight become worthless if the Soviets were, in secret, to develop a fleet of such spacecraft, capable of launching nuclear warheads from overhead positions. It would take only minutes from the moment of launching to the moment of impact. Civil defense would become meaningless.

Speaking from a background of full knowledge of our classified military research and development programs, General LeMay made these further suggestions as to the space weapons of the future:

"Perhaps they will be weapons that will enable us to neutralize earth-based ICBM's.

"Perhaps they will be weapons that strike with the speed of light.

"If a new generation of armaments operated in space can neutralize an aggressor's ICBM's, the world will enter a new era in warfare. Furthermore, war in the future may be waged and decided without a weapon being applied against an earth target. Space capabilities may bring about the technological disarmament of nuclear weapons. It may also remove major wars from the surface of the earth."

General LeMay's prophetic words may be difficult to credit, even in this age of technological miracles. But when the General spoke of weapons that strike with the speed of light, he was not speaking about things that are vague theoretical concepts.

In the vacuum of space, certain weapons whose powers are greatly reduced by the earth's atmosphere, could operate effectively, over long distance, against hostile spacecraft. Many possibilities are being explored. Nuclear accelerators could discharge concentrated beams of energy at speeds which would make it impossible for enemy spacecraft to maneuver out of the way. Projectiles launched by nuclear explosions could have a devastating effect. Also under research and development is the "Laser," an instrument that has the ability to focus a beam of light so sharply as to be destructive at a distance of hundreds of miles. And the speed of the Laser is precisely the speed of light, 186,000 miles per second. Very primitive Lasers are already in existence both in this country and in the Soviet Union.

If any of these potential weapons should be developed, as the experts believe they can be, and if they were then wedded to space vehicles, the military possibilities would be virtually unlimited.

It is against the background of these facts and possibilities that we must reassess our space program with a view to determining whether we are allocating the necessary priorities to our military space effort, and whether the mechanism of coordination between NASA and Defense cannot somehow be improved in a manner that brings benefits to both our scientific and military efforts in space.

Money is part of the problem. One of the ranking military experts told me that they could effectively use two or three times the funds now assigned for our military space program, and that such an increase in funding would produce a phenomenal acceleration in this program.

Personnel is another part of the problem. In our free society, scientific talent gravitates toward the agency which has access to the most funds, the best facilities, and the first call on the country's resources. In the current competition for space experts and supporting technological personnel, NASA is clearly in the driver's seat. This situation was dramatically and publicly underscored when NASA took over from the Army the incomparable ballistic missile team that Werner von Braun had built up at the Huntsville Laboratory, and Caltech's famed jet-propulsion laboratory in Pasadena.

Despite this combination of handicaps, the Defense effort in space has scored some outstanding successes. Only last week, for example, the press reported that, while NASA still seemed solidly wedded to liquid fuel rockets and had held back on funds for solid fuels, the Air Force had successfully test fired a giant solid fuel rocket of 600,000 lbs. thrust. The Air Force pointed out that with its five test firings to date of solid fuel rockets, it has scored a "100% untarnished record." It added, with justifiable pride, that there had been no comparable series of tests in the entire history of rocket development.

In re-examining our space program, I believe we can learn much from our recent experiences with the test ban moratorium.

We embarked on this moratorium because certain of our scientific experts and certain political advisers persuaded President Eisenhower that the only way to stop the nuclear arms race was for us to stop running. If we stopped running, so the argument went, then the Russians would stop running —and we would continue to enjoy the technological superiority which was ours on the day the moratorium began.

For three years, we adhered scrupulously to this moratorium. Despite justified suspicions of Soviet intentions, we did not even make serious preparations to test if the Soviets should first violate it.

Our good faith and our patience were rewarded by Khrushchev's unilateral termination of the test ban negotiations and by the massive series of 50 atmospheric tests which the Soviets conducted last September. According to the experts, these tests have brought the Kremlin superiority in at least several vital areas of nuclear weapons technology.

Against this background, unless the Soviets should miraculously agree to submit to an international space authority and open up their territory to inspection, we must assume the worst about their intentions in space.

We must assume that the Soviet Union's design for world conquest will be manifested in outer space as it is on earth. We must assume that they are at this very moment engaged in a massive effort to develop military space capabilities with a view to forcing the submission of the Free World.

This evaluation of Soviet intentions is in no way altered by Khrushchev's recent proposal that the United States and the Soviet Union engage in a joint space effort. It is to be noted that Khrushchev nowhere suggested that he is now willing to permit the UN or some other international authority to witness and inspect the launchings of all space vehicles from Soviet territory. He has simply proposed that *some* launchings be carried out on a cooperative basis.

The Soviets are today far ahead of us in the development of a maneuverable space vehicle. We are far ahead of them in space science and in the development of communications, navigation and weather satellites.

As it is now couched, Khrushchev's proposal boils down to the fact that the Soviets want to get their hands on American know-how in those areas where we are greatly ahead of them, while they are prepared to surrender no knowledge and no control in the one area where they are unquestionably ahead of us.

Let us not be deluded into concluding such a one-sided agreement. As President Kennedy has pointed out, our experience of the past twelve months justifies a healthy skepticism about Soviet intentions.

If there is to be an agreement of any kind on the joint exploration of space, it will have to be based, in the first instance and from the very first day, on the prohibition of secret launchings of space vehicles of any kind. This would involve prior announcement of all launchings, international inspection of all payloads, and international observation of all space shots.

Anything less than such an agreement would be an open invitation to a repetition of the kind of perfidy that the Soviets practiced on us in the case of the nuclear test ban moratorium.

The proposal that we give priority to national security projects in our space program does not mean that we would have to abandon or even seriously restrict our peaceful goals in space.

To a very large degree, especially in the first phase of space exploration, our military objectives in space and our peaceful objectives run completely parallel. Because of this, the collaboration between NASA and the Defense Department has been remarkably effective.

The Navy has been responsible for the successful development of our weather satellite program, our communications satellite program and of our navigational satellite program. NASA has been conducting our scientific probes of the space environment, many of our studies in space biology, and our Mercury astronaut program. All of these can either serve the world community in peace or can serve to enhance our national security in the event of war.

We must recognize, however, that our very access to the space environment for peaceful activities will in the future depend on our ability to protect the men and equipment we send there. If the Kremlin should ever succeed in gaining military control of near space, that is, of the regions close to earth, it would be in a position to shoot down our vehicles already in space and deprive us of future access to space.

This, I am told by the experts, is not a fantasy of worried minds. It is a serious physical probability that we dare not overlook in determining the orientation of our national space policy.

We have now reached the point in the development of space science and space technology where our scientific and our military efforts in space must begin to diverge at a number of points. Our military establishment is now confronted with the practical need to develop technologies and hardware specifically adapted to military purposes. The existing structure may have been adequate for the past. But, for the future, I believe it is essential that our military experts be made more nearly equal partners in the direction of our overall space program.

The basic problem is to so adjust and so coordinate our space programs that competition, friction and overlapping are reduced to a minimum, that priorities are established which give due consideration to both the requirements of science and the requirements of defense, that the special genius of our military for getting things done is given proper scope.

In the first place, without in any way disparaging NASA which is really an incredibly competent organization, I believe that greater military participation in the direction of our space program would automatically step up its tempo. This is so for two reasons.

First of all, military risk calculations are a great deal different from the risk calculations under which civilian agencies are, rightly, obliged to operate. Second, the sense of urgency which stimulates our defense establishment is almost impossible to duplicate in a non-military atmosphere.

In our nuclear submarine program, in the Navy's Polaris missile program, in the Air Force's Minuteman program, our armed services have repeatedly demonstrated the capability to carry out the most massive projects within time limits that exceed the most optimistic expectations. But they can only do so if they are given the necessary authority and the necessary facilities.

What concrete changes can we make in our space program to give our armed services more say than they have today?

We might consider the advisability of adding representatives of the three armed services to the National Aeronautics and Space Council.

We might further consider the advisability of appointing a qualified and selected military officer as Executive Director of the Space Council, with full powers, subject to the decisions of the Council, to assign priorities, and to coordinate and balance our military needs and scientific space program.

For this purpose, we should select a man who combines outstanding technical competence with faith in space and the military potentialities of space, and with a profound determination to make America pre-eminent in this vital new arena. I know that we have such men in our military service today.

There are, perhaps, other measures that might be taken that would also serve the purpose. But what is clear is that we can no longer indulge in wishful thinking about space.

We can no longer permit ourselves to be paralyzed by the hope that we can negotiate an enduring peace in space when we have not yet been able to negotiate a stable peace on earth.

We must have a space program that is second to none. If we must redouble our effort to overtake and surpass the Soviets in the crucial race for manned space vehicles, then I am convinced that America can find both the means and the personnel to do so.

We must have a space program that gives priority to the security of our nation.

We must provide the Defense Department with the directives and facilities to proceed, as a matter of the utmost urgency, with the development of military space systems. We must give particular priority to the building of the basic space vehicle which General LeMay has described: a craft that can maneuver into and out of orbit, and perform all essential military functions in space and the upper atmosphere.

Let us by all means strive to place space at the service of mankind.

Let us always keep the door open to an agreement ensuring that space will become a domain of peaceful cooperation between the great powers.

But in the absence of a properly safeguarded agreement, we must bend ourselves to be supreme in space power, as we are supreme in naval power and air power.

For this will be the price of preserving our freedom in the fantastic technological world of the future.

Chapter XVI

IS THE UN WORTH SAVING?*

In the very near future, Congress will be called upon to vote approval of the Administration's proposal to purchase $100,-000,000 worth of the projected UN bond issue. Before we do so, I consider it natural and proper that we should want to take stock of the recent record of the UN in world affairs, of the tendencies at work within it, of how well it has served the cause of peace, and how well it has served, or can be made to serve, our national interests.

In increasing numbers, people are beginning to ask themselves whether the UN is worth saving. I, myself, believe that the UN *is* worth saving, and that is why I cast my vote in the Senate Foreign Relations Committee in support of the revised proposal that we purchase $25,000,000 worth of UN bonds outright and authorize matching purchases up to a total of $100,000,000, subject to matching commitments by other nations.

But I also believe that the UN *requires* saving, because I fear it will doom itself if certain of the tendencies apparent in recent years are permitted to develop unchecked and if certain essential reforms are not instituted.

It is in this spirit, Mr. President, that I propose to examine the record and present status of the United Nations.

When the UN was founded, there were absolutely no limits to the enthusiasm and optimism of its sponsors.

The high sounding principles of the United Nations Charter were accepted at face value and the adherence of the

---

* United States Senate, March 22, 1962.

founding nations to these principles was taken for granted.

The United Nations was to usher in an era of peace and international order, an era in which the rights of nations, big and small, would be protected, and disputes between nations would be settled by conciliation.

War was to be banished as an instrument of policy; and the Security Council was authorized to take whatever action might be necessary, including military measures, against nations guilty of aggression or of violating the peace.

Today this dream lies shattered by events in the Congo, by India's forcible annexation of Goa, and by the Pandora's box of unilateral threats that this action has already opened: Indonesia's threats against Dutch New Guinea, Iraq's threats against Kuwait, India's renewed threats against Kashmir, and so on.

Today people throughout the free world are asking themselves whether the UN can be saved, and, for that matter, whether it is really worth saving.

They are profoundly disturbed by the UN's role in the Congo —by its seeming tolerance of Lumumbaism, by its brutal military intervention in Katanga, by its extreme tardiness in taking action against the pro-Communist forces of Vice Premier Antoine Gizenga, by the dangerous encouragement to racism implicit in the removal of white "mercenaries" and advisers.

They are disturbed by the failure of the UN to take any action to prevent or condemn India's attack on Goa and by the estimate that, had the matter been taken to the General Assembly, almost 2/3 of the present Assembly would have supported India's action. Ambassador Stevenson, I am convinced, spoke for the American people when he warned that this failure by the UN might be "the first act in a drama that could end in its death."

People are also worried over the implications for the future of the rapidly escalating membership of the UN.

When the UN was founded at San Francisco, there were exactly 50 members. Today, in consequence of the rapid liquidation of the European colonial empires, 104 nations are represented in the General Assembly, and the chances are that at least another 20 newly emergent nations will be added to this number over the next several years.

Many of the new Afro-Asian member nations were ill-prepared or hardly prepared at all for independence. They do not understand the meaning of freedom or the fundamental issues involved in the conflict between the free world and the Communist world; and they are too often prone to follow the lead of the Communist world because of their residual resentment against Western colonialism and because they have been led to believe that violent attacks against Western colonialism pay off in the form of increased foreign aid, while attacks on Soviet colonialism are best avoided because the Soviets are quick to respond in anger and to take political and economic counter measures.

The Soviets have always exercised a negative control over the actions of the Security Council through the uninhibited application of the right to veto. In 1952, under the pressure of the Korean War, the United States was able to get the General Assembly to place an apparent curb on the abuse of the veto through the enactment of the so-called "Uniting for Peace" resolution. Under the terms of this resolution, a Security Council veto can be overridden by a 2/3 majority of the General Assembly whenever a breach of the peace is involved. This victory, unfortunately, has proved to be a transitory one.

Today, thanks to the rapid increase in UN membership, the Soviets have virtually achieved *de facto* veto power over the actions of the General Assemby.

There are today few conceivable issues on which the Communist nations could not rally enough support to prevent the 2/3 majority vote required to override a Soviet veto. And when the 11 Communist nations (including Cuba) can persuade the 46 Afro-Asian nations to vote with them, they have the simple majority required to get their own way on procedural matters. If another 20 new nations were to enter the United Nations, the day may not be too far distant when the Soviets will be able to muster the 2/3 majority in the Assembly necessary to override a Western veto.

It is understandable, Mr. President, that the Western nations should be worried over the present situation in the General Assembly and even more worried over the prospect for the immediate future. It is understandable that doubts should now be expressed about a voting procedure that gives an African nation of 500,000, still emerging from tribalism, precisely the same vote as the United States and the Soviet Union. In this grotesque UN calculus, one African bushman becomes the equivalent of 100 Frenchmen or 400 Americans. And although many plans have been advanced for "weighting" votes by population and other factors, there is not the remotest chance that the jealous, sensitive nations of Asia, Africa and Latin America will agree to anything less than the present formula of "one nation, one vote."

There is also widespread concern over the declared Soviet intention of extending the power of the veto to the UN Secretariat, through the establishment of the so-called "troika" or 3-man Secretariat.

Given their veto power in the Security Council and their increasing ability to prevent any majority directed against their interests in the General Assembly, the establishment of a Soviet veto power over the Secretariat would, in effect, turn the UN into a captive instrument of Soviet foreign policy.

The Western nations were able to mobilize sufficient support to defeat the Soviet troika proposal. But, without abandoning their basic proposal, the Soviets have been able to place certain limitations on the powers of the Secretary General through the compromise establishment of an "inner-cabinet" of 8 "principal advisers" around the Secretary General.

In accepting the general concept of an "inner-cabinet" the United States had argued for a 5-member body in which the United States, the Soviet Union, Western Europe, Africa and Latin America would be represented. The Soviets had held out for a larger body in which the Communist bloc, the Western bloc and the neutrals would be equally represented. Finally, it was decided to leave the composition of the inner-cabinet to the discretion of Secretary General U Thant.

On December 30, it was announced that the Secretary General had completed the selection of his inner-cabinet. In this cabinet 3 Western nations are represented (the United States, France and Brazil), 2 Communist nations (the U.S.S.R. and Czechoslovakia) and 3 Afro-Asian nations (India, the United Arab Republic and Nigeria). This is very close to the 3-3-3 formula proposed by the Soviets. Actually, counting U Thant as a member of the cabinet, we have 4 Afro-Asian and 2 communist representatives against the 3 Western bloc representatives.

The "principal advisers" do not have the power of veto. But the establishment of this inner-cabinet unquestionably dilutes the authority of the Secretary General, while its composition can hardly be considered a victory or an augury of victory for the Free World.

Once again the Soviets have demanded the moon, settled for half the moon—and persuaded the Free World that they were being generous in compromising on their original demand. But let there be no mistake about it, the Soviets will be back for the rest of the moon when the Secretary General's term expires two years from now.

There is another situation that has many people worried, although little is said about it. I refer to the *double standard of values that governs the employment of UN personnel.*

The Security Council, the General Assembly and the Secretariat are the direct instruments of power in the United Nations. But power in any organization is transmitted through its personnel. In the process of transmitting or executing directives, their intent can be so modified by employees with strong ideological convictions that, for all practical purposes, personnel must be considered a fourth instrument of power within the UN.

Employees of the UN Secretariat are recruited according to agreed ratios, from the member States of the United Nations. Theoretically, all of these employees, at the point of joining the United Nations, abandon their national loyalties and ideological convictions and become "international civil servants." In practice this absurd concept has created a situation that is dangerously weighted in favor of the Soviet bloc.

On the one hand, in the case of Secretariat employees from non-Communist countries, the application of the "international civil servant" concept has favored those who are neutral in the struggle between East and West and militated against applicants with strongly anti-Communist views.

On the other hand, in the case of employees from the Communist bloc, it is taken for granted by everyone but the wilfully blind that all of them are Communists by conviction and that a very substantial percentage of them are espionage and secret police agents. The "Exposé of Soviet Espionage" prepared in May, 1960, by Mr. J. Edgar Hoover, Director of the FBI, presented details concerning ten Soviet nationals employed by the UN who had been obliged to leave the United States when the FBI established that they were engaged in espionage activities.

This situation was most dramatically high-lighted in the trial of Judy Coplon, whom the F.B.I. caught in the act of turning over classified government documents to Valentin Gubitschev, a Soviet citizen employed by the UN.

Since the UN is not an anti-Communist organization, a record of pro-Communist associations or other evidence which would preclude applicants from employment by the United States government or by the British government or by any free and sensible government does not, in itself, preclude an applicant from employment by the UN.

In the course of 1952, the Senate Subcommittee on Internal Security called before it 33 Americans employed by the United Nations in various capacities. Twenty-six of these invoked the Fifth Amendment when questioned about Communist activities, and these were subsequently dismissed by the United Nations. Many of those dismissed held very high rank. Perhaps the best known was Frank Coe, Secretary of the International Monetary Fund and one-time assistant to Harry Dexter White in the Treasury Department. Coe refused to answer on grounds of possible self-incrimination when he was asked: "Are you a Soviet agent, Mr. Coe?" Mr. Coe has now provided us with the answer to this question, because he is today working as an expert for the Chinese Communist government.

The hearings also developed the information that the United Nations had previously ignored adverse information concerning nine of these employees, which had been submitted to it by the State Department Security Clearance Board.

The very great majority of the Western nationals employed by the United Nations are certainly not pro-Communist. Very many of them do combine dedication to the ideals of the UN with dedication to the cause of freedom. At the worst, they suffer from the affliction of ideological neutralism which is supposed to be a virtue in the "international civil servant." But there is no question that the employment policies of the UN make things relatively easy for Communist infiltrees; and there is every reason to believe that the Communist infiltration among the quotas of the other non-Communist nations is at least as great as it has been demonstrated to be in the case of the American quota.

Needless to say, a single Communist infiltree, in a situation like the Congo, or in any other crisis situation, can do an infinite amount of damage. I know that our intelligence community has had serious reason for believing that the UN's former number two man in Katanga, Michel Tombelaine, a Frenchman, was, at the very least, a Communist sympathizer. And Tombelaine was one of the men primarily responsible for embittering relations between the UN and the Katanga government, and for launching the September action in Katanga without the approval of Dag Hammarskjold and his UN superiors.

The Soviets have, over the past year, been demanding a larger quota of Secretariat employees for the Communist countries. This is a demand that will prove difficult to resist because, on a pro-rata basis, they unquestionably are entitled to greater representation in the secretariat staff.

Finally, there is concern over the UN's seemingly hopeless financial plight and over the fact that the United States has not merely been footing 60% of the UN's bills, but may be left holding the bag for the better part of its accumulated deficit.

France, the Soviet Union, and many of the Afro-Asian nations have refused to pay any part of the Congo operation. The Soviet Union and other nations have refused to contribute to the cost of the United Nations' operation along the Israeli frontier. Most of the member nations are heavily in arrears on all of their obligations to the United Nations, even where they have not formally indicated an intention to withhold payment. British Foreign Secretary Lord Home in his recent statement on the UN charged that the refusal by so many members to bear a share of the cost of the UN brings the prospect of "power without responsibility."

The result is that the United Nations is $120 million in debt; and, in consequence of the Congo operation, it is running into deeper debt at the rate of another $10 million each month. Secretary General U Thant, in desperation, has made an internal loan of $12 million from the UN's Children's Emergency Fund—in my opinion, a highly questionable measure—and he has now proposed an international bond issue of $200 million.

The crisis of the United Nations is therefore four-fold: It is simultaneously a crisis of principle, a crisis of structure and personnel, a financial crisis, and a crisis of public confidence.

Unfortunately, Mr. President there has always been a tendency for opinions on the UN to polarize.

On the one hand, there have been those who have credited the UN with almost miraculous powers and who look upon the UN, and not upon the strength and courage and wisdom of the free nations, as the "last great hope for peace."

On the other hand, there have been those who have never been able to see anything good in the United Nations, who deny it any positive accomplishments, who are convinced that the United Nations has always worked and will continue to work in the interests of the Kremlin, and who feel that we should encourage its demise rather than attempt to delay it.

Surveying the unbroken panorama of crisis and chaos in the UN, even its staunchest friends now agree that the UN is very sick and that we must do some serious rethinking on its structure and on our role within the international organization.

In deciding whether the United Nations can be saved and should be saved, it might be well first of all to establish what the UN is and what it is not, what it can do and what it cannot do, the situations in which it has succeeded and the situations in which it has failed.

In my opinion, the United Nations has never had the miraculous powers claimed for it by its Utopian supporters.

On the other hand, there have been a number of situations in which it has clearly served the cause of freedom and the national interests of the United States.

The United Nations has played a positive role in those situations where we have frankly accepted its limitations.

There have been other situations where the United Nations unquestionably could have performed more effectively if we had displayed more vigorous leadership within the United Nations and more vigorous diplomacy outside the UN.

Finally, there have been situations in which we have completely closed our eyes to the UN's limitations and weaknesses and have made it the custodian and executive of our foreign policy.

For my own part, I believe that the UN can play a truly vital role in the preservation of peace, in the conciliation of disputes, and in the development of harmonious relations between the nations of the world. Given time, given patience, and given some basic changes in the world in which we live, the UN may some day begin to function as a limited parliament of man. But the UN is doomed if we continue to indulge in illusions concerning its nature, functions and powers at this moment in history.

The chief of these illusions is that the UN today represents a true community of nations, united in spirit and purpose, and sharing the principles espoused by the UN Charter.

If we wish the United Nations to live, and if we wish to live with it, we must first of all face up frankly to the fact that there has never been any such community of nations; that the United Nations, instead, has been from the beginning a two-headed organism, a composite organization embracing two mortally antagonistic camps, the Communist world and the

Free World; and that the Communist world is out to bury this free world by subversion, by infiltration, by guerrilla operations, by direct aggression where they can get away with it, by indirect aggression where this seems safer.

The existence of the veto is a reflection of this fundamental division within the UN.

My argument is that, once we frankly accept the fact of this fundamental cleavage within the UN and once we recognize its limitation, the UN can, on balance, usefully serve the community of free nations and the cause of world peace.

Mr. President, I think it would be useful to examine several of the most significant case histories of UN action by way of indicating both its limitations and its potentialities.

In the immediate postwar period there were two dramatic examples of how the UN could be used to serve the cause of freedom and to supplement an independent foreign policy conceived from the standpoint of national interest.

IRAN

In January, 1946, the Government of Iran filed charges with the Security Council that the Soviet Union was interfering in Iran's internal affairs by refusing to withdraw the troops that had been permitted to enter the province of Azerbaijan during the war, and by fostering the creation in Azerbaijan of a quisling separatist regime. The ensuing discussion in the Security Council served to place the facts before world opinion, even though the Council went no further than recommending that the Soviet and Iranian Governments endeavor to resolve the dispute by direct negotiations.

In early May, 1946, President Truman addressed a strongly worded note to Stalin on the question of Iran, warning that the United States would not stand idly by while Azerbaijan was annexed to the Soviet Union. On May 9, leaving behind their puppet government, the Soviet troops were evacuated. Six months later on November 14, 1946, the Iranian Army, backed up by President Truman's note, moved to reoccupy Azerbaijan. The hated quisling regime collapsed like a house of cards, and the Red Army did not lift a finger to intervene.

GREECE

In December of the same year, the Government of Greece asked the Security Council to investigate the evidence that its Communist neighbors to the North—Albania, Yugoslavia, and Bulgaria—were actively supporting the Communist guerrillas in Greece and were directly involved in the ruthless terror practiced by the guerrillas, including the abduction of thousands of Greek children.

To investigate this situation, the Security Council set up a body which paralleled its own membership, with the euphonious title "Commission of Investigation to Ascertain the Facts Relating to Alleged Border Violations along the Greek Frontier." The Soviet Union and Poland, as members of the Security Council, were included in the Commission; and the Deputy Secretary of the Commission, by agreement, was a Pole.

The composition of the Commission was a serious handicap, especially in taking the testimony of anti-Communist Greek villagers. Moreover, with Poland and the Soviet Union represented in the Commission, everything the Cominform may have wished to know about the workings of the Commission was automatically available to it. But, despite these limitations, the Commission, in balance, rendered an important service to the Free World. The majority report, with only Poland and the Soviet Union dissenting, implicated Yugoslavia heavily in the guerrilla attacks and Albania and Bulgaria to a lesser degree.

In the Security Council the Soviet Union repeatedly vetoed Western resolutions calling upon Yugoslavia, Bulgaria and Albania to desist from supporting the Communist guerrillas; and when the matter was finally taken up by the Assembly, the Soviets were able, by the sheer violence of their oratory, to prevent the Assembly from adopting a simple resolution condemning Communist aggression against Greece.

Greece was saved primarily by the Truman Doctrine, American assistance, and Tito's expulsion from the Cominform. But the massive factual evidence accumulated by the UN Commission gave important support to our rescue operation by effectively indicting the Communist satellites in the eyes of world opinion.

In both Iran and Greece the United Nations played a highly useful role. But it was able to do so, in both instances, first, because we had an affirmative national policy, backed up by power or show of power; second, because we were realistic in our appraisal of the UN's capabilities and limitations and used it primarily as a fact-finding instrument and as a forum for enlisting the support of world opinion.

In neither case did we turn the situation over to the UN and abdicate our own responsibility.

Korea

The Korean war marked the high point of the UN's activities. It marked, at the same time, the turning point of our policy towards the UN, so that what began as an affirmative act of national policy was transformed, in its final stages, into passive submission to the fears and desires of the UN majority.

United Nations intervention against Communist aggression in Korea has often been held up as an example of what the UN can do. But it was a fluke which will probably never again occur, and a greatly overrated fluke, to boot.

In the first place, the Soviets had four months previously, in February, 1950, pulled out of the Security Council and other UN organs, and there was open talk that they would formally abandon the UN. Their motives for doing so are still obscure and subject to debate. But the immediate significance of their absence was that the Security Council was free to act without being frustrated by Soviet vetos. The Soviets returned to the Security Council two months after the Korean War began, in August, 1950, and immediately set about frustrating and vetoing further UN action.

It can virtually be taken for granted, Mr. President, that the Soviets will never again make the mistake of absenting themselves from the Security Council when a critical matter is being discussed.

In the second place, the initial decision to intervene in Korea was made by President Truman and not by the UN. Had

President Truman waited for the UN to authorize intervention, it would, at the worst, never have been authorized; or, at best, it would have been authorized too late to do any good.

President Truman's action was a supreme example of the difference that affirmative leadership can make. Without waiting for the UN, he ordered American troops in the Far East into action. With American intervention a *fait accompli,* he then asked the UN for a resolution condemning Communist aggression in Korea and calling upon the member nations to render all possible support to South Korea. The resolution won overwhelming support.

There was unquestionably a great moral advantage to waging a war that was sanctioned by 53 member nations of the UN and actively supported by 16 of them. But it was a moral advantage that carried with it a serious political liability. Although the bulk of the fighting in Korea was done by American and South Korean troops, the participation of other nations in the military effort—the fact that it was a "United Nations war"—made it necessary to share the military and political direction of the Korean war with our United Nations allies.

It was in deference to our United Nations allies that we refrained from bombing the Yalu River bridges, across which the Chinese Communists were supplying their 1,000,000 man army in Korea. Because they feared that the war might be enlarged, we refrained from attacking staging areas or airfields in Communist China and even gave up the right to pursue Chinese aircraft to their "privileged sanctuary" across the frontier. And when the tide of war turned against the Chinese Communists and they went reeling back in defeat, it was primarily in deference to our allies that we consented to an immediate ceasefire instead of pressing our military advantage until the Communists had accepted certain basic conditions.

The result was that a war that could and should have ended in a decisive triumph for the Free World, wound up, instead, in an armistice agreement that enabled the Communist negotiators to rush from the tent in Panmunjom shouting: "We have won! We have won!"

The Communists had lost a small chunk of North Korean territory. But they had saved themselves from total military disaster; they had humiliated the West through the protracted negotiotions at Panmunjom; they had obtained a prisoner of war agreement much closer to their point of view than that of the West; and, finally, the Korean armistice had not even imposed the simple condition that they terminate their guerrilla activities in Vietnam.

The result was that in 1954, one year after the conclusion of the Korean Armistice, the Free World found itself obliged to sign over the 15,000,000 people of North Vietnam to Communist control. And this was only the first installment we have had to pay for our failure to grasp tne victory which was ours in Korea. We are still paying for this failure in Laos today, in the bitter war we shall have to fight for many years if South Vietnam is to be saved, and in the danger which now threatens the whole of Southeast Asia.

But before we blame the outcome of the Korean war on the UN, we must, in fairness, ask ourselves whether things might not have turned out differently if we had continued to provide the resolute leadership with which we embarked on the war, instead of following supinely after the opinions of our UN allies.

HUNGARY AND SUEZ

The Hungarian revolution and the Suez crisis, which took place concurrently, constituted a dramatic demonstration of the UN double standard in practice.

On the one hand, having abjured military force as an instrument of international policy, the United States sided *with* its enemies *against* its friends in sponsoring a resolution demanding the immediate withdrawal of the British and French forces from Suez and of the Israeli forces from Sinai. The threat of sanctions seemed implicit in the resolution.

Britain, France, and Israel complied with the demand that they withdraw.

On the other hand, the UN proved itself completely impotent to prevent or to deal with Soviet aggression against the people of Hungary. In its brutal suppression of the Hungarian revolution, the Kremlin openly flouted world public opinion; and it subsequently defied more than half a dozen UN resolutions calling upon it to withdraw its forces from Hungary. No sanctions of any kind were imposed or, for that matter, suggested as punishment for this defiance.

And, although their credentials have never been formally approved, the representatives of the quisling regime which, so said the UN resolutions, was imposed by Soviet bayonets, continue to sit in the General Assembly with full voting powers.

For the UN's many failures in the case of the Hungarian revolution, the U. S. must accept a very large portion of the blame. Once again, instead of providing vigorous leadership, we submitted supinely to the majority belief that nothing must be done to thwart the will of the Kremlin in Eastern Europe because any such action would gravely imperil peace.

There were many actions, short of war, that we could and should have taken to support the Hungarian revolution during the several brief days of Hungarian freedom.

We could have made it emphatically clear from the first minute that we recognized the government of Imre Nagy as the legitimate government of Hungary.

We could have moved immediately to make certain that his representatives were properly accredited to and seated by the UN.

We could have urged and obtained the immediate dispatch of a corps of UN observers to Budapest or, alternatively, we might have urged the appointment of a group of non-Communist ambassadors as a UN observation committee.

We could have warned that the re-entry of the Red Army into Hungary would have grave and unpredictable consequences, that it would, among other things result in the immediate imposition of stringent economic and diplomatic sanctions against the Soviet bloc.

But we did none of these things.

The failure of the UN in the case of Hungary was, in short, a reflection of our own failure.

THE CONGO

The UN's ability to uphold its charter impartially has declined with the growth of the Afro-Asian bloc and the weakening of the authority of the Secretary General. Yet for some strange reason, in proportion as the Western ability to influence the UN becomes weaker and the Soviet ability greater, we seem to be relying more heavily on the UN for the solution of cold war problems.

In the case of the Congo crisis, we have witnessed for the first time a total abdication of national policy. In the Congo we have made the sorry experiment of substituting the UN for an independent foreign policy, giving our passive assent to the will of the UN majority.

What this has meant in practice is that our policy in the Congo has been determined by such illustrious champions of freedom as Krishna Menon, Gamel Abdel Nasser, Haile Selassie, Kwame Nkrumah, Sekou Toure—yes, and at certain points, by Khrushchev and his satellite lackeys.

The history of the Congo since independence provides an interesting contrast between the rigid, blindly utopian attitude of the United States toward the UN, and the flexible, ruthlessly utilitarian attitude of the Soviet Union.

In its blind desire not to do anything to frustrate the UN, the United States has gone along with UN resolutions on the Congo even when it had grave reservations about their wisdom or when these resolutions lacked amendments that we had once considered essential. But whenever UN policy on the Congo has not completely satisfied the Kremlin, it has resorted to violent attacks, the use of the veto, and even threats of withdrawal.

It has been pointed out by defenders of UN actions in the Congo that Khrushchev bitterly assailed the UN's Congo policy at last year's session of the General Assembly and demanded Dag Hammarskjold's dismissal or his replacement by a troika, or 3-man secretariat. A careful examination of the record, however, will reveal that the Soviets have at various times supported UN actions in the Congo when they felt that these actions served their interests; and when UN policies have fallen short of the Kremlin's optimum requirements, the Communists have fumed and threatened, and have finally wound up by getting somewhat more of their own way.

The Soviets supported the original Security Council resolution on the Congo in July, 1960, because they saw in this resolution a means for forcing out the majority of the Belgian technicians and administrators and promoting a condition of general anarchy and chaos on which communism thrives.

When Colonel Mobutu in September, 1960, overthrew the government of Lumumba and ordered the Communist embassies out of the country, the Kremlin charged that Mobutu's action was illegal and it blamed the UN for countenancing this action. Khrushchev assailed Hammarskjold at the UN General Assembly in vitriolic terms for this affront to Soviet dignity and he banged his shoe on the desk.

Colonel Mobutu has publicly accused the UN of opposing his coup and undercutting his regime at every point. The record bears out Colonel Mobutu's allegations. The UN representative in the Congo, Rajeshwar Dayal, was openly sympathetic to Lumumba and later showed a strong indifference to or partiality for Gizenga. The one thing the UN could not do, however, was to overthrow the Mobutu government by force or prevent it from expelling the Soviet bloc embassies.

Khrushchev's attacks on Hammarskjold had very tangible results. Sensitive to the need for keeping his organization together, Hammarskjold offered certain concessions. He refused for many months to dismiss Dayal, despite the complaints of the Leopoldville government and the American embassy. He ignored the pleas of the Leopoldville government in ordering the dispatch of Indian troops to the Congo. He authorized, or condoned, a policy of tolerance and inaction *vis-a-vis* the illegal rival government which Gizenga set up in Stanleyville. He committed the UN to press for an early return to government by the Lumumbaist-dominated national assembly.

Hammarskjold's concessions were not sufficient to satisfy the totalitarian appetite of the Kremlin. But as UN policy in the Congo began to conform to Soviet requirements, Soviet support again became manifest. The Soviets did not oppose the Security Council resolution of February, 1961, which called for the expulsion of foreign mercenaries and advisers from Katanga and which at the same time protected the Gizenga regime by instructing the UN forces to prevent clashes between the rival Congolese factions.

Finally the Soviet Union joined the United States in actively supporting the Security Council resolution of November 24, 1961, which was directed specifically and exclusively against Katanga and which was, in fact, intended as a green light for all-out military action against the Tshombe government.

As for the story that the UN is saving the Congo from communism, I would point out that the UN forces until recently took no action against the illegal government which Gizenga established in Stanleyville; took no action to round up or to punish the Gizenga soldiers who massacred the 13 Italian airmen; took no action to punish the soldiers responsible for the massacre of the 20 Catholic missionaries at Congola; in fact, took no action of any kind against the left wing extremists for almost 18 months.

Unless we can succeed in emancipating ourselves from total subservience to UN policy, there will be no way of coping with the mounting extremist threat in the Congo.

So long as we accept the United Nations as the only instrument of policy in the Congo, so long as we abdicate our right to an area policy which reflects our national interest, so long as we back the UN in actions which please the Kremlin and the Afro-Asian extremists but which clearly violate its charter —so long as we do these things, the situation in the Congo will remain perilous and unpredictable.

The beginning of wisdom in the Congo would be a public affirmation that the Free World will not under any circumstances permit the Kremlin to take over in the Congo, either directly or through crypto-Communist agents. Such an affirmation would lay the basis for a concerted economic and political policy designed to keep the Congo free.

The Conditions of Survival

The issue of how much control over our foreign policy should be surrendered to the mercies of unpredictable UN majorities, really goes to the heart of the question of whether the UN can survive and whether it is worth saving.

The UN is worth saving as an area of contact between the Communist world, the free world, and the uncommitted nations; as a forum from which we can plead the cause of freedom and solicit the support of the world community for the objectives of our foreign policy; as a medium for the conciliation of disputes; as a vehicle for cooperative non-political activities like the World Health Organization; as an organization whose functions may be progressively enlarged if the world situation improves.

The UN *can* be saved, and *should* be saved, if we are prepared to conceive of it in these limited terms and participate in it on this limited basis.

The UN will *not* be saved if we continue to ascribe to it virtues which it cannot possibly possess and assign to it executive tasks that it is functionally incapable of fulfilling. It will not be saved if we continue to sweep its misdemeanors and weaknesses under the rug instead of airing them frankly.

The UN cannot save the Congo from Communist subversion because it is precluded, both by charter and by composition, from saving any country from Communist subversion.

The UN cannot be used as a protective apron to prevent a direct confrontation between the Communist bloc and the Western bloc, because, UN or no UN, the Communist bloc will confront when it is prepared to confront and strike when it has the ability to strike.

The UN will prove as powerless to prevent further aggression by the Soviet bloc or by the Afro-Asian nations as it proved in the cases of Hungary and Goa. In fact, the Security Council veto and the composition of the General Assembly make it inconceivable that the UN will ever again take adverse action that seriously affects the Communist bloc.

The UN cannot, except at the gravest peril, be used as a substitute for an independent foreign policy or as an excuse for not having one. Where our vital national interests are at stake, we cannot submit passively while a Communist-Afro-Asian coalition imposes its will on the Congo or on any other area.

Krushchev has publicly announced that the Kremlin does not intend to pay the least attention to the UN when UN resolutions run counter to Soviet interests. Apart from the brazenness of the statement, there was really nothing new about it; the Kremlin has after all exercised the veto against 91 Security Council resolutions and it has flouted resolutions of the General Assembly on both Hungary and Korea. Now India and the majority of the Afro-Asian nations have made it clear that they have just as little regard for the UN Charter.

The United States and the other Western nations have, up until now, observed the rules of the game prescribed by the United Nations Charter. They have abstained or backed away from the use of force, and have shunned the use of the veto in the Security Council.

There is only one way in which this dangerously unbalanced situation can be corrected: The United States and its allies must reserve for themselves precisely the same freedom of action as Khrushchev and Nehru have claimed for themselves when they felt their own interests were directly involved.

If air support is required to assure the success of a landing by Cuban freedom fighters, then air support must be given, despite the hysterical and hypocritical protests that unquestionably will be heard in the United Nations.

If Valerian Zorin vetoes Ambassador Stevenson's amendments to the Congo resolution, then Ambassador Stevenson should be encouraged to respond by imposing the veto on the version desired by the Kremlin.

In the debates in the United Nations, Soviet emphasis on colonialism, racial discrimination, and economic welfare has thus far given them both the initiative and the spotlight.

But we *can* make the initiative ours, Mr. President, by challenging the Soviets on every issue; by repeatedly counter-posing the issue of Soviet colonialism to the dying issue of Western colonialism; by demanding the right of self-determination for the captive nations of Europe and Asia; by presenting the facts about the massive Soviet antisemitism of today whenever the Communists talk about the Nazi antisemitism of yesterday; and by pursuing policies, within and without the United Nations, designed to promote the welfare and freedom of all peoples.

The adoption of such an affirmative policy, would inevitably involve certain other important adjustments in our foreign policy.

Among other things, it would require a strengthening of the community of free nations, perhaps working through the existing mechanism of NATO.

It would also involve a complete overhaul of our foreign aid policy so that we would no longer be in the preposterous position of giving billions of dollars to countries like Yugoslavia and Indonesia and Ghana, which vote with the Soviet bloc on virtually every issue in the United Nations, while we grant aid on a far more niggardly basis to staunch little allies like the Philippines and Thailand. Once we decide to make the scale of our foreign aid somehow commensurate with the attitude and voting records of recipients, there will, I am convinced, be a decided improvement in our voting strength in the UN General Assembly.

The present success of the Communist bloc within the United Nations is in large measure due to the fact that the uncommitted nations, both new and old, believe Communism to be the wave of the future. They see hostility toward the West overlooked, or rewarded by more generous aid programs, while votes adverse to the Soviets are not soon forgotten.

Such a policy as I have outlined above would, I am convinced, bring many of the newly independent nations to our side and automatically fortify our position within the councils of the United Nations.

In taking the stand that the UN is worth saving and that we should make the effort to keep it alive and to work within it along the lines I have indicated, there are several additional conditions that I feel must be observed.

Condition number one is that we must permit no further curtailment of the authority of the Secretary General. The Kremlin's proposal for a *troika*, or three man secretariat, would, if it is ever accepted, give them the power to veto within the secretariat any proposal which was not to their liking.

Condition number two is that we must not again submit to Communist blackmail as we recently did in swapping the admission of Mauritania for the admission of Outer Mongolia, the most miserable and the most dependent of all the Soviet puppet states. Each time we submit to such blackmail, we lose something of our own integrity and the United Nations loses something of its affirmative meaning.

Condition number three is that we should put the United Nations on firm notice that we will never reconcile ourselves to the admission of Red China to its ranks. Red China stands guilty of so many crimes against humanity that it is preposterous that this criminal regime should even be considered for membership in the United Nations. If the UN should ever seat the representatives of this criminal regime, it would be tantamount to going over a moral precipice. Then, I believe, nothing could save it, because it would, by its own act have forfeited the respect and confidence of honest men everywhere.

Under these conditions and with these reservations, recognizing its limitations but not ignoring or underestimating its very great potentialities for peace and conciliation, I believe that we should make every effort to save the UN.

Chapter XVII

THE INDONESIA-NETHERLANDS DISPUTE
OVER WEST NEW GUINEA*

The past few weeks have brought ominous news from Netherlands New Guinea.

Negotiations between the Netherlands government and the government of Indonesia appear to have broken down. Indonesian commando units have invaded several of the minor islands surrounding New Guinea. The Netherlands forces on the islands have taken counter measures against the invaders. Meanwhile, the cries of President Sukarno and all the other extremist leaders in Indonesia have become shriller and more threatening.

New Guinea, say the Indonesian extremists, belongs to Indonesia, and the Netherlands must cede it forthwith to Indonesia, or the Indonesian government will embark on all-out miltary action to assert its rights to the area. To this the Netherlands replies that New Guinea does not, by any stretch of the imagination, belong to Indonesia and that the only just solution would be to permit the people of West New Guinea to determine their fate in a future vote under UN auspices.

The outcome of this dispute will, to a very large degree, depend on the position taken by the United States and by the manner in which we exercise our influence. But our present policy in this matter has been defined only by rumors and by unconfirmed reports in the press. There have been no formal hearings or discussions in depth on the matter with the Senate Foreign Relations Committee; and such hearings should be held before any irrevocable decision is made.

---

* Memorandum to members of the Subcommittee for Far Eastern Affairs, Senate Foreign Relations Committee, April 16, 1962.

The island of New Guinea, half of which is administered by the Netherlands government and half by Australia, is larger than the state of Texas. It is a land of savage mountains and steaming jungles, a land of incredibly primitive peoples who still practice cannibalism and head hunting, a land whose interior areas are so inaccessible that one might well wonder why anyone should want it and why it should be of any strategic importance.

But the thousands of American boys who died in New Guinea provide the most eloquent testimony to the strategic importance which both sides attached to it in World War II. And the fierce dispute now raging over Netherlands New Guinea and the volume of Communist propaganda on the subject strongly indicate that the island remains of equal strategic importance in the present conflict between the free world and the slave world of Communism.

The voices that urge that we avoid unpleasantness with Indonesia by persuading our Dutch allies to cede West New Guinea to the government of President Sukarno do not understand the strategic significance of New Guinea; nor do they appreciate the fact that in turning over control of this territory to President Sukarno, we are turning it over to a government which, of all the governments in the non-Communist world, runs perhaps the greatest chance of falling to Communism before the decade is out.

Of all the territorial demands made by the governments of the countries that have recently achieved independence, the claim of the Indonesian government on Netherlands New Guinea is the most arrant, the most baseless, the most flagrantly imperialistic, the most threatening to the free world, and the most offensive to the spirit of the United Nations' Charter.

While we all condemned India's forcible annexation of Goa, it was at least understandable that the Indian people should wish to put an end to this foreign enclave in the territory of the Indian subcontinent. One might question the thesis that the Goan people welcomed their annexation by India; but it is understandable that the Indians should look upon the Goan people as fellow-Indians, because ethnically there is no dispute that the Goanese *are* of Indian stock.

But none of these considerations apply to Indonesia's claim to New Guinea. The Indonesian peoples have no personal nostalgia for West New Guinea, because very few of them have even visited there. They have no sense of ancestral attachment, because none of their ancestors, going back to prehistoric days, ever came from West New Guinea. They have no feelings of brotherly love for the people of Netherlands New Guinea, because there is no common bond of race or language or culture or religion. In short, none of the ingredients that have historically justified nationalist movements, enter into the fraudulent nationalist demands for West New Guinea which are now being advanced by the Sukarno government.

The Indonesian demand for Netherlands New Guinea is not anti-imperialism, as President Sukarno pretends; it is imperialism. It is not anti-colonialism; it is a new colonialism which is all the more immoral because it is being advocated by a government that has itself only recently emerged from colonialism, and that should know something of the evil of colonialism.

Geographically, New Guinea is almost a thousand miles removed from Java and the Celebes. It is, in fact, much closer to Australia than it is to the main Indonesian islands. The islands of Indonesia, geographically, are part of the great contintental shelf of Southeast Asia. New Guinea, on the other hand, is distinctly a part of the continental shelf of northern Australia.

Ethnically and culturally, the Papuan people of New Guinea have absolutely nothing in common with the Indonesians. The Indonesian peoples are of Malay stock. The Papuans are a black people of Melanesian stock who bear no affection for the Indonesians and who would, in fact, look upon Indonesian sovereignty as an intolerable form of imperialism.

Approach the New Guinea dispute from whatever standpoint you wish—from the standpoint of morality or of political common sense, or of international law or of historic tradition—and it is impossible to find a single valid argument to support Indonesia's claim on West New Guinea. That is why the Indonesian government has consistently refused to submit the case to the International Court in The Hague. And that, too, is why the Indonesian demand that the Netherlands enter into bilateral negotiations on the case of West New Guinea has been repeatedly turned down by the United Nations.

The Dutch position on New Guinea has been clear and positive and irreproachable from every standpoint. The Netherlands government maintains, and I quote from an official statement:

"That no historical, constitutional, or cultural ties ever existed between Netherlands New Guinea and the territories now known as the Republic of Indonesia; to the contrary, the facts show that the separate and distinct character of West New Guinea was always recognized under the Netherlands Indies administration;

"That far from being included in the transfer of sovereingty over territories now part of the Republic of Indonesia, West New Guinea was specifically *excluded*, and letters *acknowledging* and *agreeing* to this *exclusion* were exchanged between the Netherlands and the Republic and became part of the official records of the Charter of Transfer of Sovereignty;

"That the Netherlands administration is firmly determined to foster in West New Guinea, through a comprehensive developmental program already well underway, a free political conscience which is a prerequisite for self-determination;

"That this growth toward eventual self-determination would be automatically exterminated if West New Guinea were arbitrarily to be made part of the Republic (of Indonesia)."

Far from exploiting West New Guinea, the Dutch have been sinking many millions of dollars into the country each year to develop its economy and to educate its people toward self-government.

Considering the forbidding geography of New Guinea and considering the fact that its peoples were among the most primitive to be found anywhere in the world, the progress registered by the Netherlands administration has perhaps not been equalled in any other country.

Of the 700,000 Papuans in Netherlands New Guinea, about 400,000 live in areas that have been brought under administrative control. In these areas, fully 80% of the children are receiving education. There are almost 1,000 schools functioning in the country, including secondary and technical schools and teachers' training courses.

At the end of 1959, native Papuans held 52% of the civil service posts, and the government of the Netherlands had committed itself to raise this percentage to 95% by 1970.

The Netherlands administration has also been moving rapidly to provide the Papuans with an adequate economic base for ultimate self-government. There have been vast increases in the production of nutmeg and cocoanut and cocoa and other crops, a lumber industry has been built up, and geological surveys have turned up promising deposits of minerals.

All of this progress would be lost if, through the delinquency of the United Nations and the weakness of the Western powers, the Netherlands were forced to cede New Guinea to the Indonesian expansionists.

But much more than this would be lost. As the Right Honorable R. G. Casey, former Australian Minister of External Affairs, has pointed out, "If West New Guinea passed to Indonesia, the native inhabitants would lose once and for all any opportunity of determining their own future."

Why is the Sukarno government so insistent in pressing its claims to this remote island territory? One would imagine that Indonesia had problems enough of its own. Her economy is bogging down. There is galloping inflation. The *Christian Science Monitor* of April 9 pointed out that Indonesia's financial-economic situation has slumped to one of the lowest points since the proclamation of independence in 1945, and that the price of rice, which is the staple food of the Indonesian diet, had reached the all-time high of $1.10 per kilogram. This is a price which spells near-starvation for most of the Indonesian people.

Political parties, with the exception of Sukarno's party and the Communist party, have been suppressed and many prominent members of the opposition parties have been thrown into prison. And there are large areas of Sumatra and the Celebes and even Java that are not under the firm control of the Central Government.

Why, in the light of all its own difficulties, does Indonesia want to add to her island territories a new territory, peopled by alien and hostile tribes, a territory that can only be developed into an economic asset with substantial capital investment and which, at the best, will remain an economic liability for a period of many years?

The answer to this question is easy to find if one takes the trouble to examine the output of the Communist propaganda apparatus on the subject of New Guinea over the course of the past few years.

The fact is that Indonesia's strident claims to West New Guinea are primarily due to the agitation of the Indonesian Communist Party, the largest Communist Party outside the Soviet bloc, and of the international Communist apparatus. If there were ever any doubt on this score, it should have been dispelled by a UP dispatch from Indonesia which appeared in the *Washington Post* this last Thursday, April 12. The dispatch described a mass meeting in the city of Jambi, addressed by President Sukarno. After he had whipped the crowd up into a fury with a fiery speech demanding "freedom for West Irian" (the Indonesian name for Netherlands New Guinea), President Sukarno called to the podium one after another, the Ambassadors from the Soviet Union, Hungary, Poland, Yugoslavia and Communist China. To roars of approval from the crowd, the Communist Ambassadors all shouted: "Meredeka Irian barat!" (Freedom for West Irian). They were joined in this dismal and undiplomatic display by the Ambassadors from India and Burma.

Before we commit ourselves to the support of Indonesia's demands, it would be well to ponder the significance of this demonstration.

As in so many other cases, the Communists have pointed the way to an ultra-nationalist position, and they have been able to carry the extreme nationalists along with them in agitating for this position. And in Indonesia the Communists have found this particularly easy because President Sukarno has been so willfully shortsighted with regard to Communism, and because he is so desperately seeking to divert popular attention from the problems begotten by his own administration.

This leads us to the next question: Why are Moscow and Peiping so intensely interested in this remote underdeveloped jungle territory? The strategic and political significance of West New Guinea becomes immediately apparent from a look at the map of the southern Pacific.

New Guinea lies athwart the trade routes between Southeast Asia and Australia, from which it is separated by only 150 miles of water. It lies squarely between the two most important and most reliable SEATO nations—Australia and the Philippines.

Less than a year ago, when I was in the Far East, I discussed the situation in Southeast Asia with a member of the Australian Senate. Australia and New Zealand were very worried over the situation in Laos, he told me, and that was why they had taken a stand in favor of SEATO intervention in Laos to prevent a Communist takeover. They were afraid that the fall of Laos would pave the way for Communist takeovers in Cambodia, Vietnam, Thailand, Malaya and Burma. And once the mainland of Southeast Asia was firmly under Communist control, Indonesia, they felt, would be a pushover; it would be a pushover because the Communist party there was already so powerful and because President Sukarno had done so much to weaken and destroy the anti-Communist forces.

"We see the tide of Asian Communism creeping down toward us," said the Senator from Australia, "and we know that if it succeeds in conquering Southeast Asia and Indonesia, we are doomed." In a future that may lie only several decades ahead, he warned, Indonesia and New Guinea might be used as springboards for an Asian-Communist invasion of Australia. But long before this came about, he pointed out, the entire strategic position of the free world would be gravely

271

compromised if the forces of world Communism held control of the whole Pacific littoral, from the Bering Straits to Singapore, and of the southern island chain from Sumatra to New Guinea. For if this ever came to pass, the Communists would, in effect, have cut the world in half.

The Communists are inciting and supporting the Indonesian agitation for West New Guinea because they *do* look far ahead, because they *do* have long range strategic aims, and because they *are* confident that the time is not too far distant when the hammer and sickle of Communism will fly throughout the lands of Southeast Asia and the islands of Indonesia.

For the moment, the Indonesian Government takes the stand that its claim extends only to West New Guinea, and not to the eastern portion of the island which is a non-self-governing territory under the Commonwealth of Australia. In fact, President Sukarno has gone out of his way to assure the Australians that Indonesia has no pretensions of any kind to east New Guinea. But the Australians are skeptical about these assurances; and who can blame them for being skeptical?

It is in the interest of the free world, it is in the interest of the people of New Guinea, it is in the ultimate interest of the United Nations, that the people of New Guinea, after an appropriate period of preparation, be given the right to determine for themselves what form of government they wish to have and what political affiliations they wish to enter into.

To deny this right to the people of New Guinea would be to abandon the cardinal principle on which the United Nations is based; the right of all peoples everywhere to determine for themselves the form of government desirable to them.

To accede passively to the hysterical demands of the Indonesian Communists and nationalists by surrendering New Guinea to them would gravely imperil the future of Australia and the Philippines and of all the free world's positions in the west Pacific.

Many people have been disturbed by the fact that we have taken no action and made no protests when the Indonesian government has flouted the United Nation's Charter by its repeated public announcements that it planned to take West New Guinea by force, if it were not ceded peacefully.

They have been even more disturbed by the fact that when our Dutch NATO allies sought to transport troops to New Guinea in order to defend a non-self-governing territory of which they are recognized as the legal administrators by the UN, against a threatened invasion in violation of the UN Charter, we reacted to this situation by denying our NATO allies the right to land and refuel their transport planes at American Pacific bases.

But they have been most disturbed, by the persistent reports that we are endeavoring to persuade, or perhaps I should say, to pressure our Dutch NATO allies to cede West New Guinea to Indonesia without a fight. Only last week, the *Washington Star* carried an AP story which spoke of a reported United States proposal that the administration of West New Guinea be switched from Dutch to Indonesian control over a two-year period. According to this story, the reported proposal met with stiff opposition from The Hague, which still insists that self-determination under UN auspices is the only proper way to dispose of the fate of the Papuan people. According to the same story, President Sukarno told a cheering crowd in South Sumatra that he holds to his pledge to put his government in control of the disputed territory by the end of the year. "Who said I want to accept a two-year condition?" he asked rhetorically.

I earnestly hope that these reports, at least as they relate to the attitude of the United States government, are in error.

I earnestly hope that we are not endeavoring to appease Sukarno and his Communist supporters at the expense of our NATO and SEATO allies.

I earnestly hope that we will not seek thus to ingratiate ourselves with Sukarno, Nehru, Nasser and Nkrumah, despite the fact that this action would break the hearts of our staunch allies in Australia, the Philippines, New Zealand and Thailand; despite the fact that it would place further serious stress on NATO; despite the obvious peril it would create to the free nations in the area and to the strategic position of the free world.

I earnestly hope that in any action we take with regard to West New Guinea, we will be guided above everything else by considerations of morality and by the basic principles on which the United Nations is founded. For in this situation, as in so many other situations, the path of morality coincides with the enlightened self-interest of the free world.

Since the United States first achieved its own independence, it has remained a staunch friend and supporter of the cause of national liberation and of every nation, young or ancient, seeking freedom from foreign bondage. In the post World War II period, the moral influence of the United States has played a role of central importance in bringing about the peaceful liberation of the great majority of the colonial countries. The colonial countries have had no better friend than the United States: our record in this respect is something of which we have every reason to be proud. But having supported the colonial countries in their struggle for independence, we can not be indifferent to the new and infinitely greater danger of Communist colonialism which now threatens many of these countries. Nor can we, out of our long-standing sympathy for the national aspirations of these countries, permit or assist these new-born countries to establish their own systems of imperialist and colonial subjugation in neighboring territories.

In approaching the dispute over Netherlands New Guinea, we should say these things frankly but firmly to our friends, to our enemies, and to the recently liberated neutralist nations, some of whom, unfortunately, are not prepared to concede the same rights to other peoples that they demand for themselves.

Chapter XVIII

SENTIMENTALITY AND NATIONAL POLICY*

The United States, up to now, has had a success as a nation which is unique in history. By every index of national achievement our country is unrivaled in the world today. Whether the standard be industrial production, agriculture, military strength, or standard of living, our country is truly the giant among the nations of the world.

Moreover, important as our physical resources and material wealth and military strength are, even more important is the fact that our national heritage has been an honest one; our national ideals are valid and have universal appeal; and the causes we uphold in the world are right causes, right for ourselves, and right for all peoples.

If all this is true, and it is, what we have seen in the world in the past seventeen years represents a strange paradox. For we have seen the wealthiest, strongest, most successful nation in the world, a nation which has used its wealth and strength not to enslave others but to assist them, losing round after round against Communist opponents who are markedly inferior in every index of real success.

There are many reasons for these defeats. Tonight I would like to speak about only one of the reasons.

On a variety of crucial issues we have allowed sentimentality to displace realism in the formulation of our national policies.

By sentimentality I mean a fuzzy emotionalism which approaches complicated problems either with the rapture of an ardent lover or the indignation of a dragon-slayer.

* Pittsburgh, Pennsylvania, Saturday, April 14, 1962.

I mean a chronic optimism about the motives and nature of the Communists.

I mean the Hollywood-style approach to world problems; the placing of what we would like to believe ahead of the facts; the preferring of sentimental assumptions to cold unpleasant realities.

I refer to the lop-sided state of mind which is so entranced with such general goals as peace, disarmament, brotherhood, and reform (with a capital "R"), that it ignores the real obstacles in the path of each of these goals.

Harold Ickes once said of Henry Wallace that he considered himself so firmly in possession of the truth that facts did not matter. So it is with the sentimentalists of today.

Sentimentality can be a very endearing trait in a personal relationship.

Surely it is a comforting thing to have some friend or loved one look at our faults not with the cold eye of reality, but with an attitude that sees only the good and ignores the bad. But this quality than can be so consoling in personal relationships can be very deadly in the conduct of national policy.

During World War II for instance, we allowed ourselves to get emotional about the Russians. We began to think of Red Russia as a land of happy peasants and brave soldiers, united under heroic leaders. Even our movies depicted scenes of colorfully dressed, singing peasants, parading arm in arm toward their collective fields as though they dwelt in some sort of paradise.

The direct result of swallowing all this moonshine about Russia was that in the later stages of World War II we formed a postwar foreign policy on the assumption that the Communists were all right after all, that they would honor their commitment to freedom for Eastern Europe, and would cooperate with us in building a free and democratic world.

One would have thought that the postwar Russian treachery would have punctured the balloon, and for many it did; but sentimentality has a way of enduring and regrouping, and of attaching itself to other fads.

We have always had a sort of Robin Hood complex in this

country. We made a national folk hero out of Jesse James, who was really nothing more than a common thief, a murderer and a pillager, on the false ground that he took from the rich to give to the poor. This kind of nonsense gave a hand to Communists propagandists in the late 1940's and helped them to get away with fooling the American people when Communist thieves, murderers and pillagers appeared in China under the guise of agrarian reformers who were to take fom the rich and give to the poor. By the time we had gotten the dust out of our eyes, a nation of half a billion human beings had been enslaved.

Yet, ten years later, the sentimentalists fell for the same thing all over again when Fidel Castro came on the scene, and they confused the whole nation, from the White House on down, until a Communist dictatorship had been fastened upon our neighbors in Cuba.

Sentimentality has left its distorted mark on domestic issues as well. Let me use as an example what, for lack of a better name, I shall call the underdog sentimentality.

This approach views the criminal, the delinquent, the irresponsible person as the helpless victim of society rather than as a threat to society, or a drag upon it.

Here we encounter a frequent aspect of sentimentality, that of seizing upon an idea which has some merit and pushing it too far.

We have taken some wise measures in the field of probation of prisoners, rehabilitation, retraining and humane sentencing. But in many places, the sentimentalists have gone overboard and pushed the soft approach so far as to severely hamper law enforcement and water down the principal deterrent to crime, which is the fear by the would-be offender that he will be swiftly apprended and promptly punished.

Starting with the praiseworthy desire to take the "big brother" approach to juvenile delinquents, to shield them from the blot of a criminal record, to safeguard them from procedures that would throw them in with adult criminals, we have established a privileged sanctuary for many hardened criminals who are young only in years, and this soft treatment of them has served only to multiply the number of hideous crimes committed each day on our streets.

The sentimental desire to shield people from the results of their own actions has spilled over into a number of other fields.

Parental discipline seems to have gone out of style in many homes with the result that a growing number of young people are approaching maturity without any sense of responsibility, or respect for authority, or concern for the rights and interests of others.

Discipline in some schools has deteriorated to the point where a teacher recently told me she was prohibited from even making a disobedient child put his head down on his desk, as a mild discipline, because this might contribute to the growth of some mental complex.

In many schools, the child who fails to do his work and pass his examinations is no longer kept back and made to repeat the year but is passed along from grade to grade as though he had met the qualifications.

This sort of thing can have no other effect than to encourage in the future citizens the idea that no matter how irresponsible he may be, no matter how dismally he may fail even the modest tests of life, he can expect to be taken care of and shielded from the results of his own incompetence and lack of effort. Nothing could be more dangerous to a free society than the growth of this sentiment.

Another variety of sentimentality is the persecution complex which afflicts many and which has had a lamentable influence on public policy. The victim of this persecution complex looks at the world and sees a few noble dissenters appealing vainly to a benighted, apathetic public, with the vicious forces of government lurking in the background ever ready to pounce upon the noble ones.

To these people Alger Hiss was and, I think, still is, a hero, and Whittaker Chambers and J. Edgar Hoover are still villains. The left-wing press, which is addicted to most forms of sentimentality, fairly wallows in this variety.

When a Congressional investigation begins into Communist activities, the left-wing press and its sympathizers always try to picture the various individuals who are willing or witless collaborators in the Communist conspiracy, as helpless, defenseless underdogs who are being put upon by an irresponsible publicity-seeking group of Congressmen.

If the investigative hearings are to be in public session, the committee is charged with smearing the witness.

If it is to be in private session, the committee is charged with "star chamber" proceedings.

If a long list of Communist-front affiliations is substantiated, the committee is charged with promoting guilt by association.

If pro-Communist and anti-American statements are correctly attributed to the witness, the committee is charged with persecuting a person for expressing his ideas.

And so it goes. The danger is that those who investigate the Communist conspiracy are threatened with personal vilification and political destruction. This drives good men away from anti-Communist work, it impedes the struggle against subversion and espionage, and it endangers the security of the country.

Internationalism makes sense, it is a blessing, when combined with a hard-headed realistic attitude. But when internationalism is perverted by sentimentalism, it gives birth to the most exotic plants and flowers, and, I might add, the most dangerous.

For the danger of the exaggerations and misrepresentations and emotionalism of the international sentimentalists is compounded by the fact that they frequently parallel the goals of the Communist world propaganda apparatus. I refer to such groups as the various peace marchers, the disarmament agitators, the "better Red than dead" crowd.

Let us take up the peace marchers. They demonstrate against the launching of our nuclear submarines as though these submarines were threats to peace instead of the guardians and protectors of the security and peace of the Free World.

They parade in front of the White House and make a public

scene, the effect of which is to produce the impression that somehow the President of the United States is not interested in peace, or is less interested than he ought to be.

They parade through the halls of Congress with half-baked appeals to legislators against our defense budget or against the development of weapons that are necessary to give our military forces the supremacy they need to prevent an enemy attack upon us.

There are among the peace marchers and picketers many sincere, dedicated pacifists, people of unquestionable integrity who simply cannot believe that communism is totally evil or completely proof against the force of moral example. For the genuine pacifists I have respest, even though I believe that their philosophy is dangerously starry-eyed. But I must say, in all frankness, that they frequently do not show very much discretion about those that accompany them in these demonstrations.

Some of their companions are Communists and professional Communist-fronters.

Others are publicity seekers.

Others are screwballs, the kind who attach themselves to any demonstration movements.

Others are merely gullible and deluded people who, unwittingly or half-wittingly, allow themselves to be manipulated and used by the Communist world propaganda apparatus.

But, whoever they are, the effect of their demonstrations and marches is not as negligible as it ought to be.

This strange amalgam of idealists and communists, of fellow travelers, and innocents, succeeds somehow in leaving the impression that they are *all* honest idealists, and perhaps the United is as guilty as the Communists for the lack of real peace in the world.

They command a degree of attention from the American press and the world press that is altogether out of proportion to what they represent in terms of American public opinion.

They have a certain intimidating effect upon our policy planners, an effect which is revealed in the apologetic manner in which we invariably announce new defense measures or such necessary steps as the resumption of nuclear testing following the recent Russian treachery.

Even the President feels compelled to invite these demonstrators in for tea.

One recurring theme is that if the women and mothers of the country made their influence felt more, we would move toward peace.

I do not at all resent the uncomplimentary inference about men implied in this; it is not important.

What is important is that this sort of thing promotes the belief in the world that the cause of tensions and possible war is the ignorance or perverseness of willing men in our country and in other countries, when the truth is that Communist aggression and the Communist blueprint for world conquest is the only real threat to peace in the world.

Any attempt to lay the blame equally on both sides is not only a smear upon our leaders and our country, an evidence of a basic lack of commonsense or patriotism, but it tends as well to immobilize our people, it confuses them as to the real danger and thus makes more difficult the task of arousing them to the effort which must be made to preserve our freedom.

Another form of internationalist sentimentality is the worship of that nebulous thing called "world opinion." Again and again we are cautioned against taking steps that would strengthen ourselves or our allies because of the adverse effect it would have on so-called "world opinion."

"World opinion" was probably the principal factor in our tragic abandonment of nuclear development and testing three years ago. This so-called "world opinion" to which we have deferred is little more than the organized propaganda of Communists and their neutralist sympathizers around the world.

We are told, for instance, that this or that course of action will offend the sensibilities of the Indian villager, or the Burmese peasant.

Yet if we think about it, the Indian villager does not even

know what is going on in the next village, let alone having an opinion about our moves on the international scene.

Even if he did have an adverse opinion, it would be our duty to take those measures which we felt were necessary to our own just interests.

But we are gulled again and again through our desire to cater to something that does not exist.

One of the greatest myths of the sentimentalists, and one which is rapidly being exploded by events, concerns the neutralists. Neutral nations have been pictured as being somehow above the cold war, as being the final arbiters of the dispute between East and West and of being the people to whom we must make an idealistic appeal. Neutralists are held up as the moral leaders of the world.

The sentimentalists have lionized people like Nehru and Sukarno.

The fact is, of course, that the neutral in today's world is one who for reasons of self-interest refuses to take a side in the gravest and most clear-cut struggle between right and wrong in history.

The neutralist has been a sort of pawnbroker between good and evil, playing both sides of the street, trying to get as much as he can out of both sides. Some neutralists are not even neutral, but are disguised pro-Communists.

The Communists have used the neutrals when it suited their purpose and slapped them down when they got in the way of Communist plans.

The United States has pampered them, catered to them and shown them a deference and a consideration out of all proportion to their merit or their influence in the world.

Nehru's aggression against Goa and Sukarno's declaration against West New Guinea have exploded a lot of misconceptions about the neutralists in the minds of all but the most hopeless sentimentalists. But myths die hard and the sanctification of the neutrals will continue to hamper our efforts for a more realistic foreign policy.

The mecca of the sentimentalists appears to be the United Nations. The overflow of emotion concerning the United Nations has acted against the interests not only of that body but of the Free World.

The United Nations represents one of the hopes we have for eventual world peace based upon law and international justice.

I have supported the United Nations. I support it now, and I demonstrated this only a few days ago by voting for the United Nations Bond Issue proposal.

But the United Nations has grave structural defects at the present time and principal among those defects are the veto power of the Communist bloc and the inordinate strength in that body of the new nations, nations which do not have the population, the wealth, the strength or the responsibility to match their influence in the United Nations.

It should be clear that reforms will have to be made if the U.N. is to become equal to the task of preserving peace in the world. Yet, any attempt to objectively analyze the U.N. is greeted with howls of protests by the sentimentalists. Any criticism of unjustified U.N. action is condemned as an attack upon world peace.

To the sentimentalists, the U.N. is the answer to most world problems. Whatever the crisis may be, there is an impulse to turn it over to the U.N.

The danger here is two-fold: first, the U.N. is so ill-equipped to deal with some crises that it would doubtless fail, make itself look impotent and ridiculous, and could discredit itself; second, there is the danger that resort to the U.N. will become a substitute for United States foreign policy, rather than an instrument of it. We must not let control of policy affecting our vital interests and our survival, slip out of our hands. We must not shirk our responsibility for decisive action, and we must not burden the U.N. with problems it is not equipped to handle.

I make these criticisms of the sentimental approach to national problems not because I fancy myself as a critic, nor because I enjoy singling out any group for criticism.

I do it because the time has come to try to undo the damage which sentimentality has done to our national policy.

The moony assumptions that are so often allowed to go unchallenged must be met head-on so that they can be isolated and will cease to exert harmful influence on the conduct of our affairs.

There is a hope that the honest sentimentalists can be brought back to reality.

It may be possible to prove to them that sentimentalism is not idealism, that the goals they seek can be achieved, not by emotion but by reason; and that, while dealing with the hard realities of national and international life may not be as exciting as pursuing sentimental phantoms, it can in the end be more rewarding.

Sentimentality can affect public policy only in a free country. Communist regimes are certainly the least sentimental of all governments.

We may hope that the free interplay of ideas which permits sentimentality to influence policy will at the same time provide the antidote to it.

Jefferson once said, "Error of opinion can be tolerated where reason is left free to combat it." It is time to put our reason to work. It is time to dethrone sentimentality and to restore truth as the guide and the molder of our national policy.

Chapter XIX

THE POLITICS OF LIBERATION*

One of the first rules of statesmanship is that one must prepare for all contingencies, including the worst. Whether we call the Soviet bluff on Berlin or meet an actual military challenge, we must be prepared for war as the alternative to capitulation. If we are to plan our strategy intelligently, however, it is important that we try to estimate, on the basis of the known facts, whether the Soviets, in forcing the Berlin crisis, are leading from strength or weakness; whether their martial talk and missile-rattling are plain bluff or really serious; or whether bluff and seriousness are so intermixed that the outcome of these threats is impossible to assess.

The Soviets may indeed be emboldened, to a certain extent, by their missile lead, by their overwhelming superiority in conventional arms and by the anticipation of Western disunity. But I believe they are also motivated, to a very large degree, by a serious weakness in their own position.

The Soviet puppet regime in East Germany is suffering from a chronic social disintegration that the Kremlin has found no means of arresting. Although increased production has been achieved in some areas, East Germany, compared with the prosperity and well-being of West Germany, has since the end of the war become an economic wasteland. If the flight of skilled workers, teachers and professionals from East Germany continues at the rate of the past 10 years, and if the East Germany population continues to decline, Soviet Germany may within the next decade become a near-desert.

The Communist leaders have apparently decided that this

---

* United States Senate, June 11, 1959.

Freedom and Foreign Policy

process of attrition must be stopped. To accomplish this, a quadruple operation will be necessary:

1. Surgery must be performed on West Berlin to eliminate it as a showcase of democracy in the heartland of Communist Germany and as the Number One escape route for East German refugees. Berlin is, in Khrushchev's words, "a malignant tumor which must be cut out."

2. The East German satellite regime must be bolstered internationally, and domestic opposition to it must be discouraged by compelling the Western powers to grant it recognition.

3. Since the proximity of Western troops, even in the absence of an active liberation policy, must be considered a potential stimulus to the liberation of Eastern Europe, West Germany must be disarmed and the North Atlantic Treaty Organization divisions must be obliged to retire as far to the west as possible.

4. To consummate the consolidation of Soviet power over the satellites, the Kremlin proposes a European security pact, under which the West would, in effect, guarantee the maintenance of Soviet control of Eastern Europe.

This is an ambitious program: but Khrushchev apparently believes that he has everything to gain and nothing to lose by demanding a summit conference on these issues.

Was Khrushchev bluffing, or did he really mean it, when he said that once control of the Berlin routes is turned over to the East Germans, any clash between them and NATO troops would automatically result in war? A factor in this ultimatum may be Khrushchev's conviction that the development of Soviet nuclear and missile power has already succeeded in canceling out, or will soon be able to cancel out, the deterrent power of American nuclear superiority. Indeed, he may have made his threats and he may be using the present negotiations for the purpose of testing this conviction. There may be much wisdom in the observations which Joseph Alsop, writing from Geneva, made in the May 13, 1959, issue of the New York *Herald Tribune*:

"What Andrei Gromyko and his vast Soviet delegation are

here to find out, if they can, is whether the Western nations really are ready to fight for Berlin. If they conclude the contrary, as they well may, there will be no end to the concessions which the Soviets will demand. Nothing but the clearest, most decisively proven Western willingness to fight for Berlin will promote the kind of compromise that would be acceptable to the West."

"Western willingness to fight," in the given situation, means our willingness to employ our nuclear and thermonuclear weapons. Khrushchev may be right in reasoning that the responsible Western leaders will hesitate a long time before hurling the first nuclear bomb and involving the world in a war of mutual devastation. But he ought not to underestimate the free world's will or courage if he confronts us with a choice between war or capitulation.

In this connection, the Gallup Poll published March 29, 1959, is most significant. The question asked was: "Do you think we should keep American forces in Berlin—along with British and French forces—even at the risk of war?" Eighty-one per cent of those queried felt that we should remain in Berlin even at the risk of war; 8 per cent had no opinion; and only 11 per cent felt that we should not stay in Berlin. The consistency of American public opinion on the Berlin question is as remarkable as its strength. A Gallup Poll in 1948, at the time of the Berlin blockade, showed 80 per cent of the American people in favor of staying in Berlin and 11 per cent opposed. Another Gallup Poll in December 1958, just after Khrushchev's ultimatum, showed 78 per cent favored remaining in Berlin and, again, only 11 per cent opposed.

The American people know if war should come, it will almost certainly be a nuclear war. And yet, in the face of this, they have given an overwhelming mandate to the Administration and Congress to pursue the firm and unyielding policy to which they have committed themselves. Why does the average America think as he does? Gallup quoted this typical comment: "Russia wants to take over all Germany, and then Europe, and then the world." The understanding and fortitude which the American people have always displayed in times of crisis constitute an element of national strength which must be weighed heavily in any comparison of American and Communist power.

In coping with Khrushchev's blustering threats we need not —indeed, we must not—rely only on our power of nuclear deterrence. The fact is that we have in our grasp a deterrent potentially even more effective than our arsenal of atom and hydrogen bombs. It is a deterrent of which, regrettably, we appear almost wholly unaware, and which we have thus far not employed as an instrument of diplomacy. But it is one of whose potential effectiveness the men in the Kremlin have been made painfully aware and which will cause them to shrink from putting us to the test of military action, if the West remains united and firm. The flaw in Soviet armor is the hatred which the people behind the Iron Curtain feel for their tyrannical regimes.

There was a time, perhaps, when the Soviet leaders may have imagined that, given an increase in their nuclear strength, they would possess the potential to wage a war against the West. But the successive events in East Germany in 1953 and in Hungary and Poland in 1956 have seriously weakened this potential: and this is something that is perhaps better understood in the Kremlin than it is in the Western capitals. The succession of uprisings in the satellite area, in particular the Hungarian Revolution, has demonstrated three things: (1) that the satellite army divisions are totally unreliable; (2) that the Soviet Army itself is dangerously unreliable; (3) most important of all, that the masses of the people under Communism share a mortal hatred for the regime which oppresses them.

If Moscow were to launch a general war in Europe, the 100 divisions which the Soviet Army maintains in Europe would not be supported by the 75 satellite divisions of the Warsaw Pact. At best, the Soviet Army would be able to enforce the neutral inactivity of the satellite divisions and exercise a perilous control over the bitterly hostile populations, some 100 million strong, of all the satellite countries. The strength of the Soviet divisions would have to be dissipated in garrisoning the satellite nations, in guarding their routes of communication against nationalist guerrillas, and in policing the satellite divisions to prevent their disaffection. At worst, the Kremlin would have to contend with a chain reaction of Hungarian-type rebellions throughout the satellite empire.

The passionate desire for liberation that exists in all the satellite countries constitutes a serious deterrent to Soviet military aggression; it would make war against the West a very hazardous undertaking even assuming that the Kremlin could count on the loyalty of its own Army. But the 64-ruble question which Khrushchev must ask himself is: *Can* the Soviet Army be counted on in a war against the free world?

While it is now a commonplace that Communism is unpopular, we in the West still fail to comprehend either the degree or the universality of the hatred which the people who have been subjugated by Communism feel for their Communist masters. It is understandable that we should find such comprehension difficult because this hatred is far more intense, far more explosive than anything we of the non-Communist world have ourselves experienced

During my participation in the Nuremberg war crimes trials in the postwar period, I learned something of the desperation and hatred and terror of the hundreds of thousands of Russian war prisoners and slave laborers held by the Nazis whom we, through incredible ignorance, returned against their will to the Soviet authorities. My soul is still tormented by the nightmarish accounts of mass suicides, in which men slashed their wrists with tin cans and women jumped with their children from upper story windows rather than face return to Soviet Russia.

Since the end of the war, a whole series of events in many parts of the world has demonstrated that this incredibly intense hatred was not confined to one moment in history or to the specific variety of Communism that existed in the Soviet Union under Stalin.

What kind of fear and what kind of hatred was it that induced four million North Koreans—one-third of the pre-war population of this Communist satellite—to abandon their land-holdings and their belongings and seek refuge in South Korea?

What kind of hatred was it that compelled one million North Vietnamese to flee from the so-called liberation regime of Ho Chi Minh, most of them under conditions of terrible danger and hardship, racing against the armistice deadline?

What kind of hatred was it that induced 15,000 of the 20,000 Chinese prisoners of war taken in Korea to refuse to return to their homeland—despite the blandishments of the Communist representatives, despite the discouraging attitude of the West, despite the bleak prospects of resettlement elsewhere, and despite the overwhelming importance of family and homeland to Chinese generally?

What kind of hatred and desperation was it that produced the East German and Polish uprisings and the incredible heroism of the Hungarian Revolution, in which an unarmed and unorganized citizenry triumphed over both the Hungarian Secret Police and the Soviet Army in the first round of battle?

And, within the past few months, what kind of hatred was it that led two million Tibetans, virtually without arms and with no friendly armies on their frontiers, to rise up against the overwhelming might of the Chinese Red Army?

In the evolution of the hatred of tyranny, there is a point where this hatred becomes a blind and all-possessing passion; and no regime in history has been so outstandingly successful in fostering this special breed of hatred as has the Communist regime in Russia and its satellite regimes in other countries.

In evaluating the present situation, it would be helpful to recapitulate certain established facts of World War II and of the Hungarian Revolution. An entire literature on the subject of Soviet defections in World War II has grown up—Eugene Lyons' *Our Secret Allies*, George Fischer's *Russians Against Stalin*, Boris Shub's *The Choice* are outstanding in this category. But the memory of man is short, and many of the facts that were so painstakingly set forth have been forgotten.

When the *Reichswehr* invaded the Soviet Union in June

1941, the Red Army enjoyed overwhelming superiority in manpower, aircraft, tanks and artillery. Within the first eight months of the war, the German Army took 3.6 million military prisoners and destroyed or captured immense quantities of war material, including more than 16,000 guns and over 17,500 tanks. These are truly colossal figures. By the end of the war, the Soviets had only succeeded in rebuilding their tank corps to a total of 13,400 tanks, while the Germans on the Eastern front opposed them with no more than 3,500.

Wherever the German troops came, the civilian population greeted them as liberators and received them with enthusiasm and with garlands. This was particularly true in the Ukraine and other areas where nationalist feeling was superimposed on hatred of Communism. But it was by no means confined to these areas. In the streets of Moscow there was spontaneous singing, for the first time since the Revolution, when the German Army penetrated to the suburbs and the Government and the Secret Police fled to Kuybishev, in the interior of Russia. The warm greeting accorded the German Army had nothing to do with pro-Nazism. Nor can it be equated with treason, since the great mass of the Soviet peoples regarded themselves as patriots and the Bolsheviks as traitors.

The *Wehrmacht* officer, Herwarth von Bittenfeld (now, incidentally, the German Ambassador to Great Britain), pointed out that the invading German Army received as friendly a reception at Smolensk, Viasma and Bryansk, in Great Russia, as it did elsewhere. Said von Bittenfeld:

"With all the handicaps created by the brutal, senseless Nazi racist policy, we raised more than 500,000 soldiers for our side among war prisoners and among the peoples of occupied territory. With an intelligent political policy, we could have won the war in the East simply because the Russian people themselves would have overthrown the regime. Especially in the first months of the war, surrenders were on a mass scale and were political, not military. At that time I would go out as a cavalry officer on a patrol and would come back with thousands of altogether voluntary prisoners."

Supporting von Bittenfeld's finding from a civilian point

of view was the wartime opinion, recorded in the Nuremberg record, of Dr. Otto Bräutigam, official of the Reich Ministry of the East:

"Were the war being conducted only for the purpose of smashing Bolshevism, then it would have been decided long ago in our favor, for, as all experiences of this war have confirmed, Bolshevism is hated to the utmost by the Eastern people, above all by the great mass of peasants. In the Soviet Union we found on our arrival a population weary of Bolshevism, which waited longingly for new slogans holding out the promise of a better future to them. It was Germany's duty to find such slogans, but they remained unuttered. The population greeted us with joy as liberators and placed themselves at our disposal willingly and freely with body and life. Wherever Ukrainians, Russians, White Ruthenians and members of the Baltic peoples enlisted in the German *Wehrmacht*, they proved themselves and fought excellently without exception."

The amazing success that General Andrei A. Vlassov had in raising his "Army of Liberation" from the ranks of Soviet POWs and forced laborers in Germany is something that no amount of Soviet rationalization can explain. Despite the brutality that the Nazis had practiced on Soviet civilians and POWs alike, Vlassov succeeded in a very short time in building up an army of 500,000 men who mistakenly believed that they could fight against Stalin for the liberation of their homeland in the ranks of the German Army.

According to a letter which Eugene Lyons received from a Russian refugee in Germany, the matter of joining the Vlassov army was discussed in one Russian POW camp on November 19, 1944, at a time when it was obvious to everyone that Germany was headed toward disastrous defeat. Only 15 out of 200 prisoners did not join. In addition, it is estimated that at the end of the war, Vlassov's enlistment bureau had applications from some 2.5 million civilian and POW volunteers.

True, the Red Army finally did defeat the Germans. It defeated them first, because of the tremendous military pressure applied by the Western allies on land and in the air; second, because of the massive military assistance it received from the United States; and third, because of its utterly overwhelming superiority in men and equipment. Toward the end of the war, the Red Army on key fronts outnumbered the Germans by almost eight to one in infantry, seven to one in artillery, ten to one in mortars, and five to one in tanks. But the Red Army could not have achieved victory if there had not been a fundamental reversal of attitude on the part of the Russian peoples. It was not any increase in affection for the Bolshevik regime that brought about this change, but, very simply, the brutality of the Nazis.

Now, it is conceivable that the Khrushchev regime has succeeded in reducing popular disaffection by curbing some of the worst terroristic practices of the Stalin regime and by making some concessions to the Soviet consumer. On the other hand, despite the minor attenuation of terror, the Soviet Union still remains a totalitarian police state. To the growing class of Soviet intellectuals and professors, in particular, the rigid state control of thought must be a constant source of outrage. For example, there is evidence that the overwhelming majority of Soviet intellectuals were even more indignant than we in the West over the treatment of Boris Pasternak and the suppression of *Doctor Zhivago*.

Hungary provided the most significant revelation. The Soviet divisions initially stationed in Budapest had to be withdrawn because in the first round of battle they proved either reluctant to fight the Hungarian people or else openly sympathetic to them. The free Hungarian radio stations broadcast repeated messages from Soviet defectors, up to the rank of colonel, to their comrades in the Soviet Army. Broadcasting over Radio Gyor on October 28, 1956, Soviet Colonel Vladimir Novikov said:

"My unit has forcibly overpowered the attacks of the Security Police. Now the most urgent problem for the Soviet Army is to uphold the good name of the Russians with arms in the spirit of Russian-Hungarian friendship. We, the Soviet people, have found out by our own lives that it cannot go on like this any more. We see that the Stalinists are hated not only at home but everywhere. We call upon all real Russian patriots, for whom the honor of our nation is dear, to extend a brotherly hand to the Hungarian people and, together with them, to pave the road for a new and better future."

No accurate account may ever be available of the scale of defections from the Soviet forces that were first deployed against the Hungarian people. But certainly it was substantial. This was something on which all Western observers were agreed.

Seymour Freidin reported in the New York *Post* on November 18, 1956: "I know of three specific cases and obtained reports of countless others where Soviet soldiers came over to the revolutionaries to capitulate with their equipment." Reuters carried the report that 3,000 Soviet troops and 60 Soviet tank crews had deserted and fought with the Hungarians. On December 15, 1956, the Hungarian expert of the highly reputable London *Sunday Observer* estimated the number of Soviet deserters in Hungary at 15,000. Joseph and Stewart Alsop reported on December 6, 1956, that a high percentage of the defections took place from the elite Soviet Second Guards Division which, as they carefully pointed out, "is as though soldiers in the American Marines or the British Guards had gone over to the enemy."

And on December 22, John MacCormac reported in the New York *Times* that soldiers of the Soviet 83rd Motorized Infantry had revolted when ordered to fire into a crowd of demonstrators at Tokaj, that five Russian soldiers had been shot in the fray, and that after the fighting two entire companies had melted away to join the rebels. When the fighting in Hungary was almost over, the American press carried a report that a large Hungarian training camp had been converted into a prison camp for Soviet Army defectors. According to Hungarian sources this camp housed almost 10,000 prisoners.

Perhaps all of these estimates are somewhat exaggerated. But even allowing for a four- or five-fold exaggeration, the defection of several thousand Soviet soldiers—defection to a side that seemed foredoomed to defeat—must be considered symptomatic of the most basic and deeply rooted discontent. It is a matter of common knowledge that the Soviets found it necessary to replace their occupation troops with fresh troops ordered into Hungary from the USSR and the surrounding satellites. These were indoctrinated to believe that they were about to fight the American imperialist invaders, either on the Elbe River in Germany or at Suez.

It is particularly interesting that for the initial assault on Budapest, the Kremlin saw fit to use some 5,000 tanks unsupported by infantry. Without infantry cover, the tanks were especially vulnerable in street fighting, and the revolutionaries took a heavy toll of them with grenades and Molotov cocktails.

In using massed tanks without any infantry protection, the Soviets violated all the tactical rules. Why did they do so? One explanation is that they were seeking to intimidate the people of Budapest, as they were able to intimidate the people of Berlin in 1953, by a show of armored strength. Another and more probable explanation is that they feared the possible effect of contact between Soviet foot soldiers and the Hungarian people, at least until the back of the Revolution had been broken. Even in their easy war against the Hungarian people, the men in the Kremlin were obviously tormented by the ghost of General Vlassov and his "Army of Liberation."

FOR A POLICY OF LIBERATION

What if it should come to a war with the West? There are certain things that can safely be predicted: We would not wage the war for purposes of imperialist aggrandizement. We would not practice the bestial master-race policies of the Nazis. *Our political traditions, our code of morality, and the logic of our position would lead us, on the very day that war broke out, to proclaim the restoration of freedom to the peoples of the satellite countries and of the Soviet Union as our only goal, and to set up the first cadres of national liberation movements and liberation armies.*

It is of course not feasible for the Secretary of State or the President to say these things, for the simple reason that they must guide themselves by the etiquette of diplomacy. But there are certain things a Senator may properly say and should say that a head of state may not. We should let the Soviets know that we are not deceived by the recent bluster of the Warsaw Pact powers; that we are aware of the existence of massive popular discontent in all the satellite countries; that we have not forgotten the questionable performance of the Red Army in Finland and in Hungary, and in the early stages of the war against Hitler; that if the Soviet Union provokes war, we know it would have to devote much of its strength to enforcing the obedience of the satellite peoples; that we are certain the great majority of the Soviet Army would be demoralized if ordered to wage war on the workers and peasants of other countries; that if war is forced on us, we would wage it from the first day as an all-out war of liberation for the peoples of the Soviet Union as well as for the peoples of the satellite countries.

We should tell Moscow bluntly that, if it comes to a crisis, we know we shall not have to contend with a monolithic armed force consisting of the 100 Soviet divisions stationed west of Moscow and the 75 divisions maintained by the satellite countries. The 33 divisions which the Kremlin maintains in Eastern Europe—22 in East Germany, 7 in Hungary, 2 in Rumania, and 2 in Poland—would have their work cut out performing occupation duties. At best, only a portion of them would be available for offensive action. And, if the chronic unrest in these countries were again to erupt, the Kremlin might have to augment these divisions with reinforcements drawn from the Soviet Army in Russia.

We can call the Soviet bluff on the Warsaw Pact. Not in our lifetime will they be able to use against us the 300,000 members of the Polish armed forces, the 250,000 Rumanians, the 200,000 Czechoslovaks, the 160,000 Bulgarians, the 150,000 East Germans and the 90,000 Hungarians. On the contrary, there is a much greater chance, if it comes to war, that the armies of the Warsaw Pact will wind up on the side of the free world. Certainly this would be our goal—a very realistic goal.

We should let Khrushchev know, too, that we have studied and digested some of the lessons of the Bolshevik Revolution; that we know how effectively—and how fraudulently—the Bolsheviks employed the slogans of "national self-determination" and "land to the peasants"; that we are convinced these slogans correspond today, as they did in 1917, to the deepest desires of the Soviet peoples and the Soviet peasantry; and that we are confident these slogans, despite their abuse by the Bolsheviks, would enlist the trust and support of the peoples of Russia if they carried the guarantee of the West. In short, we should let the men in the Kremlin know that, if they force a war over Berlin, it will be an all-out political war, with no holds barred. And we should perhaps inform them, in some precise detail, of the plans that already exist for the creation of national liberation armies and liberation movements.

If our diplomacy is to be conducted in these terms, we must be prepared to place certain chips on the table. Some of these chips, by the nature of things, will be military. Quietly, and without ostentation or panic, but in a manner that spells business, we must increase the combat readiness of the NATO forces in Europe. But, more important, we must devise a carefully thought-out policy that will give encouragement to the liberation movements in all the captive countries, and we must find ways of sharpening our ideological impact on the enslaved peoples.

Liberation is indeed a pipe-dream, if the word is used to signify an external initiative using subversive movements under the aegis of the Western governments. But it is *not* a pipe-dream if one accepts the premise that liberation will have to come from within, that the role of the West must be limited to keeping the spirit of liberation alive through its propaganda and supporting it through its diplomacy, and that it can only be achieved given a highly favorably conjuncture of circumstances. It is not a pipe-dream if one considers the significance of the Hungarian Revolution which, despite the absence of Western support, came within an ace of promoting uprisings throughout Khrushchev's satellite empire.

[*Editor's Note:* The lessons of the Hungarian Revolution are discussed in detail in Chapter V.]

Khrushchev was able to crush the Hungarian Revolution by massing his armored divisions against the people of Budapest. But the Revolution, in defeat, exposed the lie of Communism for all peoples to see and overnight converted the Warsaw Pact from a diplomatic asset into a military and diplomatic liability.

Thus, the most effective deterrent to Communist expansion in Europe at this juncture would be to place our basic diplomatic emphasis on the ultimate freedom of the captive peoples of Eastern Europe. If we are not prepared to do so for their sake, then we must do so in order to save ourselves.

Both of our political parties in the 1952 election committed themselves to the liberation of the subjugated nations. But unfortunately the word was used more as an electioneering slogan than as a name for a carefully thought-out foreign policy that is vital to our own national security. Because of this, the word "liberation" is today somewhat compromised in the eyes of the captive peoples and of the millions of their compatriots who are now American citizens.

To use the word again as a slogan, or simply to pay lip service to it, would be the height of irresponsibility. Let us, therefore, spell out what such a policy means in practice and, if we use the word again, let us do so as a serious act of self-dedication.

"Liberation" does not mean that we confront the Soviets with an ultimatum and launch a war if they reject it. Nor does it mean that we organize subversive movements and foment revolutions in the captive nations. Either proposal would be irresponsible folly, in addition to running counter to our entire tradition. Liberation, as I have pointed out, will have to come essentially from within. *But what we say and what we do can encourage or discourage the spirit of liberation and, in this sense, can exert a decisive influence.*

How do we go about encouraging the liberation movement? The first step would be to demonstrate the earnestness of our concern by raising the issue of the captive nations at every diplomatic conference and at every UN session. In enslaving the captive nations, the Soviets were guilty of violating a whole series of international agreements that guaranteed free elections. In imposing their regimes and maintaining them in power, they have used the Soviet Army in the most flagrant manner as an instrument of political intimidation; and when intimidation failed in Germany and in Hungary, they resorted to open military intervention and repression. They have violated the UN Charter repeatedly and at almost every point. Let us spread the facts about Soviet imperialism upon the record at every available opportunity. Let us continue to demand that the Soviets respect all their obligations.

To raise the issue of liberation in this manner would by itself have a great impact on the other side of the Iron Curtain. But the issue must never be permitted to degenerate into a simple propaganda device. We must, in all earnestness, make liberation a cardinal goal of our diplomacy. I do not underestimate the difficulty of persuading the Kremlin to liberate its satellite empire. But I can conceive of a situation where a combination of division within the Kremlin, unrest in the satellites and hard bargaining on the part of the West will induce the Soviets, in their own interest, to grant freedom to the unyielding, troublesome, hostile, captive peoples.

Let us say to Khrushchev: "You say that you desire peace and that you wish to reduce tensions. No one in the free world wants war, and everyone would be happy to see tensions reduced. But the tensions are the symptom and not the cause. You do not cure pneumonia, Mr. Khrushchev, by placing ice packs on the patient's forehead. You diagnose the disease and you prescribe a remedy in accordance with this diagnosis. What are the causes of the tensions that exist in the world today?

"No one believes, not even you, that the world is tense because the 17 NATO divisions are planning aggression against the Soviet Union. There is tension, Mr. Krushchev, because of your ultimatums and blustering threats, because of the massive armed aggressive strength which the Soviet Union and Communist China maintain, because of the subversive activities of the Communist parties in every country, because you have flagrantly violated so many covenants that the world can no longer have any confidence in your pledged word. And there is tension because the Soviet Union has ruthlessly imposed its rule on the peoples of Estonia, Latvia, Lithuania, East Germany, Rumania, Bulgaria, Czechoslovakia, Hungary and Albania.

"Let us remember that armed force has been used only twice in Europe since the end of the war: the first time, by the Soviet Army against the people of East Germany, and the second time, by the Soviet Army against the people of Hungary. Here is the proof of the real source of tension. You wish us to reduce tensions? If the Soviet Union could have the wisdom to withdraw to its pre-war frontiers, tension would disappear overnight and the whole world would sleep better."

To ease the way for the Communists, we should make it clear in advance that, in exchange for liberation, we would be prepared to make some concessions to Soviet desires in other areas. If Khrushchev truly wants a reduction of tensions, there is no more effective measure he could take than to negotiate a package agreement with the West in which liberation is exchanged for such concessions as a European security pact, increased East-West trade, partial disarmament, and conceivably, even some long-term credits.

In short, the active commitment to the ultimate liberation of the captive peoples, in addition to endowing our diplomacy with a power of deterrence it does not now possess, would strengthen our position politically, because it is in harmony with the moral principles on which our faith and civilization are based. Beyond this, it is the only conceivable way in which we can recapture the political offensive. It is a military maxim that a side which defends itself when attacked but never takes the offensive is ultimately doomed to defeat. The same is true in politics.

Admittedly, the Kremlin might not like it if we began to wage the cold war as a war of liberation. But only by doing so can we effectively cope with Khrushchev's hydrogen missile diplomacy. Only by doing so can we rekindle the flagging faith of our scores of millions of allies behind the Iron Curtain.

In the long run, it may not be too much to say, only by doing so can peace be preserved and freedom under the rule of God prevail on earth.

Chapter XX

FREEDOM OR COMMUNISM *

When I received your invitation to come to Atlanta, I was grateful for the opportunity to take part in a significant and perhaps historic event. Here, for the purpose of studying the Communist menace, are gathered the principal leaders of this great State in the fields of government, jurisprudence, education and journalism.

This distinguished assembly is both a demonstration and a symbol of the deep concern that is spreading throughout this land, concern about the continuing failure of the Free World to defend itself successfully against the ceaseless onslaught of Communist aggression.

Some of our esteemed pundits scornfully dismiss this concern and lay it to the inability of simple-minded, ignorant people to adjust to the new, mysterious complexities of foreign affairs. But this meeting is further proof, if any were needed, that the discontent with our posture in the cold war stems from responsible, enlightened men and women who are deeply disturbed, not by the mysteries of the cold war, but by the clear, simple, demonstrable fact that our policy is failing, and we are losing.

My purpose today is to lay before you three propositions which, I believe, explain why we are losing.

First, World Communism and Western Civilization are totally opposed to one another in everything that is basic and important; freedom cannot survive a major infection by com-

---

* Board of Regents of the University System of Georgia, Atlanta, Ga., January 16, 1962.

munism, and communism certainly cannot survive any injection of freedom.

Second, because of this total irreconcilability, because of the dedication to destruction which is at the heart of communism, because the continued flourishing of Western society makes a mockery of Marx, communism is compelled to destroy us to justify itself, to fulfill itself and to save itself from contradiction and collapse.

Freedom and communism therefore cannot live together under the same roof; and the Communists will not permit us to exist apart from them, if they can help it, for to do so will result in their own undoing.

Third, the long and gloomy series of Free World defeats, incredible in the face of our overwhelming superiority in wealth and in power, has resulted from our refusal to accept these truths as the bases for our policy.

Let me attempt to demonstrate my first proposition, that of the irreconcilable conflict between civilization and communism.

We believe in God. We believe in a Creator who ordained the natural laws governing the Universe and proclaimed the moral laws which should govern the conduct of man. We believe that He has revealed to us the purpose of society and the eternal destiny of each human being.

The Communists contend that God is a myth, that belief in Him is a fraud intended to assist in the exploitation of the working classes. They insist that society has no God-given purpose and that man has no eternal destiny.

Thus we are in total disagreement over the most important matter of our lives.

We believe that man has an ingrained knowledge of right and wrong and a free will enabling him to choose either, and and upon this concept of free will we have built a structure of rights and freedoms to safeguard and implement the sacred principle of free choice.

They contend that free will does not exist, and that free choice must not exist, because man has neither the knowledge to act wisely nor the virtue to act honestly.

We believe that man is essentially good and that the just society aims at encouraging that goodness, developing it and benefiting from it. .They contend that man is essentially evil and that unless he is remolded and rigidly controlled by the state he will only seek to exploit and debase other men.

We believe that the growth and fulfillment of the individual human being is the all-important end and that the institutions of our society are but means to this end. They contend that society is the all-important end, that the individual is but a means toward that end, and that the self-fulfillment of the individual is hostile to the welfare of society.

We believe that our policy toward nations, like our attitude toward individuals, should be to help them work out their own destiny in peace and justice, through the process of free choice.

They contend that independence is an illusion, that revolution, bloodshed, and fratricidal wars are inevitable and desirable, and that non-Communist nations must be destroyed, enslaved and rebuilt on the Communist pattern.

The reigning idea of Christian civilization is love; the reigning idea of communism is hate.

We are thus involved not in a simple conflict between nations or power blocs or economic or political theories. What is at stake here is everything that has made us what we are, as individuals, as families, as a nation, as a civilization.

To lose is to lose everything.

My second proposition is that this basic irreconcilability compels the Communists to work ceaselessly toward our destruction.

Our world haunts the Communist. He cannot be content just to deride us and wait for our collapse. He has invested his whole life, his whole being, in communism. He will live in jungles or deserts, accept the most cruel and odious discipline, commit any crime, betray any friend, surrender even his hope of eternal life to advance the world revolution.

If our truths are real, then his life is a senseless nightmare.

He abhors the present world and is driven on by a desperate inner compulsion to seek its destruction.

The only priority ahead of the destruction of our system is the building and preservation of his own. The only restraints upon his designs against us are his fears for the safety of his own system.

The threat of Communist subjugation, therefore, differs from all previous attempts to conquer the world. Here is no tyranny which seeks domination only for the sake of power, or spoils, or exploitation, or even the gratification of limitless ambition. Here is a depraved Samson who seeks to pull down the pillars of the present world and raise in its place a structure such as man has never seen.

We need not trace the history of this previous aggression to prove this point. We need only cite the present, in Berlin, in Laos, in Vietnam, in Cuba, in Tibet, in the Congo, along the Indian border. We need only cite the subversion being carried on in every nation of the Free World. We need only cite the demonstrations and riots which erupt wherever it serves their cause, even in our own country.

All of this seems to me so obvious as to be self-evident. The Communists have reaffirmed their intentions to destroy us by a thousand words and a thousand deeds. Yet our policy has consistently refused to recognize both the utter irreconcilability between Communism and Western Civilization and the compulsive necessity which drives the Communists on to bury us.

Our leaders ignored this when they charted a post-war policy based upon the assumption that the Russians were prepared to live at peace with the rest of the world.

Our leaders ignored the fact that Communism and freedom cannot co-exist peacefully when they sponsored coalition governments which inevitably fell one by one under Red control.

Our hasty demobilization after World War II certainly indicated a complete failure to see in the Communists an aggressive conspiracy more dangerous even than that of the Nazis.

Our folly in entrusting the freedom of Eastern Europe to the good intentions of the Russians could only have resulted from a complete failure to see the Communists as they were, and as they had always been.

As old illusions were dispelled by the cruel logic of events, new ones were invented to take their place.

When the Reds made their bid to take China, we did not treat it as merely the latest chapter in their book of aggression. We talked of "agrarian reformers", and of "waiting until the dust settles".

We fooled ourselves into believing our conflict arose from misunderstandings that could be resolved through summit conferences, only to find that each summit conference resulted in a carefully planned propaganda victory for the Russians.

We deluded ourselves into believing that the Russians would observe in good faith a nuclear test ban moratorium, and halted our own development in this crucial field, only to find that they first tested in secret, and then in the open, gaining substantial scientific advantages over us.

We deceived ourselves into believing that Castro was a latter-day Simon Bolivar who would deliver his people from a hated dictatorship, only to see him establish a Communist base 90 miles from our shores.

And we are convincing ourselves at this very moment that Cheddi Jagan in British Guiana is another agrarian reformer, only to find, as I am quite certain we will, that he is building still another Communist base in this hemisphere.

And so, the first step toward the building of an effective foreign policy, the indispensable step, is to accept the basic facts of our existence as they are, and to clear away the illusions that have obscured those facts.

If we can free ourselves from the illusion that Communism and Western Civilization can get along, we will give up vain hopes of an easy way out and begin to make the stupendous effort in the field of Free World armament and mobilization that must be made.

If we can free ourselves from the illusion that the temporary easing of this or that individual crisis will bring about an era of good feeling or another "spirit of Camp David," we will scrap the patchwork foreign policy of the past which has been essentially a policy of short-term reactions to Communist initiatives, and adopt instead a consistent long-range program aimed at the expansion of freedom and the defeat of communism.

If we can free ourselves from the illusion that communism is accepted by its subject peoples, we will institute policies aimed at encouraging resistance behind the Iron Curtain, with the consequent demoralization of the Red empire.

If we can free ourselves from the illusion that Polish Communists or Yugoslav or Cuban Communists are less the enemies of freedom than Kremlin Communists, we will stop pouring out our substance in aid to Red dictatorships, which have received almost $4,000,000,000 from the American people in recent years, and instead divert that aid to those allies who are manning the front lines of freedom.

Freed from the illusion that the hard-core Communists who rigidly dominate the Communist World can be influenced by friendly demonstrations on our part, we will bring to an end all practices which blur and obscure the nature of the life or death struggle that has been forced upon us.

Freed from the illusion that we improve the world climate by soft-pedaling our criticism of Communist infamy, we can for the first time institute an effective program of bringing to the world the truth about Communists, by each day dragging them before the bar of world opinion, indicting them again and again for the atrocities and crimes they have committed in enslaving one billion human beings, and convicting them in the minds of men for what they have in fact made of themselves, the moral outcasts of humanity.

Freed from the illusion that the way out of each enemy aggressive act is a coalition government which includes Communists, we will at last recognize that the government which includes Reds today will be controlled by them tomorrow, and that there is no substitute for standing firm against aggression from the beginning.

Freed from the illusion that the Communists are seriously interested in negotiating a just peace or indeed in seeking any honorable common objective with us, we will never again fall for such a ruse as the nuclear test ban negotiations which paralyzed our own technological development for three years while our enemies secretly moved ahead.

Freed from the illusion that the Communists can take part

in any international organization or court without either poisoning it or subverting it to their ends, we will begin to think less and less in terms of utopian worldwide international organizations and more and more in terms of Free World cooperation and unity.

Freed from the illusion that there is some easy way out of the present crisis of civilization, we will adopt a policy of strength, of risk, of sacrifice, of effort for every American.

I have tried to outline some beginnings of an effective foreign policy.

No one can predict with certitude that his set of policies will give us the victory over World Communism that will save Western Civilization. No one, least of all myself, can foretell the hour or the manner or even the generation in which this victory will be achieved.

Our task is to stop losing. Our task is to start the tide running in our favor.

If we can do that, if we can bring to bear upon the cold war the inherent superiority of our system, then we will have set in motion the triumph that we ourselves may not see.

What will save us, in the end, is this:

A free man is better than a slave; a free economy is more productive than a slave economy; a free university, in the long run, will achieve more than an indoctrination center; a free nation which governs through consent is stronger than a dictatorship which governs through fear; a coalition of independent states banded together through a common cause will, in the end, prove stronger than an artificial slave empire held together with bayonets.

We meet here today to try to find a path that will lead us to the victory that the justice of our cause deserves and the superiority of our civilization makes possible.

I am confident that through this meeting and through thousands like it across this land, we will find that way because we have now begun to do what must be done. We have begun to look.

Chapter XXI

CAN LIBERALS AND CONSERVATIVES UNITE FOR FREEDOM?*

There is a developing mood of anger and frustration in our country today, and there ought to be. For we are losing round after round in the cold war, and our people do not like it.

At the close of World War II, our forces stood triumphant on land and sea and in the air. We had at our command the mightiest array of military power in history. The flags of freedom were unfurled on every continent.

Had we the understanding and the will, our diplomacy, backed up by this military and moral power, could have assured the freedom of the peoples of Europe and Asia and laid the basis for a stable peace. Of this I am convinced.

Yet, the past 16 years have witnessed a calamitous retreat from victory. During all these years, we have suffered defeat after defeat at the hands of international Communism; we have retreated from position after position; we have committed folly after folly.

Everywhere we are on the defensive. Everywhere we find ourselves being pushed back.

We have retreated so far that we now stand perilously close to the brink of total disaster. Speaking in Paris last December, I said that if there were another 15 years like the previous 15 years, there would be no more Free World left to defend. In the light of what has happened over the intervening eight months, I feel compelled to revise the timetable.

We do not have 15 years left to us. The next 5 years, I

---

* Los Angeles, California, August 28, 1961.

feel will witness a series of decisive battles between Communism and the Free World. The outcome of these battles will determine for centuries to come whether mankind is to live in freedom or in slavery.

We now stand with our backs to the precipice. We have no ground to give, no time to lose, no margin for error.

It is not in the tradition of the American people to accept defeat, or to respond to threats and bullying with mere paper protests. That is why they are restive today.

That, I believe, is why you are here today.

Our people are convinced that the trend must be reversed and can be reversed. In their overwhelming majority they believe that we must stand up to the threat of Communist aggression and Communist subversion, even at the risk of war. They suffer from a sense of deep frustration because they feel that something is wrong, but do not know what is wrong.

If this national dissatisfaction can be channeled into concerted action to restore the supremacy of freedom, it will be a national blessing. But if this sense of anger and frustration were to vent itself in bitter feuding between liberals and conservatives here at home, it would be a national curse. This we must seek to avert.

This situation confronting us calls imperatively for two things:

First of all, it calls for a frank analysis of the lessons of the past. If we are to reverse the trend of recent years, if we are to force the Communist world back on the defensive, if we are to set our sights on the victory of freedom over tyranny, we must first of all restudy the strategy and tactics of World Communism and we must draw all the hard, bitter lessons of the postwar era. We must decide where we have erred and where we have failed and what might have been done to avoid these failures. We must all be brutally frank with ourselves. Nothing less than this will suffice.

Secondly, I believe that the situation calls imperatively for national unity, for unity between Democrats and Republicans, liberals and conservatives, Catholics, Protestants and Jews. When I speak of unity, I do not mean unity for the sake of unity. I mean unity behind a program designed to assure the defeat of Communism and the world-wide triumph of freedom.

The differences that exist within our society are important, inevitable and, indeed, proper. But we all share the same basic beliefs in freedom and justice, in the God-given nature of man's rights, in the destiny of our country. And these basic beliefs that unite us are ten thousand times as important as the controversies that divide us.

In this moment of grave national peril we can no longer afford the luxury of exaggerating our political differences, of racial or religious bigotry, of emotional extremism on the right or emotional extremism on the left.

Although there is a growing recognition of the need for national unity, I believe that there is far too much accusation of party by party and group by group.

I am particularly worried by the growing bitterness of the debate between our liberals and our conservatives. In speaking about liberals, I do not mean the totalitarian sympathizers of the Soviet Union who disguise themselves as liberals; and in speaking about conservatives, I do not mean those who have so completely abdicated their belief in freedom that they still regret the defeat of Nazism. In both instances, I refer to the great mass of decent Americans whose adherence to these respective philosophies of government falls within the framework of the American political tradition.

Let me give you one example of the price we pay for this suspicion and division between liberals and conservatives.

For several months there has been languishing in a pigeonhole in the Senate Committee on Foreign Relations a bill that would establish a Freedom Academy, designed to train thousands of Free World leaders in the science of successfully waging the cold war against Communism.

Nothing is more demonstrable than the need for this legislation. Last year this bill passed the Senate but failed in the House because of suspicions by hard anti-Communists there that the Freedom Academy would be infiltrated and taken over by pro-Communists or by liberals who were soft on Communism. And this year the bill has been buried in the Senate, largely, I am inclined to believe, because of the fear of liberals that the Freedom Academy would become a sort of fortress of militant anti-Communism, manned by conservative thinkers.

Thus do we let our differences rob us of the unity to do those things that must be done if we are to survive. And it need not be so.

The fact is that on the question of Communism and how to deal with it, neither Republicans nor Democrats, neither liberals nor conservatives, have had a monopoly on wisdom or on folly.

There have been a few situations, but only a very few, in which one party has been more right than the other. There have been other situations in which apparent differences boiled down to the dismal fact that both parties were wrong, but for different reasons. But by and large, our foreign policy has been a bipartisan policy.

When we have had victories, they have invariably been accomplished with bipartisan support. When we have blundered with good intentions, we have blundered hand in hand.

When we have suffered defeat or accepted retreat, the policies that resulted in failure have in most cases enjoyed the active or passive support of both parties.

As for the acrimonious debate between liberals and conservatives, as I see the matter, there is, on both sides, some truth, a good deal of exaggeration, and far too much self-righteousness.

THE EXTREMES OF CONSERVATISM

There are some conservatives who believe that the problem of Communism is essentially a problem of a domestic nature and, if we could get rid of the Communists in government, then the problem of Communism would somehow cease to exist. They are sometimes disposed to look upon liberals and all others who deny this thesis as abettors of the Communist conspiracy.

This, of course, is a dangerous oversimplification.

Communism is a massive international movement which has in its arsenal many weapons.

Communism means the Soviet Army and the Chinese Red Army and all the other armies that march under the hammer and sickle.

It means Radio Moscow and Radio Peiping and a propaganda network a hundred times the size of the combined propaganda resources of the Free World.

It means a science of political warfare that has been systematically developed in the Red academies in the 45 years since Lenin seized power.

It means scores of thousands of trained practitioners of political warfare, distributed through every country in the world.

It means proven techniques for confusing public opinion in the Free World and every conceivable device for exploiting differences within each country and among the countries of the Free World.

It also means subversion and espionage and infiltration in government.

But the point I want to emphasize here is that infiltration in government is only one of many means by which Communism operates.

Even if some miraculous method could be found for screening every last Communist infiltree out of government, international Communism would still constitute a formidable menace to the Free World.

THE EXTREMES OF LIBERALISM

But those liberals who decry all talk of Communism in government as "witch-hunting" are just as wrong as those conservatives who see in it the only real or the major danger to our society. Communist infiltration in government has been a very real and very serious problem, and it will, I am convinced, remain a problem so long as there is a Communist movement.

Let us look at a few facts from the record.

Alger Hiss, one of the top officials of our State Department was convicted of perjury for denying that he had turned over secret State Department documents to Whittaker Chambers, a self-admitted Soviet agent.

Harry Dexter White, the number two man in our Treasury Department, according to incontrovertible evidence in the hands of the FBI, was also a Soviet agent.

Frank Coe, who was deputy to Harry Dexter White in the Treasury Department, later moved up the ladder to become head of the International Monetary Fund. Called before the Senate Subcommittee on Internal Security in 1953, Coe took the Fifth Amendment in reply to the question, "Are you a Communist agent, Mr. Coe?" This terminated Coe's career as head of the International Monetary Fund. Today he is working for the Chinese Communist government.

Laurence Duggan, one-time head of the Latin American Division of the Department of State, was also identified in sworn testimony as a member of the Communist network in government, before his mysterious suicide in 1952.

And for every one of these infiltrees of top rank, there were a dozen infiltrees of lesser rank.

Communist infiltration in government may at no time constitute more than a tiny fraction of one percent of all government employees and officials. The potential danger of such an infiltration, however, is obvious. It will never be able to take over the American government from within, as some exaggerated fears have had it. But it is a matter of record that this tiny fraction of one per cent has done a lot of damage by purveying state secrets to the Kremlin and by mis-directing American policy.

In July 1953, after extensive hearings, the Senate Subcommittee on Internal Security issued a report on "Interlocking Subversion in Government Departments." Speaking about the Communist infiltrators in government, this report stated: "They colonized key committees of Congress. They helped write laws, conduct Congressional hearings, and write Congressional reports. They advised Cabinet members, wrote speeches for them, and represented them. They staffed interdepartmental committees which prepared basic American world policy. They traveled to every continent as emissaries and representatives of the American people. They attended virtually every international conference where statesmen met to shape the future."

It would be prudent to assume that Communist infiltration of government offices did not come to an end with the Hiss hearings and the hearings held over the next several years. It would be prudent to assume this and to take the necessary precautions. In doing so, however, we must be careful to avoid extremes and careful to protect the civil rights of government employees.

LIBERAL-CONSERVATIVE UNITY IS POSSIBLE

The ultra-liberal extremist and the ultra-conservative extremist in a sense beget and encourage each other.

On the one hand, the extremist conservative is sometimes too prone to accuse everyone with whom he disagrees of being a Communist or a Communist sympathizer. The extremist liberal, on the other hand, is able to use every untrue or unsubstantiated allegation to prove, according to his own lights, that Communism is a non-existent menace which has been dreamed up by the "reactionaries", and to defend those whose complicity in the Communist conspiracy is unmistakable. The extremist conservative reacts in turn by damning all liberals as pinks and crypto-Communists.

And so it moves, in a vicious circle.

I believe that the extremists on both sides have received far more attention than they merit, perhaps because all extremists are vociferous, and because extremism is news, whereas moderation is not news. This unfortunate emphasis on the extreme elements on both sides has had the effect of driving both the liberals and the conservatives further apart, because it has distorted the impression they have of each other.

To my conservative friends I would point out that party labels really mean very little, that conservatives have sometimes been very foolish in their relations with the Communists and that liberals and, for that matter, socialists, have often conducted themselves with wisdom and courage. Rather than judging any man on the basis of party label, he *should* be judged on his record of principle and of opposition to Communism.

It was one of the great liberal Senators of our time, the late Robert M. LaFollette, Jr., of Wisconsin, who first became aware of the seriousness of Communist infiltration in government and brought it to public attention.

It was the liberal New York weekly, *The New Leader,* which, during the heyday of our wartime alliance with the Kremlin, swam against government policy and the current of editorial opinion, challenged the Yalta and Teheran agreements and warned against our over-trustful attitude toward our Soviet allies.

While there are a few unions in our country that are under Communist control, and some union leaders who suffer from fuzzy thinking, on the whole you will find more solid understanding on the subject of Communism in the American trade union movement than you will in any other major sector of our society. In the fight against Communism, President George Meany, in particular, has shown himself an articulate spokesman and a statesman.

It was a tough old European Social Democrat, Vaino Tanner, who saved Finland from Communism in the difficult postwar years, while the Finnish Agrarian Party, which was supposed to be more conservative, collaborated with the Communists.

In Berlin, the Free World has been fortunate to have as allies and spokesmen, first Mayor Ernst Reuter and now Mayor Willie Brandt, both of them Social Democrats.

I could go on and on with the listing. Among the moderate Socialist statesmen who have played an outstanding role in resisting Communism in Europe, were the late Ernest Bevin and the late Herbert Morrison in Britain; Paul-Henri Spaak, the recent Secretary General of NATO; Jules Moch, the first French Interior Minister to crack down seriously on the Communists; and Guiseppe Sarragat, the leader of the anti-Communist Socialists in Italy.

I would ask my conservative friends to examine and weigh

the record of liberal anti-Communism with an open mind. I am confident that, if they do so, it will lead them to reapraise the possibilities of conservative-liberal cooperation.

To my liberal friends I would also appeal for less self-righteousness and more tolerance. The liberals may lay claim to men like George Meany and Robert LaFollette in this country and men like Mayor Willie Brandt and Paul-Henri Spaak in Europe. But on the other side there have been giants like Winston Churchill, Premier de Gasperi of Italy, Chancellor Adenauer of Germany and General Douglas MacArthur, all of them conservatives.

I would urge the liberals, too, to show more balance in their political attitudes. Few of them will challenge the statement that Communism is the great menace of our time, that the Communists are cheats, liars and murderers and that they are out to cut our throats. But for some reason there are liberals who expend a hundred times more energy combatting right wing extremism than they ever seem able to put forth in the fight against Communism.

Show them an extremist movement on the right, and they are off like chargers, anxious for the fray. Show them a movement like the Fair Play for Cuba Committee, organized under Communist direction and with Communist financial support, but still able to attract and mislead thousands of innocent students, and these self-same liberals are just not interested.

This completely imbalanced political attitude is, I am afraid, reflected in our press. If it is a matter of exposing some right wing extremist movement or some movement which is accused of right wing extremism, many of our newspapers will devote column after column to the subject, day after day. In such cases they display amazing investigative resources. But these investigative resources lie dormant and unused when there are movements like the Fair Play for Cuba Committee waiting to be exposed. And when committees of Congress expose these Communist front movements for what they are, with overwhelming and incontrovertible evidence, the reports of these committees are frequently ignored or buried.

I report this to you on the basis of experience.

In appealing for liberal-conservative unity in the struggle against the mortal peril that confronts us, I do not underestimate the difficulties. There are ancient prejudices to be overcome, there are areas where agreement will be difficult to achieve. But I believe that such unity *is* possible because there have already been several highly successful experiments in liberal-conservative unity on specific issues.

Take the issue of the admission of Red China to the UN. This is a basic issue of principle and morality on which the American people have from the first been united. Congress has repeatedly gone on record, by unanimous votes, as opposing the admission of Red China to the UN. The broad unity which exists on this issue is further reflected in the remarkably representative membership of the Committee of One Million Against the Admission of Red China to the United Nations. On the roster of this Committee you will find names as diverse as Governor Charles Edison and the late General George C. Marshall, Ambassador Joseph C. Grew and the late Ambassador Warren Austin, Senator Paul Douglas and Senator Styles Bridges. It is this broad Democratic-Republican, liberal-conservative composition that has made the Committee of One Million so effective an organization.

Let me give you another example, closer to home. During the forties, the Communists were able to establish a virtual stranglehold over the motion picture trade unions. Recently I had a conversation with Roy Brewer, one of the courageous trade union officials who helped to break this stranglehold. Mr. Brewer told me that they were successful in driving out the Communists because they were able to establish an anti-Communist coalition that embraced both liberals and conservatives. Without this kind of unity, he said, they could never have succeeded.

Now, as Ronald Reagan recently told the press, the Communists are again crawling out from under the rocks in Hollywood, and the anti-Communist forces must close ranks once again or risk losing the ground they so painfully gained.

WHAT YOU CAN DO

What is it that you as private citizens can do to combat and defeat Communism? There is a lot that you can do. Perhaps more than in any other country of the world, the people of America have the power to help determine government policy on critical issues.

Before you do this, you must inform yourselves. You must attend lectures. You must read books recommended by competent authorities on Communism. You must engage in discussions with your friends. You must give this matter the most serious study and thought of which you are capable, because your own future and your country's future are at stake.

You must shun those who are prone to damn everyone with whom they disagree as Communists, or who impugn the motives of everyone who has blundered in the fight against Communism. For there are very few who have not blundered, even among our greatest men. I am reminded of the fact that it was Winston Churchill, himself the soul of British conservatism and one of the immortal political leaders of all time, who was responsible for installing a Communist regime in Yugoslavia.

If you are to be a true fighter for freedom, you must shun the amateurs and quacks and extremists, whose anti-Communist activities only compromise the cause of anti-Communism.

You must assiduously attend the meetings of the trade unions and of the other organizations to which you belong, raise issues, encourage discussions and submit proposals and resolutions.

You must try to remember what you learn. You will find it helpful to follow the proceedings of the Senate Subcommittee on Internal Security and of the House Committee on Un-American Activities. You must be careful about your facts and careful about making charges and allegations that you cannot prove to the hilt.

You must be tolerant, and err on the side of giving people the benefit of the doubt. You must all endeavor to make it as easy as possible for those who have joined front organizations

319

in innocence or good faith to extricate themselves from their associations and come back to the side of freedom.

Finally, you must make your views known to your representatives in Congress, and to your local press and politicians.

We must all give our utmost to the struggle, because we are now passing through the gravest and most perilous period in our history.

WANTED: A FOREIGN POLICY BASED ON FREEDOM

I would be less than frank with you if I pretended that I was altogether satisfied with the conduct of our foreign policy.

Foreign policy must be based on an understanding of the enemy that confronts us; and by our successive follies and successive defeats under both Republican and Democratic Administrations, we have demonstrated that we do not have this understanding. Over and over again we have indulged in pipe dreams and wishful thinking and shied away from the hard fact that we are locked in a life and death struggle with an incredibly cunning, ruthless and totally evil enemy.

It requires resourcefulness to meet the many-sided aggressions of this ruthless and cunning opponent; but we have come up with nothing more original than bigger defense budgets and bigger foreign spending programs.

It requires the courage and understanding to seize the initiative to challenge the enemy, to exploit every opportunity and press every advantage, to strive unrelentingly for the world-wide victory of freedom. But no such proposals have yet been made that would extricate us from the fatal defensive posture of the postwar period.

We must find a foreign policy that will lead us to victory over the evil forces of Communism, because the alternative to this is the static, defensive, do-nothing foreign policy that has led us from disaster to disaster since the close of the war.

I believe we can find common ground for such a foreign policy in the timeless words of Thomas Jefferson, "I have sworn upon the altar of God eternal hostility against all forms of tyranny over the mind of man." There is no reason why all of us, Republicans and Democrats, liberals and conservatives, cannot rededicate ourselves with these words.

If we so rededicate ourselves, in deed as well as in word, I am confident that the American people and their elected representatives can devise a foreign policy that will point the way to the world-wide triumph of freedom.

29-101